FIRST LOW-PRICED
EDITION OF

Julia Child
& More Company

W9-DAY-354

Also by Julia Child
Published by Ballantine Books:

JULIA CHILD & COMPANY

Julia Child & More Company

Julia Child

IN COLLABORATION WITH E. S. YNTEMA

BALLANTINE BOOKS • NEW YORK

Library of Congress Catalog Card Number: 79-2226

ISBN 0-345-31450-6

This edition published by arrangement with Alfred A. Knopf

Printed in Canada

First Ballantine Books Edition: October 1984

Introduction

Julia Child's Company

Like its predecessor and companion, *Julia Child & Co.*, this is a menu cook book. Last time we began thinking of the kind of parties we give; this time we pondered the components: What'll we do with mussels? Could a classic onion soup be better still? We kept a thrifty budget and a tight schedule in mind, but allowed for occasional splurges—like rack of lamb, or taking time to enthrone wine-poached pears in macaroon-cushioned chocolate cups, to be swathed with caramel sauce. We cosseted an old fowl and made pork dressy; we got fanciful with fresh Rock Cornish hens, and we turned *pâté en croûte* and a tri-colored fish terrine into everyday pleasures. Along the way, we gave a whirl to almost everything we thought of, taking no conventions for granted.

Finding solutions to these problems meant much research and testing. Our team consisted of executive chef, Marian Morash (Straight Wharf Restaurant, Nantucket Island); associate chef, Sara Moulton, (recently of Cybeles' Quincy Market, Boston); food designer and super cook, Rosemary Manell; assistant cooks Bess Coughlin, Jo Ford, and Temi Hyde; Elizabeth Bishop, executive associate sommelier, and right hand; our marvelous and spirited writer for the two J.C. & Co. books, E.S. Yentema; office and personal secretary, Gladys Christopherson; Jim Scherer, official photographer; and Paul Child, husband and officially unofficial photographer. Other members of our family were Lorraine Ferguson and Stuart Darsch, both skilled in layout; Marilyn Ambrose, Judith Avrett and Avis Devoto, who helped so much in the office and with patient, persistent research. For meat lore and for fish stories, we relied on our unofficial mentors, Jack Savenor and Roger Berkowitz, both generous with technical know-how and with on-loan specimens, often of heroic scale, like Jack's entire lamb and Roger's monster monkfish. Russell Morash produced the first French Chef television series, and the two J.C. & Co. series; our director was Russ Fortier. Finally, my collaborator, Ruth Lockwood, known officially as talent coordinator, she was my personal director. Knopf editor Judith Jones and book designer Chris Pullman contributed much to the look of the original hardcover version of the book.

Whether we were devising a quick ice-cream glorifier or judiciously comparing versions of a new lobster soufflé, the whole team pondered, cooked, and tasted together, joined sometimes by spouses or offspring. (See page 150 for one 12-year-old's contribution.) Serious artist or weekend amateur, it's more fun cooking *for* company *in* company.

Certainly I've never enjoyed better company than our team. To each and every one of them this book is affectionately dedicated.

J. C.

Cambridge, Mass., August 15, 1979

Note: throughout this book,
- ❷ *indicates a stopping point in the recipe, and*
- ● *indicates further discussion under Remarks.*

Contents

Contents

UFOs in Wine

Menu

For 6 people

Moules Marinière—Steamed mussels
Hot French Bread

Rock Cornish Hens Broil-roasted with Garlic, Cheese, and Wine
Giant Straw Potato Galette
Cherry Tomatoes Tossed in Butter and Herbs

Fresh Orange Blueberry Bowl

Suggested wines

A Chablis, Pouilly-Fuissé, Pouilly-Fumé, Sancerre, or dry riesling with the mussels; a red Bordeaux or cabernet with the birds; and there would be nothing wrong in serving a Champagne or sparkling wine with the dessert

Eating this meal demands fingers, and cooking it demands loving, last-minute attention. The right people to ask to this dinner party are knowing, sensuous eaters whom you welcome backstage because they understand and enjoy what's going on there. Dine in the kitchen, if you have room, so your friends can breathe in that first waft of perfumed steam when you uncover the mussel pot. Let them await in suspense that soul-satisfying plop when the big potato pancake is flipped in sizzling butter. And don't feel rushed arranging the main course stylishly; it only takes a moment, and is served all on one platter except perhaps for the cherry tomatoes. (Big tomatoes wouldn't, I feel, be in the right scale for these small birds on their neat round nest.)

A *paillasson*, or straw mat, is what the birds' nest looked like to Fernand Point when he used to serve the straw potato *galette* at his legendary restaurant, La Pyramide, in southern France. According to Point's former apprentice, chef Joe E. Hyde, in his engaging cookbook *Love, Time, and Butter* (New York: Richard W. Baron, 1971; out of print), Point's version was cooked first on the stove, and then the frying pan was moved to the oven. But that was before the blessed advent of nonstick cooking utensils.

As to the Flying Objects, they truly are Unidentified, as this recipe works well for many kinds of small birds. But since squab pigeons, partridge, quail, etc., are rather hard to come by, and the season for game birds is short anyway, I chose Rock Cornish hens. Just for fun, I looked up their origin in the *Encyclopaedia Britannica*, and discovered that in the late eighteenth century cocks were imported here from Cornwall and mated with our Plymouth Rock hens. So it's an old breed, though we didn't hear much about it until the middle of this century. I think the first person to have raised Rock Cornish commercially was the humorist-cum-pianist Victor Borge, at his farm in Connecticut. For some years you could buy them only frozen, but growing demand has made fresh Rock Cornish hens more and more available. At about a pound, a hen serves one jumbo or two standard-sized guests. Mussels, though not a bit fattening, are so filling that I figure, for the next course, half a hen is better than one.

These elegant birds have a slightly more pronounced flavor than does chicken, but it's still mild; so I step it up with a marinade (which you wouldn't need with a squab or a wild bird) and intensify it by cooking them under a light blanket of shredded Swiss cheese. That might sound odd, but you don't taste the cheese as such—you just taste the bird more, and of course it browns beautifully. I use a good nutty Gruyère, sometimes mixed with mozzarella, almost as freely as butter—not so much for its own very unassertive flavor as for the way it enhances others. (See the crêpe-and-vegetable gâteau on page 192, for instance, where the custard binding is fortified and enriched with cheese, and the stuffing for the stewing hen on page 138.) The marinade is quickly turned into a savory little sauce, and the mushrooms and garlic are strewn over all. Don't worry about the garlic: blanching and roasting tame it down.

Fresh fruit is a perfect follow-up to such richly flavored first and second courses, and it should be something not too sweet, with the tang of citrus and a soft plumpness for contrast. Above all, after such an artful, even whimsical dish as the birds on their nest, the dessert should be pretty but matter-of-fact. Even something like the charming *vacherins* on page 43 would be a bit much this time. There are lots of possibilities, but we finally elected to layer fresh oranges and blueberries strewn with glossy amber shreds of home-candied orange peel.

Our friend Rosie said delightedly, "This is such a *foody* meal!" and it is, if you see what we mean. The precise word for it, though, occurs only in French—*raffiné*, meaning 1 part refined, 2 parts canny, 3 parts subtle, plus 1 dash amusing: a nice cocktail of an adjective.

Preparations and Marketing

Recommended Equipment:

To steam the mussels, use an 8-quart (8-L) soup kettle with a lid; enamel or stainless steel is preferable to aluminum, which turns wine gray. You'll need something to dip the mussels out with.

For the potato *galette*, a nonstick frying pan 11 or 12 inches (28 to 30 cm) in top diameter, with some kind of cover, and a long-handled pancake turner. Be sure the well of your serving platter matches or exceeds the frying pan in size.

The tomatoes should have a sauté pan just big enough to hold them in one layer.

Before clarifying butter, don't forget to check your cheesecloth supply.

Staples to Have on Hand:

Salt
Peppercorns
Sugar
Optional: fragrant dried tarragon
Imported bay leaves
Flour
Optional: olive oil
Corn syrup
Chicken stock or broth •
Shallots or scallions
Butter
Clarified butter •
Carrots (1)
Onions (4 or 5)
Celery (1 small stalk with leaves)
Parsley
Port or Madeira wine
Dry white French vermouth or dry white wine
Orange liqueur

Specific Ingredients for This Menu:

Mussels (5 to 6 pounds; about 4 quarts or 4 L) •
Rock Cornish hens (3), fresh preferred
Swiss (Gruyère) cheese mixed with mozzarella (1 cup or ¼ L, grated; about ½ pound or 225 g)

Garlic (2 or more heads)
Mushrooms (1 pound or 450 g)
Potatoes (6 medium), "baking" type preferred
Ripe cherry tomatoes (36 to 48) ●
Fresh green herbs, such as parsley, chives,
    tarragon, or chervil
Seedless oranges (5 or 6 large "navel" type)
Blueberries (1 pint or ½ L), fresh or frozen

● Remarks

Staples to have on hand

Chicken stock or broth: the recipe for making it is in this chapter; you can, however, use canned broth. *Clarified butter*: the recipe for it is on page 368. We treat it as a staple because it's so good to have on hand all the time, and it keeps for months refrigerated.

Specific ingredients for this menu

Mussels: moules marinière begins with fresh, live mussels in their shells. Before you buy them, please read the note preceding the recipe; a few hints on gathering your own mussels are given in the Postscript to this chapter. *Cherry tomatoes:* since you can rarely buy them perfectly ripe, allow a few days' lead time. For tips on tomatoes generally, see page 188.

Mussels

Quantity note: for the average-sized mussels commercially sold, you can figure that 1 quart equals 1½ pounds (675 g) equals 25 mussels in the shell equals 1 cup (¼ L) mussel meat. This rule of thumb comes from Sarah Hurlburt.

Preparing mussels for cooking

Mussels are perishable, and you should plan to cook them as soon as possible after buying or gathering them. The latter will need more cleaning than cultivated mussels. First, wash the mussels. Then, with a short, stout knife, scrape off any seaweed, barnacles, etc. Pull off their wispy beards. Discard any mussels that do not quickly close when tapped, any mussels with cracked or broken shells, any that feel unduly light (they may be empty), or any that feel unusually heavy (they may be full of sand).

Soak the mussels (whether cultivated or gathered) in a bowl of cold water, swishing and knocking them about with your hands for a few seconds, and let them sit for 5 minutes. Lift them out, and if there is any sand at the bottom of the bowl, rinse out and repeat the process, doing so several times if need be. Since there is nothing worse than sandy mussels, I also take a final step: I put 4 or 5 tablespoons of flour in the bottom of a bowl, blend it with cold water, then fill the bowl with 4 quarts or so (4 L) cold water, add the mussels, swish about again, and let them sit for 15 to 20 minutes— the theory being that they eat the flour and while doing so disgorge the rest of their sand. (I am sorry to report that despite all you can do, you will once in a while run into a batch of mussels that are gritty—Sarah Hurlburt, author of *The Mussel Cookbook* (Cambridge: Harvard University Press, 1977), tells me this is caused, strangely enough, by eider duck droppings in the sea water near mussel beds. Some kind of a chemical reaction then irritates the mussels, and they produce calcium granules in their flesh. Too bad, if this happens; but you can steam them open, as in the following recipe, and use their juices, and perhaps even purée and strain the meat.)

Moules Marinière

Mussels steamed in wine, minced onions, and parsley

For 6 people as a first course

5 to 6 pounds (about 4 quarts or 4 L) mussels,
   prepared as in the preceding directions
3 to 4 Tb butter
1 cup (¼ L) minced onion
3 to 4 Tb minced shallots (optional)
1 or 2 cloves garlic, minced (optional)
A large handful of fresh chopped parsley
About 2 cups (½ L) dry white wine or dry white
   French vermouth

Equipment:

An 8-quart (8-L) stainless-steel or enamel (not
   aluminum) soup kettle with lid, and a perforated
   scoop

Prepare the mussels as described. A few minutes before
serving time, melt the butter in the kettle, stir in the onion
and optional shallots and garlic, and cook slowly for 4 or 5
minutes, until wilted. Then add the parsley and the mussels;
cover kettle and shake to mix mussels with the rest of the
ingredients. Pour in the wine or vermouth, and shake again.
Turn heat to high, cover kettle tightly, and let steam for 3
to 4 minutes (do not shake again or you may toss sand into
the mussels), until the mussels are open. As soon as 'hey
open, they are done.

Dip the mussels, shells and all, into a big serving bowl or
into individual soup bowls. Let liquid settle for a minute in
kettle, then pour liquid, and spoon onion and parsley, over
mussels, being careful not to add any sand that may be in
the bottom of the kettle.

To eat the mussels

To eat the mussels, use your fingers, plucking the mussels
out of their shells. Or, for slightly more elegance, after eating
one with your fingers, use the shells from that mussel as

pincers to pick the meat out of the rest. Either pile the shells neatly interlaced at the edge of your bowl or have a shell dish at your side, then spoon up their delicious juices, like a soup.

❂ Mussels should be served as soon as they are cooked; they will toughen and dry out if you attempt to keep them warm. However, this recipe is a starting point for many other delicious preparations, including the mussel soup and the mussels in mayonnaise on the half shell described later in the chapter.

Rock Cornish Hens Broil-roasted in Wine

This is a fine recipe for any small young birds—like pigeon, quail, partridge—and is particularly good with fresh Rock Cornish game hens.

For 6 people

3 Rock Cornish hens (1 pound or 450 g each)

Ingredients for Brown Poultry Stock and Sauce:

1 medium carrot and onion, chopped
1½ cups (3½ dL) chicken stock or broth
½ cup (1 dL) dry white wine or dry white
  French vermouth
1 imported bay leaf
1 small stalk celery with leaves

Ingredients for Optional Marinade:

Salt and pepper
1½ tsp fragrant dried tarragon
2 Tb finely minced shallots or scallions
About ½ cup (1 dL) dry white wine or dry white
  French vermouth
3 to 4 Tb light olive oil (optional)

Other Ingredients:

Salt and pepper
Melted butter, or clarified butter
1 or more heads garlic
About 1 cup (¼ L) coarsely grated Swiss cheese
½ cup (1 dL) or so Port or Madeira wine, or
  dry white French vermouth
1 pound (450 g) fresh mushrooms, trimmed,
  washed, and quartered
2 Tb or more butter for sauce enrichment
  (optional)

Preparing the hens

(The birds are to be split down the back and spread out, browned under the broiler on both sides, then sprinkled with cheese, surrounded with wine and garlic cloves, and baked until done. The mushrooms are added during the last minutes of cooking.) With shears or a sharp knife, cut down each side of the backbone from neck to tail, and remove backbone. (Chop the backbone into 2 or 3 pieces and reserve for stock, later.) Turn the birds skin side up and pound breast flat with your fist. To tuck drumsticks into slits in lower breast skin, first bend knees and push up to shoulders, then tuck ends in. Fold wings akimbo behind backbone each side.

Brown Poultry Stock for Sauce:
For about 1½ cups (3½ dL)

Brown the reserved backbones, necks, and giblets (if any) and the chopped carrot and onion in a frying pan with a little oil or clarified butter (page 368). Scrape into a saucepan, discard browning oil, and rinse frying pan with the stock or broth to dislodge all flavorsome browning particles; pour liquid into saucepan. Add the wine or vermouth, ingredients from the optional marinade, bay leaf, and celery. Bring to the simmer, skim off surface scum for a few minutes, then cover pan loosely and simmer slowly for 1 to 1½ hours. Strain, skim off surface fat, and stock is ready to use.
❷ May be prepared ahead; refrigerate in a covered jar when cold, or freeze.

Plain Poultry Stock—Chicken Stock:

To make a plain stock simply omit the browning of the ingredients. You may even omit the vegetables altogether, and simmer the carcass bones and scraps, raw or cooked, in lightly salted water.

Optional Marinade:

A simple wine marinade will give the usually mild Cornish hens more flavor. Salt and pepper them on both sides and sprinkle with tarragon. Arrange in a bowl, sprinkling each with shallots or scallions, wine, and optional olive oil (oil distributes the flavors of the marinade). Cover and, if kitchen is warm, refrigerate. Marinate for 3 to 4 hours (or longer), turning and basting the birds with the marinade several times.

When you are ready to proceed, scrape off marinade and reserve in bowl; dry the birds with paper towels.

Browning under the broiler

Having dried the birds (salt and pepper them lightly if you did not marinate them), brush with melted butter and arrange in one layer skin side down in a broiling or roasting pan. Preheat broiler and set pan so surface of meat is about 3 inches (8 cm) from heat source; brown, basting several times with melted butter, for about 5 minutes on the flesh side; turn, and brown nicely on skin side.

❂ Recipe may be completed several hours in advance to this point. Although you can refrigerate them, it is best to leave the hens at room temperature if wait is not too long and kitchen not too warm.

Other activities before roasting

Separate garlic cloves and drop into a saucepan of boiling water; simmer 3 or 4 minutes to soften slightly, then slip off the skins and reserve garlic in a small bowl. Grate the cheese, set out the wine, and prepare the mushrooms.

Roasting
About ½ hour at 400°F/205°C

Preheat oven in time for roasting, and plan to roast 30 to 40 minutes before serving. Salt and pepper the skin side of the birds lightly, divide the cheese over them, and strew the garlic around them. Pour in enough wine to film pan by about ¼ inch (¾ cm). Place pan in upper middle level of oven. Baste every 6 minutes or so with the liquids in the pan as the birds slowly brown on top. After about 20 minutes, strew the mushrooms around the birds, basting with liquids in pan. Continue until birds are tender when thighs are pierced with a sharp-pointed fork; juices should run clear yellow with no trace of rosy color.

Finishing the sauce

(I didn't have time for this on our television show, but here is how I would have liked to have done it.) Remove the birds to their platter, arrange around them the mushrooms and half the garlic, scooped out with a slotted spoon. Keep warm for a few minutes in turned-off oven, door ajar, while you complete the sauce. Pour the brown poultry stock into the roasting pan and set over high heat to dislodge any roasting juices, scraping them up with a wooden spoon. Strain them into a small saucepan, leaving garlic in sieve. Skim surface fat off liquid, and rub garlic through sieve with wooden spoon, scraping it off bottom of sieve into the liquid—garlic purée will thicken the liquid as you rapidly boil it down for a moment to concentrate its flavor. When lightly thickened, taste sauce carefully for seasoning. Off heat, if you wish, beat in the enrichment butter by spoonfuls.

Serving

For this menu, the birds are arranged on a giant potato *galette* (following recipe), with the mushrooms and garlic. Either spoon the sauce over the hens, or pass in a warm bowl.

Giant Straw Potato Galette

An enormous pancake of matchstick-sized potato pieces

Potatoes cut into matchstick-sized pieces and pressed into a layer in a large frying pan with hot butter, cooked to a fine walnut brown on each side— what a beautiful bed for our little birds, or for many another morsel, like chops, tournedos, or even fried eggs.

Manufacturing Note:

Potatoes are odd creatures indeed, and one of their peculiarities is that some turn brownish or reddish almost while you are cutting them. Although a sojourn in cold water usually brings them back to white again, the water soaks out the starch—which you need for this recipe because you want the potatoes to stick together and form a mat as they cook; no starch and they tend to separate. Thus potato cutting must be a last-minute affair. The cooking of the galette is, too; if it sits around, its tender inner core begins to discolor, and the whole galette slowly loses its buttery freshly cooked potato taste. Finally, clarified butter is really a must here, since ordinary butter, with its milky residue, can make the potatoes stick to the pan, which spells certain disaster. An excellent way to clarify butter is described on page 368.

For a 9- to 10-inch (23- to 25-cm) galette serving 6 people

About 6 medium potatoes, preferably "baking"
6 Tb or more clarified butter (page 368)
Salt and pepper

Equipment:

A nonstick frying pan 11 to 12 inches (28 to 30 cm) top diameter; a cover of some sort for the pan; a long-handled pancake turner; a round serving platter to hold the galette.

Just before you are to cook the *galette*, peel the potatoes, drop into a bowl of cold water, and then cut them into matchstick-sized pieces: either using a big knife, slicing them first, and cutting the slices into sticks; or use the coarse side of a hand grater; or use the grating attachment of a food processor. Do not wash the potatoes once cut; simply dry them in a kitchen towel.

As soon as the potatoes are cut and dried, film the frying pan with a 1/16-inch (1/4-cm) layer of clarified butter, and heat to very hot but not browning. Turn in the potatoes, making a layer about 3/8 inch (1 cm) thick. Sprinkle with salt and pepper, and 2 or 3 spoonfuls more butter, then press them down firmly all over with the spatula so they will mat together as they cook. Frequently press them down while they slowly brown on the bottom, and shake pan gently by its handle to be sure potatoes are not sticking to the pan.

When browned, in 2 to 3 minutes, cover the pan and lower heat to moderate. Cook for 6 to 8 minutes, or until the potatoes are tender on top, but watch they do not burn on the bottom. Press them down again, and the *galette* is ready to brown on its other side.

To turn it: either slide it out onto an oiled baking sheet, turn the frying pan upside down over it, and reverse the two so the *galette* drops into the pan, browned side up; or flip the *galette* in its pan, which, of course, is much more fun and faster—just have the courage to do it! Raise heat slightly, and brown lightly on the other side (which will never show, but browning crisps it). Slide the *galette* onto its platter, and plan to serve it as soon as possible.

❂ May be kept warm, uncovered, but the sooner you serve it, the better.

Cherry Tomatoes Tossed in Butter and Herbs

Cherry tomatoes, for this delicious recipe, are peeled and then tossed gently in butter, salt, pepper, and herbs just to warm through but not to burst, before serving. A labor indeed it is, but well worth it for beloved family and special friends.

For 6 people—6 to 8 tomatoes apiece

36 to 48 ripe red firm cherry tomatoes
2 Tb or more butter
3 to 4 Tb fresh green herbs, such as parsley,
**   chives, tarragon, and chervil—alone or mixed**
Salt and pepper

Equipment:

A nonstick stainless-steel or enamel frying pan just
**   large enough to hold tomatoes in one layer**

A handful at a time, drop tomatoes into a saucepan of boiling water and boil 3 or 4 seconds, just enough to loosen the skins. With a small sharp-pointed knife, cut around each stem to remove it, and slip off the skin.

❂ May be done several hours in advance; place tomatoes in one layer in a glass or enamel plate, cover, and refrigerate.

Just before serving, heat the butter to bubbling in the frying pan, turn in the tomatoes, and roll over heat (shaking and twirling pan by its handle) with the herbs and seasonings just until warmed through. Turn into a hot vegetable dish (or spoon around your meat or vegetable platter); serve at once.

Orange Blueberry Bowl

For 6 people

5 or 6 large fine bright firm ripe seedless "navel"
  oranges
Sugar syrup: 1 cup (¼ L) sugar, 5 Tb water,
  and 1 Tb corn syrup
1 pint (½ L) blueberries, fresh or frozen
Sugar, as needed
2 Tb or more orange liqueur

Candied Orange Peel—for Decoration:

With a vegetable peeler, remove in strips the orange part of
the peel of 3 (or all) of the oranges, and scrape off any white
residue from underside of peel. Cut the peel into very fine
julienne strips—as fine as possible. Drop into 1 quart (1 L)
simmering water and simmer 10 to 15 minutes, or until tender.
Drain, and rinse in cold water; pat dry in paper towels.

Meanwhile, bring the 1 cup (¼ L) sugar, water, and corn
syrup to the boil in another saucepan (doubling syrup ingredients if you have used all the orange peel), twirling pan by
its handle until sugar has dissolved completely and liquid is
perfectly clear. Then cover pan and boil over high heat for
a few minutes until syrup has reached the soft-ball stage,
238°F/115°C (bubbles are big and thick, and droplets of syrup
form soft balls in cold water). Drop the peel into the syrup
and boil slowly for several minutes, until syrup has thickened
again. Set aside until ready to use.

◗ May be done weeks in advance, and stored in a covered
jar in the refrigerator.

Preparing the oranges and blueberries

Not more than a few hours before serving, neatly trim off
the white part of the peel from the oranges to expose the
orange flesh. Cut the oranges into neat crosswise slices, and,
if you are not serving for more than an hour, place slices in
a bowl, cover, and refrigerate. Defrost the blueberries if
necessary; if they need sugar, toss in a bowl with several
tablespoons of sugar and let macerate, covered, in the refrigerator.

Assembling the dessert

Not more than an hour before serving, drain the candie
peel, reserving the syrup. Choose an attractive glass servin
bowl or individual coupes, and arrange a layer or 2 of orang
slices in the bottom, spoon over them a little of the orang
peel syrup, and add a few drops of orange liqueur. Drain th
blueberries and sprinkle a layer on top of the oranges. Cor
tinue to build up the dessert in layers, ending with a handf
or 2 of candied orange peel strewn on top. Cover and re
frigerate until serving time.

❶ If the dessert is assembled too soon, the blueberries exud
purple coloring down into the oranges—in case that bother
you! And sliced oranges lose their fresh taste as they s
about.

❶ Timing

This is not at all an ahead-of-time meal, and that is certainl
one of its charms. Your guests will be getting the finest kin
of food freshly cooked and served at once. That means ther
will be last-minute work for the cook before every cours
except the dessert. If you have a big family-style kitcher
dining room, you can finish practically all the main cookin
right there with your guests, doing only the preliminarie
before they come—such as the marination of the birds, th
cleaning of the mussels, the peeling of garlic, and the car
dying of the orange peel. But if you haven't that kind of
kitchen, you'll need to do some planning, as follows.

Last-minute items are the mussels, but they take only
minutes or so to steam, plus 4 to 5 minutes to wilt the onions
and while you are cooking them you can finish the sauce fo
the birds and give the potato *galette* its final flip.

The roasted birds can wait, so they can be finished jus
before the guests arrive; keep them warm in a turned-of
oven, its door ajar, reheating them briefly if need be jus
before serving. The potatoes could be started at this time
too. And the tomatoes could be given a preliminary toss
but set aside off heat—to be finished just before you serv
them.

You'd start roasting the birds half an hour before th
guests are to arrive, and preheat the oven 15 minutes befor
that. Since you need to be around to baste the birds fre

quently, you could be arranging the dessert at that time, and getting out anything else that you will need.

Scrub the mussels and start their soaking in mid-afternoon. Peel and slice the oranges at this time, too.

This brings us up close to dinnertime again. Backtracking to midday or even morning, you can give the birds their preliminary browning (or marinate them at this point and brown them later), prepare the garlic and mushrooms, peel the cherry tomatoes, and defrost the blueberries, if you're using frozen ones.

The day before, you can buy fresh Rock Cornish hens, prepare them for their cooking, and marinate them. Also, you could simmer their backbones, necks, and giblets for stock; otherwise, make it any time and freeze. If you can buy only frozen birds, be sure to allow 2 days for defrosting in the refrigerator—always the best way. The orange syrup can be prepared now, or even weeks before, from the skins of oranges you may be using for other things.

Even though the cooking of each dish is done at the last, this is not a tricky meal. There are no surprises, and it's unusually delicious as well as being special.

❹ Menu Variations

Moules marinière: there's a variant recipe, thickened with bread crumbs, in *Mastering I*, which has several other classic mussel recipes. That book was intended to explain the dishes and methods my co-authors and I thought most important in traditional French cooking, where mussels count for a lot. But I didn't do anything more about mussels until the frabjous day when they became generally available in this country. Now, joyously making up for the lean years, I have tucked in two more mussel recipes at the end of this section. However, if your fish dealer is still in a rut and you can't get these wonderful shellfish but like the *marinière* idea, you might try clams, as the Italians do: use steamers. I do think a hot, fairly substantial shellfish dish makes an exciting opener for the little birds, but I wouldn't come on too strong. Bouillabaisse, for instance, would be just too much garlic at one meal, but a small serving of Mediterranean fish soup, scallop soup, broiled oysters or a small oyster stew, or a little crab or lobster in mayonnaise would be fine.

Game hens: for a classic dish, *coquelets sur canapés*, roast the birds and serve them with a deglazing sauce on sautéed bread *canapés* (sofas, literally), spread with a pâté made of their livers. Substitute other birds, as the recipe explains, or you can use Rock Cornish hens in many chicken recipes. They're nice served cold, with liver stuffing and Cumberland sauce.

Potato galette: with small birds, crisp potatoes are classic. Homemade potato chips are exquisite, as are waffled potatoes (you need a special cutter), or sautéed potatoes or *pommes soufflées*, for which you can do most of the work beforehand; the final frying in very hot fat goes fast.

Cherry tomatoes: I love the trim look of each guest's plate at this party; but any other lively-tasting, lively-looking vegetable would be nice with the birds.

Fruit desserts: surely you'd want something cold and fresh after *moules marinière* and roast birds with garlic; it's just a matter of the season. Fresh pineapple (see "Cassoulet for a Crowd" on how to buy, cut up, etc.) might be lovely; or a basket of perfect ripe fruit, such as pears, peaches, apricots—it's about the most voluptuous dessert you can offer, yet has a country air like the birds on their nest. Or a bowl of cherries layered with ice to make their skins snap when you bite.

❶ Leftovers

You won't have much in the way of leftovers in this meal. Mussels can go in a salad or soup, as described in the next section.

Bird bones and tomatoes, mushrooms and garlic are also candidates for soup. The potatoes have no future but—oranges and blueberries for breakfast? And now for more mussels!

Soupe aux Moules

Mussel soup

Moules marinière *can turn themselves into a perfectly delicious soup, delicate, fragrant with a variety of thinly cut vegetables, and tasting subtly of wine and cream with a tiny spark of curry for the* je ne sais quoi *chic a good soup should have.*

For about 2 quarts (2 L)

2 large carrots
2 medium onions
1 or 2 leeks (optional)
2 or 3 celery stalks
6 Tb butter, more if desired
2 cucumbers
Salt and pepper
The recipe for mussels steamed in wine, mussels
    removed from shells, and cooking liquid with
    onion and parsley warmed (without sand!)
2 tsp curry powder
4 Tb flour
2 cups (½ L) or more milk, or as needed
2 egg yolks
5 Tb or more heavy cream
Minced fresh parsley

The vegetables

Cut the carrots into julienne matchsticks, and the onions into slices about the same size. Discard roots and tough green parts of leeks, slit leeks lengthwise halfway from root end, turn and slit again; wash, spreading leaves under cold running water, and cut into julienne; cut the celery likewise. Simmer these vegetables slowly in a heavy-bottomed saucepan with 2 tablespoons butter, until wilted but not browned. Meanwhile, peel the cucumbers, cut in half lengthwise, scoop out seeds with a teaspoon, and cut cucumbers into julienne. When other vegetables are almost done, stir in the cucumbers, and salt lightly to taste. Continue cooking for 3 to 4 minutes, then stir in a cupful of mussel-cooking juice and simmer 5 minutes to blend flavors.

The soup base

In a 3- to 4-quart (3- to 4-L) heavy-bottomed stainless-steel saucepan, melt the rest of the butter, blend in the curry and flour, and stir over moderately low heat until butter and flour foam and froth together for 2 minutes without coloring. Remove from heat, and when the *roux* has stopped bubbling, pour in a ladleful of warm mussel liquid; blend vigorously with a wire whip. When smooth, beat in the rest of the liquid, adding enough milk to make about 2 quarts (2 L). Bring to the simmer, stirring slowly with wire whip, and simmer 2 minutes. Fold in the cooked vegetables, simmer several minutes; taste and carefully correct seasoning.

Blend the egg yolks in a medium-sized bowl with 5 tablespoons cream. By dribbles beat in a ladleful of hot soup, then pour the mixture back into the soup. Bring just to the simmer, stirring, so that the yolks may cook and thicken in the soup. Fold the mussels into the soup.

❷ May be completed to this point. Film top with a spoonful or 2 of milk or cream to prevent a skin from forming. When cool, cover and refrigerate.

To serve

Bring just to the simmer. Correct seasoning again, thin out with milk or cream if necessary, and, if you wish, stir in a little more cream and/or butter. Ladle into soup bowls or a big tureen, and decorate bowls or tureen with a sprinkling of parsley.

Variations:

This soup is very good in itself, even without mussels, using chicken stock or clam juice. Or you could add oysters and fish stock, or diced raw sole or trout fillets that cook for a few minutes in the soup. Or poach scallops in wine and shallots, dice them, and add with their cooking juices to the soup.

Moules Farcies

Mussels on the half shell with herbed mayonnaise

For 54 mussels, serving 6 people as a first course

**About 3½ pounds (2½ quarts or 2½ L)
   mussels steamed in wine (about ½ the recipe
   given earlier in the chapter)**
**1½ cups (3½ dL) homemade mayonnaise
   (page 237)**
½ cup (1 dL) sour cream
2 Tb finely minced shallots or scallions
1 tsp curry powder (optional)
2 Tb very finely minced parsley
**1 Tb very finely minced fresh dill (or a big pinch
   dried dill weed)**
Salt and pepper
Drops of hot pepper sauce

Remove the cooked mussels from their shells but save one
of the shells from each mussel. (Save mussel liquid for soup
or sauce, or freeze it.) Blend the mayonnaise in a mixing
bowl with the sour cream and other ingredients, and taste
very carefully for seasoning, adding what else you think
would enhance the mayonnaise without masking the delicate
taste of the mussels. Place mussels in another bowl, and fold
in as much mayonnaise as needed to enrobe them.

❷ May be prepared in advance several hours before serving;
cover and refrigerate.

Shortly before serving time (so mayonnaise topping will
not crust over), spoon a sauced mussel into each shell and
arrange on special shellfish plates, or on plates lined with
shredded lettuce.

❷ *Ahead-of-Time Note:* Because of the mayonnaise crusting
problem, you often find, on buffet setups, that the mussels
are prepared with the mayonnaise and then coated with a
film of aspic, which seals them. Another solution is to spread
finely chopped hard-boiled eggs and parsley over each, on
a rack set over a tray, then to arrange the mussels on their
dish or dishes.

Variations:

Instead of serving the mussels in their shells, heap them into serving shells and decorate with watercress, or with whatever else you wish. Or mound them into tomato shells, or serve them in a dish as part of a cold platter. Or spoon them around a cold poached fish, or make them part of the cold fish platter. Or fold them into cold cooked rice or pasta. And so forth . . .

Postscript: More on mussels

This chapter's so long I'll try telegraphese. Mussel is: *Mytilus edulis*, edible bivalve, familiar foodstuff worldwide. Consumed in U.S. by coastal Indians, witness prehistoric shell middens; appreciated by Pilgrims, early settlers. Seemingly forgotten, eighteenth to mid-twentieth centuries. Rediscovered, now sold quick-frozen, canned, pickled.

Why? Many virtues. Mussel is: (1) *Delicious*! and adaptable; (2) Not an acquired taste—liked even by shellfish neophytes; (3) Satisfying. Dieters note: 25 mussels (1 quart or 1½ pounds in shell) = 235 calories meat, feels like big meal; (4) Profuse. Cultivated by Spanish method (ropes hung from rafts), 1 acre sea gives *1,000* times as much meat as 1 acre pasture gives beef. Diet of future Americans need not be algae, bean sprouts. Absurd neglect of great resource.

Mussel life-style: efficient. Low on food chain, all bivalves filter seawater; mussels especially "good doers," since filter more. Plankton, other nutrients, unwastefully converted into flesh. Unfussy mussel tolerates high or low salinity; has freshwater, riverbed cousin, also edible but used chiefly for mother-of-pearl shell lining; all mussels also make pearls, not valuable.

Natural beds often several acres, containing millions; occur on Atlantic coast south to Cape Hatteras, on Pacific, south to Mexico. U.S. should cultivate on large scale, like Spain, France, Holland. To harvest own mussels: plumpest to be found below low-tide mark, where submerged, hence eating, all day. Seek on rocks, sandbanks, pilings; mussels cling to them, or to other mussels, by "byssus threads" or "beards," extruded steel wool–type filaments, very tough. Gather in cleanest, purest water only. Avoid "red tides," common on West Coast in summer, less common East: sudden proliferations of reddish dinoflagellates, micro-organisms making mussels fat, people sick. Red tides monitored by U.S. Coast Guard, U.S. Fish and Wildlife Service. Check.

Check locally. Unposted areas not necessarily safe. Inquire town shellfish warden, if any, re sewage outlets, etc. If license to gather is required, try town hall. Then help self. Recommended equipment: screwdriver or chisel, gloves if sea cold, carrying bag, rinsing bucket. Best harvest only for immediate use. For storage—2 days at most—refrigerate clumps as in plastic bag; don't separate or disturb.

Country Dinner

Menu

For 6 people

Mediterranean Hors d'Oeuvre Platter—Sliced Green and Red Peppers in Oil and Garlic, Anchovies, HB Eggs, Olives, Syrian String Cheese
French Bread, or a Braided Loaf

Leek and Rabbit Pie with Buttermilk-Herb Biscuit Topping
Snow Peas Tossed in Butter

Petits Vacherins—Individual Meringue Cases Filled with Ice Cream and Topped with Sauced Fruits

Suggested wines:

A strong dry white with the hors d'oeuvre, such as a Mâcon, Châteauneuf, or pinot blanc; a rather mellow red with the rabbit—Beaujolais, Châteauneuf, Bordeaux, or cabernet; Champagne, a sparkling wine, or a Sauternes with the dessert

The marketing list for this meal looks terribly jumbled, for the menu draws on the very different cuisines of the Mediterranean and the Orient, on down-home American cooking, and on the classical French tradition. Nevertheless, the piquant red-green-gold-black appetizer, the cozy, fragrant rabbit pie, the fresh snow peas, and the delicate dessert make a lovely harmony. Nothing very fancy about it, but it's hard to think of a restaurant where you could order all of these dishes. Restaurants tend to specialize. And most restaurants seem needlessly conservative, lagging far behind the supermarkets' resources, which increase constantly in bounty and variety. The supermarkets, in turn, lag behind seedsmen and gardeners, who prove every day that all sorts of "exotics" can flourish almost anywhere.

Though a good market can, in fact, furnish you with all these ingredients, this menu is designed especially to honor the gardeners who grow their own, sometimes on lots half the size of a tennis court. For very little money, they can eat heavenly food like this all summer long. In all but the hottest weather, they can harvest snow peas for months, by making successive plantings; since they pick their snow peas—ordinary peas too—in the dewy morning and refrigerate them at once, the quality is superlative. (If peas are harvested too old, or if they sit even a few hours in the heat after picking, they taste flat. Either way, their natural sugar has been converted into starch.) As for leeks, while you certainly can buy fine ones, the price is shocking except in the fall. That's when the crop is mature, and commercial growers harvest and sell it all at once. The rest of the year, markets must import their leeks from wherever they're mature at the moment. But leeks are good at any age, and home gardeners pick them when they please. Peppers are expensive because they don't store well, and since they become more fragile as they ripen, the red or fully ripe ones are relatively scarce.

Like most of the Victorian houses where we live, ours sits on a lot big enough to feed us—if we would only cut down all the big old trees, that is. On our one sunny spot, the top front doorstep, we grow pot herbs, but otherwise our crops are restricted to shade-loving things like lily of the valley and a wisteria vine that reaches out to the sun. So it's a great treat for us to dine out with our gardening friends and enjoy their exquisitely fresh vegetables and fruit. Amazing what ingenuity can do in a city backyard! To save ground space, our friends grow strawberries and cucumbers and tomatoes on trellises, and espalier fruit trees on sunny southern walls. Their ripening melons, groaning with juice, hang heavily in little net hammocks suspended from fence posts. Peppers, so beautiful and bountiful, are grown as ornamental plants on patios. And grapevines flourish on pergolas built over heat-reflecting concrete driveways.

And livestock! A very elderly resident, who grew up across the Common from us, on so-called Tory Row, says that at the turn of the century would-be ten-o'clock scholars like himself were roused daily at dawn by cackles and squawks and cock-a-doodle-doos. No such rustic racket around here nowadays; maybe too many sleepyheads took their troubles to city hall. But we do see an occasional rabbit hutch, and their numbers are growing. Few cities have ordinances prohibiting rabbits, since they have zero nuisance value: no smell, clean habits, no diseases in most climates, and no noise at all.

Living all over the world, wherever the State Department sent us, we got used to rabbit as a staple and a delight. The meat is delicate and fine-textured, pearly pink when raw but all white when cooked, with a flavor something like chicken, but richer and meatier. You can use it in any recipe designed for chicken. It's high in protein, low in fat, and, according to the U.S. Department of Agriculture, no other meat is as nutritious. When we first returned to this country, rabbit was hard to find in markets, but now most of them carry it, usually cut-up and frozen.

It's nice to see city people raising their own for home consumption, as country people always have. In these days of scarcity and high prices, it's worthwhile pondering the fact that "one doe, in one hutch, can produce 70 to 95 lbs. of dressed, edible meat in one year," and that a hutch can be less than a yard square. By the age of 2 to 3 months, a "fryer" rabbit weighs 4 to 5 pounds, more than half that when dressed; by 7 to 9 months, a "roaster" rabbit gives you over 4 pounds of meat. Fryers are more easily found but twice as expensive; it's a mystery to me why market rabbits should cost so much anyway, since they're incredibly cheap and easy to raise. We got these inspiring facts from the American Rabbit Breeders Association, which estimates that about half its members are backyard farmers, raising rabbits for the pot. If you're inspired too, you can write to the association at 1925 South Main Street, Box 426, Bloomington, Illinois 61701, and ask for their free *Beginners Booklet*, enclosing 50 cents for postage, or you can purchase their *Official Guide to Raising Better Rabbits*. And should you wish to go commercial, be advised that Pel-Freeze Rabbit Meat, Inc., of Rogers, Arkansas, will set you up in business if you ask for a franchise.

Except, perhaps, for the eggs for our meringue dessert, this really could be called a Backyard, rather than a Country Dinner. Wonderful what you can do right in town, I mused, as I cooked this lovely food. My imagination blazing with possibilities, I wandered out into my own yard seeking what might be devoured. Any stuff is potential foodstuff to a cook. (My friend Chef Cazalis of the fine Restaurant Henri IV in Chartres, hearing once of an elephant that would have to be destroyed, acquired and cooked the trunk...250 servings, he says; delicious too.) Wisteria! I thought; lily of the valley? But my gardening neighbor stayed my hand. "Are you mad?" he inquired. "They're both poisonous."

Preparations and Marketing

Recommended Equipment:

You need a large platter on which to display the hors d'oeuvre.

To brown the rabbit, a large frying pan; to simmer it, a 4-quart (4-L) covered pot or flameproof casserole; to bake the pie, the same pot or a big baking-and-serving dish. Obviously, the wider the baking dish, the more crust. The one we used on TV was of American-made earthenware, with a smoky-blue glaze inside; I think it's a beauty.

For the peas, a wok is nice, but you could use your rabbit-browning frying pan.

For the *vacherins*, you need a pastry bag fitted with a cannelated (toothed) tube whose opening is ⅛ inch (½ cm) in diameter. It's very important to have the right kind of pastry bag; it makes things so much easier. The best one I have run into is of lightweight, waterproof, flexible vinyl, as yet not manufactured here but imported from France. Also 2 or 3 large pastry sheets, preferably nonstick, and a 3-inch (8-cm) circular something for marking them.

Staples to Have on Hand:

> Salt
> Peppercorns
> Sugar, preferably superfine granulated
> Flour (3½ cups or ⅘ L; 1 pound or 450 g)
> Optional: dried rosemary leaves
> Optional: fennel seeds
> Optional: imported bay leaves
> Pure vanilla extract
> Optional: soy sauce
> Olive oil
> Optional: cooking oil
> Vegetable shortening
> Chicken stock, or chicken and beef bouillon (3 cups or ¾ L)
> Small black olives ●
> Double-acting baking powder
> Baking soda
> Cream of tartar
> Butter

Chives
Parsley
Onion (1 large)
Garlic (1 head)
Optional: lemon (1 large)

Specific Ingredients for This Menu:

Rabbit (4½ to 5 pounds or 2 to 2¼ kg), cut up ●
Chunk of bacon (8 ounces or 225 g)
Red or yellow bell peppers (2 or 3) ●
Green bell peppers (2 or 3) ●
Anchovies (1 can)
Fresh snow peas (1½ to 2 pounds or ¾ to 1 kg) ●
Leeks (5 to 6 pounds or 2¼ to 2¾ kg) ●
Celery (1 pound or 450 g) ●
Syrian or Armenian string cheese (one third to
    one half of a 1-pound or 450-g package)
Buttermilk (1½ cups or 3½ dL)
Eggs (6 "large" plus 4 whites)
Fillings and toppings for *vacherins* (see recipe,
    pages 33 and 34)
Dry white wine or dry white French vermouth (2
    cups or ½ L)

---

❷ Remarks:

Staples to have on hand

Small black olives: I like the "Nice" type of olive packed in
brine, or the small Italian olives, also in brine, both of which
are full of flavor. You might also try the imported, dry, oil-
packed ones. Taste one, and if it seems too salty, simmer
them in water for 10 minutes or so.

Specific ingredients for this menu

Rabbit: for your pie, use the "roaster" size, about 4½ pounds
(2 kg) dressed weight, if you can find one. The small "fryer"
rabbit is twice as expensive and is really too young and
tender for stewing; but it can be used if that's all you can
buy. If you have frozen rabbit, which comes already cut up,
it's best if you allow 2 or 3 days' thawing time, in the refrigerator. Do not soak it. Rabbit meat can absorb up to 25

percent of its own weight in water. *Bell peppers*: the green or immature ones keep better than the red, mature peppers, but in any case I'd use bell peppers within 3 or 4 days of buying or harvesting, because they soften and spot quite rapidly. Refrigerate them, wrapped in plastic. *Leeks*: buy them fresh-looking, with firm green leaves. They keep well for a number of days when stored in a plastic bag in the refrigerator.

Mediterranean Hors d'Oeuvre Platter

Peeled sliced green and red peppers in oil and garlic, anchovies, HB eggs, olives, Syrian string cheese

For 6 people

2 or 3 green bell peppers
2 or 3 red bell peppers (and/or yellow peppers)
Salt and freshly ground pepper
2 or 3 cloves garlic
Olive oil
Syrian (or Armenian) string cheese
3 hard-boiled eggs
1 can anchovies packed in olive oil
A handful or so of small black olives

The peppers

Place the peppers on a piece of foil in a broiling pan and set them so their surface is 2 inches (5 cm) from a red-hot broiler element. When skins have puffed and darkened on one exposed side—in 2 to 3 minutes—turn with tongs onto another side, and continue until peppers have puffed and darkened all over. At once, while still warm, cut 1 of the peppers in half and drain its juice into a bowl. Scrape seeds from insides, and cut the pepper into finger-width strips—for easier peeling. Pull off the skin—which should come off easily enough if really puffed and darkened. Cut the strips in half, and place in the bowl with the juice. Rapidly continue with the rest of the peppers.

Note: The preceding system works well for me, but there are other pepper peeling methods listed on page 36 that you might try if you are having difficulties.

Oil and garlic sauce

Place ½ teaspoon or so of salt in a small mortar or bowl, and purée into it the garlic. Mash with a pestle or the end of a wooden spoon to make a perfectly smooth paste, then whisk in several tablespoons of oil. If the pepper slices are swimming in too much of their juice, pour some of it out, then fold the peppers with the garlic and oil.

❷ Peppers may be sauced several days in advance of serving; cover and refrigerate, but let come to room temperature (to decoagulate the oil) before serving.

The string cheese

The cheese comes in a tightly twisted 1-pound/450-gram hank, as you can see in the photograph. Untwist it, and cut as many pieces of it as you think you will need into 8-inch (20-cm) lengths—one third to one half the package. Pull strands of cheese down the length of each piece—picky work but worth it. Taste several strands, and if cheese seems too salty, rinse in a sieve under cold running water, drain well, and toss in paper towels to dry. Before serving, you may wish to toss the cheese in a bowl with olive oil and freshly ground pepper.

❷ Cheese may be strung, but not sauced, in advance; wrap loosely in slightly dampened paper towels, and refrigerate in a plastic bag. Will keep nicely for a day or 2 at least.

Assembling the platter

One idea for assembling the platter is to have one side for red peppers and the other for green; wedges of egg at the two ends, anchovies over peppers, cheese in the middle, and olives (rolled in olive oil) at the sides.

❷ Platter may be assembled several hours in advance except for the anchovies, which go off in taste if opened more than a few minutes before serving—at least that is so in my experience. Cover platter closely with plastic wrap, and refrigerate, but let come to room temperature before serving so that olive oil will liquefy.

Leek and Rabbit Pie

Serving 6 to 8 people

About 5 pounds (2¼ kg) rabbit, cut up

Optional Marinade:

6 Tb light olive oil, or other fresh fine cooking oil
4 cloves garlic, finely minced
1 tsp dried rosemary leaves
2 Tb soy sauce
**The strained juice and the zest (yellow part of peel)
    of 1 large lemon**
½ tsp fennel seeds
2 imported bay leaves

Other Ingredients:

An 8-ounce (225-g) chunk of bacon
1 large onion, sliced
Olive oil or cooking oil
**5 to 6 pounds (2¼ to 2¾ kg) leeks, to make 6
    to 8 cups (1½ to 2 L), julienned**
**About 1 pound (450 g) celery, to make 2 cups
    (½ L), julienned**
Salt and pepper
Flour
**If rabbit was not marinated, add the garlic,
    rosemary, fennel, and bay as indicated in those
    directions**
**2 cups (½ L) dry white wine or dry white
    French vermouth**
**About 3 cups (¾ L) brown chicken stock (or
    chicken and beef bouillon)**
**Beurre manié (4 Tb soft butter blended to a paste
    with 4 Tb flour)**

Biscuit Crust:

**3 cups (430 g) all-purpose flour (measure by
    dipping dry-measure cup into flour container
    and sweeping off excess)**
2 tsp salt
4 tsp double-acting baking powder

1 tsp baking soda
8 Tb (½ cup or 1 dL) chilled vegetable
    shortening
4 Tb fresh minced chives, or 2 Tb freeze-dried
4 Tb fresh minced parsley
2 eggs
1½ cups (3½ dL) buttermilk, plus drops more
    if needed
Egg glaze (1 egg beaten with 1 tsp water and a
    pinch of salt)

Equipment:

A stainless-steel or glass bowl large enough to hold
    cut-up rabbit if you are to marinate it; 1 or 2
    large frying pans (nonstick recommended), for
    browning the rabbit; a 4-quart (4-L) flameproof
    casserole or covered pot for simmering the
    rabbit; the same casserole or another for final
    baking; a pastry brush

Optional marinade
6 to 24 hours

If you wish to marinate the rabbit, which will give it a more
interesting flavor, beat the listed ingredients together in a
bowl large enough to hold the rabbit pieces. Turn the rabbit
in the marinade; cover and refrigerate, turning and basting
the rabbit several times with the marinade. Before using,
scrape marinade off rabbit pieces back into bowl, and reserve.

Preliminaries

Remove and discard the rind, and cut the bacon into *lardons*
(sticks 1½ by ¼ inches, or 4 by ¾ cm) and blanch them
(drop into a saucepan containing 2 quarts or 2 L water,
simmer 5 to 7 minutes, drain, rinse in cold water, and dry).
Set aside.

Cook the onion slowly in a small saucepan with 1 tablespoon oil until tender, then raise heat slightly and cook,
stirring frequently, until a light mahogany brown—this is to
color and flavor your cooking liquid, later. Set aside.

Trim and wash the leeks—cut off and discard root ends,
and cut off the green part a finger width or so from where
the white begins, where the green is still tender. Slit length-

wise 2 or 3 finger widths from root, give a ½ turn and slit again, as shown. Spread leaves apart as you wash the leeks under cold running water. Cut into 2-inch (5-cm) lengths, and then into julienne (strips ⅛ inch or ½ cm wide). Trim, wash, and cut the celery also into julienne.

❷ All of these preliminaries may be done even a day in advance; cover and refrigerate.

Browning and simmering the rabbit—Rabbit stew

Cook the blanched bacon slowly in a large frying pan filmed with oil, browning it lightly and rendering out its fat; remove bacon to a side dish, leaving fat in pan. Meanwhile, dry the rabbit pieces in paper towels, season lightly with salt and pepper, dredge in flour, and shake off excess. Brown the rabbit pieces on all sides (as many as will fit comfortably in one layer) in the bacon fat, and place in the cooking casserole as each is done (add oil to pan if you need it during browning, and regulate heat so fat is always hot but not burning or smoking). Stir the leeks and celery into the frying pan. Toss and turn to blend ingredients; cover and cook slowly 5 to 7 minutes, stirring up once or twice, until softened. Spread them over and around the rabbit pieces, with the browned onions and bacon, and ingredients from the marinade. (If you did not marinate the rabbit, stir in the garlic, rosemary, fennel, and bay.)

Pour in the wine, and enough chicken stock or bouillon barely to cover the rabbit. Bring to a simmer, cover and simmer slowly until rabbit is tender when several pieces are pierced with the sharp prongs of a kitchen fork. (Older and heavier rabbits may take as much as 1 or even 1½ hours of simmering to cook tender; young ones as little as 30 minutes.)

Arrange the rabbit pieces in a cooking-and-serving casserole. Skim any accumulated fat off surface of cooking liquid, and taste liquid very carefully for seasoning, adding more salt and pepper if needed, more herbs, etc., etc. You should have about 3 cups or ¾ L. Off heat, beat the *beurre manié* into the liquid, and bring to the simmer, stirring with a wire whip. Sauce should be lightly thickened. Pour it (with its vegetables, but without bay leaves) over the rabbit.

❷ Recipe may be completed to this point even 2 days in advance (and may be served as is—a rabbit stew). If you are not serving or proceeding, let cool, then cover and refrigerate—heat to the simmer before final baking.

Biscuit dough for crust

Place the flour, salt, baking powder, and baking soda in a mixing bowl and cut in the chilled shortening—using 2 knives or a pastry blender—continuing rapidly until fat is broken up into pieces the size of coarse (kosher) salt.

● May be done to this point several hours in advance; cover and refrigerate—liquid is added only the moment before using, because the baking powder starts its action immediately.

Stir the herbs into the flour mixture. Blend the eggs in a large measure, beat in the buttermilk, and mix rapidly into the flour with a rubber spatula, turning and pressing the ingredients together to form a dough. Scoop out onto a lightly floured work surface, and with the floured heels of your hands rapidly knead the dough to give it enough body so that you can pat or roll it out—the less you work it the more tender it will be, but it must have enough body to hold its shape softly.

Food Processor Note: To make the dough in a processor, first blend dry ingredients and chilled shortening briefly with on-off spurts, then, with the processor going, pour in the mixed liquids and blend again in spurts just until dough has massed. Turn out and knead briefly as described.

● Dough must now be used immediately.

Final baking
About 20 minutes at 400°F/205°C

About half an hour before you plan to serve, have the oven preheated and set rack in lower middle level. Then, with the contents of your casserole well heated, place the dough on a lightly floured work surface. Either pat it or roll it rapidly out to a thickness of about ½ inch (1½ cm), and cut it into the size and shape of your casserole top. Flour dough lightly, fold in half, then unfold over the rabbit, pressing dough lightly against the sides of casserole. (Brush off any excess flour from top of dough.) Paint dough with a coating of egg glaze, and set in oven. Bake for about 20 minutes, or until topping has risen nicely and browned on top.

● May be kept warm for half an hour or so, as long as casserole contents are kept below the simmer so rabbit doesn't overcook.

Serving

Serve right from the casserole, cutting down through the biscuit crust and including a nice piece of it at the side of each serving; baste the rabbit with a good spoonful or 2 of the sauce—and extra sauce and biscuits are nice to have on hand, too, as in the following suggestions.

For extra sauce

Either simmer the rabbit in a larger amount of liquid than you need, or make a separate sauce with the same flavorings—chicken stock enriched with a little beef bouillon, and simmered for half an hour with leeks, rosemary, fennel, wine, and garlic; then strain it if you wish, and thicken with *beurre manié* (about 1½ tablespoons each flour and butter per 1 cup or ¼ L liquid). Serve in a gravy bowl.

Buttermilk-Herb Baking Powder Biscuits:
For about 36 biscuits 2 inches (5 cm) in diameter

The same dough you used for the crust makes very nice biscuits, too—although if you are only making biscuits you may wish to cut the recipe in half.

Preheat oven to 450°F/230°C, and set racks in upper and lower middle levels. Make the dough as described in the crust recipe, and after its brief kneading on a floured surface, roll it out ½ inch (1½ cm) thick; use a 2-inch (5-cm) cutter to form the biscuits. Place them on lightly floured pastry sheets, leaving about 1 inch (2½ cm) between the biscuits. Gently knead dough into a ball after each series of cuttings, roll out again, and continue thus until all dough is used.

Bake at once in preheated oven for about 10 to 15 minutes, or until biscuits are nicely puffed and lightly browned on top. Serve as soon as possible, while they are hot and fresh. ❹ Biscuits may be kept warm, and leftovers may be frozen and reheated, but nothing has quite the taste of biscuits freshly baked.

Plain Buttermilk Baking Powder Biscuits—for Shortcakes:

This same formula, without the herbs, also makes a very fine biscuit, and is particularly recommended for strawberry shortcakes. In this case, you might want to add a tablespoon or so of sugar to the dry ingredients before the buttermilk goes in.

Snow Peas Tossed in Butter

For 6 servings

1½ to 2 pounds (¾ to 1 kg) fresh snow peas
About 4 Tb butter
Salt and pepper

Equipment:

A wok is especially useful here, but a large frying pan, preferably nonstick, will do; a long-handled spoon and fork for cooking.

To prepare the snow peas for cooking, pull the tips off and down each side to remove strings. Wash rapidly in cold water.

❷ May be prepared hours ahead of cooking; wrap in slightly dampened paper towels and refrigerate in a plastic bag.

Since snow peas cook so rapidly, it is best to do them really at the moment of serving so they will retain their fresh taste, texture, and bright green color. Melt 2 tablespoons butter in your wok (or frying pan) over high heat; when bubbling, toss in the snow peas. Toss and turn with spoon and fork constantly for several minutes, until the peas turn a bright green. Taste one as a test for doneness—it should be crisply tender. Sprinkle on salt and pepper, toss with another spoonful or so of butter, and turn out onto a warm serving platter.

Petits Vacherins

Individual meringue cases

For 10 cases, the 4-piece assembled kind

4 "large" egg whites (½ cup, or 1 dL plus)
¼ tsp cream of tartar
Pinch of salt
⅔ cup (1½ dL) sugar, preferably superfine
granulated—to be beaten in
1½ tsp pure vanilla extract
⅓ cup (¾ dL) sugar—to be folded in

Equipment:

Very clean and dry egg-white beating equipment
(see page 236 for illustrated details); a 12-inch
(30-cm) pastry bag with toothed tube opening
⅛ inch (½ cm) in diameter; 2 or 3 large
pastry sheets, preferably nonstick, buttered and
floured; a 3-inch (8-cm) cutter or any circular
marker

---

❷ The meringues will take about 2 hours to bake, in all, or you can start them in the evening for 1 hour, turn off the oven, and leave them there overnight to finish baking.
Oven Note: Gas ovens are more tricky for meringues than electric ones—perhaps, I suppose, because the gas surges on and off, coloring the meringues if you are not careful. You may find that 200°F/95°C is best in a gas oven, but that 225°F/110°C is right for an electric one. But you will judge that for yourself after a meringue session or 2—ideally meringues should hardly color at all; at most they should be only a light ivory when baked. They are, actually, not baking; they are only drying out in the oven.

Preliminaries

Prepare the egg-white beating equipment, pastry bag, and pastry sheets. With the cutter, mark circles on the sheets to guide you in forming the meringues. Preheat oven to 200°F/95°C—if you have 2 ovens, so much the better.

The egg whites and meringue mixture

Pour the egg whites into the bowl of your electric mixer (or into a stainless-steel or copper beating bowl). If egg whites are chilled, stir over hot water until barely tepid—they will not mount properly if too cold. Start beating slowly for a minute or so until they are foaming throughout, then beat in the cream of tartar (not needed if you are using copper) and salt. Gradually increase speed to fast and beat until egg whites form soft peaks. Continue beating while sprinkling in the sugar, and keep beating for a minute or more until egg whites are stiff and shining—a spatula drawn through them will leave a distinct path, which remains. Beat in the vanilla, then remove bowl from stand and fold in the remaining sugar by large sprinkles.

❶ Meringue should be used at once.

Forming the vacherins

You may from the *vacherins* all in 1 piece or in 4 pieces—a bottom and 3 rings that are baked then glued together with leftover meringue and baked briefly again to set. This latter method produces a so much better-looking meringue in every way that I shall describe it alone—and it takes about the same total time to bake as the 1-piece model.

Form 10 bottom disks in circle outlines on the baking sheets, then form 30 rings; the meringue should be about the thickness of your little finger or less. (Reserve 3 tablespoons meringue for gluing, later.)

Baking
About 1 hour plus 30 to 40 minutes

Set at once in oven or ovens, switching baking sheets from lower to upper racks several times, and watching that the meringues do not color more than a light ivory. Raise or lower oven heat if you think it necessary. Meringues are not done until you can gently push them loose—they will loosen when they have dried out and are ready to come off.

To assemble the cases, spread a thin coating of reserved meringue on the bottom of 1 ring, and set it on a bottom disk; continue with 2 more rings. Assemble all in the same way, and return to oven for another 30 to 40 minutes, until the meringue has dried and glued the pieces of the case together.

❷ Baked meringues may be kept in a warming oven for a day or 2 to prevent them from getting soggy, but the safest place for long storage is the freezer. You may take them directly from the freezer for filling and serving. If meringues are left out on a damp day they will soften and even collapse.

Fillings for Vacherins:

You may fill *vacherins* with fruits or berries; with whipped cream and a topping; with Bavarian cream mixture, which can then be chilled and set; or with ice cream and various fruit toppings. You can use either vanilla ice cream or a sherbet, and the *vacherins* can go back into the freezer until serving time—the meringue softens after a day or so, but is equally delicious either soft or crisp, at least that is what I think.

Peach topping

Use fresh peaches, or canned clingstones (more flavorful than freestone). For fresh peaches, slice them and sprinkle with a little sugar and lemon juice and let stand 10 minutes or so, until their juices have rendered out; drain the juices and simmer with a little arrowroot or cornstarch to thicken lightly. Taste carefully for seasoning, adding a few droplets of rum or Cognac if you wish, and fold in the peaches. Use the same system for canned peaches, although they will probably need no sugar—only lemon juice, thickening, and perhaps a few drops of liqueur.

Berry topping

Use the same system described for peaches.

❷ Timing

You do have some last-minute work for this menu, but not too much. Just before serving the main course, cook the snow peas—a matter of only 2 or 3 minutes. At this time too, if you filled and froze the *vacherins*, put them in the refrigerator so the ice cream will soften a little. If your ice cream is in bulk, however, it may need a good half hour in the refrigerator to soften—unless it is the nonhardening type.

Open the anchovies just before serving the Mediterranean platter.

Set the rabbit pie in the oven when you expect your guests to come; it can wait safely if need be. Baking time is 20 minutes or so, and you must mix and roll the dough right before it goes in the oven; but the dry ingredients can be mixed long beforehand.

Several hours before dinner, you can assemble the hors d'oeuvre platter, and wash, trim, and refrigerate the fresh snow peas. Now's the time to sauce the cheese, if you wish to, and to make the fruit sauces for the *vacherins*.

A day or 2 before the party, you can string the cheese (but not sauce it)—a longish job, so allow for that. At this time, you can make the rabbit stew. If you want to marinate the rabbit pieces, start from 6 to 24 hours earlier.

Several days beforehand, you can peel and sauce the peppers.

The meringues can be made anytime and frozen. Or you can keep them for several days in a very dry place; damp weather collapses them.

Menu Variations

Hors d'oeuvre platter: for other ways to use peppers, see pages 48-50. Instead of bread, serve the platter with pita pockets, so guests can make their own sandwiches (a recipe for homemade pita is in *J.C. & Co.*). If Syrian string cheese is hard to find, try julienned pieces of mozzarella or crumbled feta. Or you could use celeriac instead (see page 57). A somewhat similar hors d'oeuvre is a platter (or several small dishes) of cold, cooked vegetables in a vinaigrette dressing or *à la grecque*, page 348: ideal for the gardener-cook who might, in late summer, prefer to offer a leaf-lined basket of home-grown sliced melon.

The main course: cassoulet (see page 115), the farmer's joy and catchall, would be a hearty substitute for the rabbit pie. You can make this same dish with chicken, or with the garlicky duck ragout in *J.C. & Co.* Or leave the crust off and serve your rabbit stew over rice, or make a different rabbit stew, like the one with lemon in *J.C.'s Kitchen*. Or make a puff pastry crust by the new fast method in *J.C. & Co.*, or use the pâté crust here on page 245; see also the suggestions in the Q & A section, page 371. No other vegetable is quite like snow peas, except the recently developed sugar snap pea with edible pods and full-sized occupants; but green peas or broccoli flowerettes would be nice with the rabbit.

The dessert: instead of topping your ice cream-filled *vacherins* with fresh or canned peaches or berries (see the recipe), you could use chocolate sauce (page 370), or shaved chocolate. Or caramel sauce (see page 222), or simply use frozen raspberries or strawberries puréed in a blender or processor and, in the case of raspberries, strained. Stewed fresh rhubarb is another idea, as is a nut brittle that you have pulverized, or even our old favorite—a spoonful of rum or bourbon poured over the ice cream followed by a generous sprinkle of powdered instant coffee. For a supremely festive look and a delicious prickle on the tongue, you could swathe each little case with spun caramel, or cover each with a caramel cage, as in *J.C.'s Kitchen*. Or set a poached pear or peach (see page 216) in each *vacherin*, and top off with caramel, chocolate, or raspberry sauce. Or make the classic Mont Blanc, and fill each case with a sweetened purée of chestnuts forced through a ricer and surmounted by whipped cream. And so on, and so forth . . .

Leftovers (and Bumper Crops)

Hors d'oeuvre platter: though the anchovies are through for the day, all the other ingredients will keep for several days, well covered, in the refrigerator. For ways to use peppers, see page 48. If unsauced, already-strung string cheese keeps well when properly wrapped (see recipe), and is delightful used like feta (the soft, snowy Greek cheese) in salads and on other vegetable platters. Spare hard-boiled eggs, or egg pieces, can be sieved to top hot vegetables or salads (see the mimosa salad on page 214). Or you can stuff cherry tomatoes with egg salad.

The main course: rabbit quickly becomes stringy if overcooked, so if you want to reheat the stew, keep it below the simmer. The stew can be frozen, or used as a soup (bone and mince the rabbit pieces; add stock). And what about too many rabbits, the classic bumper crop? Australia solved the problem by importing mongooses, which prey on rabbits. More economical would be to find a butcher who rents freezer lockers. *Baked biscuits* can be frozen and reheated, though with some loss of texture. Raw biscuit dough doesn't keep; but see the recipe for ways to use it. *Leeks*: if you bought and cooked extra leeks, use them in quiche (see *Mastering I*), or a leek-and-potato soup (*Mastering I*, *J.C.'s Kitchen*), which you can turn into vichyssoise, or vary with watercress or celery; or serve your vichyssoise *à la russe*, with beets, as in *The French Chef Cookbook*. Extra raw leeks would be delicious braised, and you can serve them sauced and gratinéed (*Mastering I*). Any soup stock is improved by tossing in a leek. And they are delicous cold, *à la grecque* (page 348). *Snow peas:* reheated cooked ones lose their crispness; but extra raw ones will keep a few days wrapped in paper towels and refrigerated in a plastic bag, or invest in Irene Kuo's *The Key to Chinese Cooking* (New York: Alfred A. Knopf, 1977), for all the delicious Chinese ways of cooking them. Or adapt them to a soup designed for ordinary pea pods, in *Mastering II*.

The dessert: extra raw meringue must be used up promptly, and you could change to a large star or rosette tube and make one-squirt meringue kisses, to bake along with the *vacherin* cases. Once it's baked, meringue freezes well. You can even fill cases with ice cream (see recipe) and freeze them that way. But don't let baked meringue stand around in damp weather. Any fresh fruit toppings should be used quickly; they don't freeze well.

Postscript: Pecks of peppers

Why peel peppers, when they're so good with the skins on? They're lovely and crisp raw, in salads; unpeeled, they can be seeded, sliced, and sautéed with onions, or cooked with tomatoes, onions, and bits of ham for a *pipérade*, page 84, so delicious with eggs, hot or cold. You can cook and marinate them *à la grecque*, for a cold hors d'oeuvre, or serve a casserole of peppers and eggplant, with plenty of garlic and fresh basil in season. They can help to stuff beef rolls, or zucchini, and with leeks they make a fine soup. Even after publishing pepper recipes in all my previous books, I'm still exploring.

But a peeled pepper is another matter. You have to heat it to get the peel off, so the flesh is slightly cooked; but it has a flavor completely different from what you taste in, say, a baked stuffed pepper. It's very subtle and tender, with an exquisite texture, and the color remains very bright.

Peeling is worthwhile, but it's quite a job. Years after my peeling experiments for *Mastering II*, I did another series which brought me back to my original conclusion, that the broiling method (see the recipe) works best. To get others' views, though, in November 1978 I asked the helpful readers of my *McCall's* column for further suggestions. They offered several. 1) Dip the peppers in boiling water, then pop them into a paper bag for a few minutes. 2) Freeze, then peel. 3) Freeze, then put the frozen pepper in boiling water for 20 to 30 minutes, take off heat, leave for another 5 minutes, and wash with cold water before peeling. 4) Sauté them in a nonstick pan, with or without oil, for 10 to 20 minutes over a very low flame, covered; shake often to prevent sticking. 5) Drop the peppers into hot fat, then into cold water as soon as the skins change color. 6) Use a potato peeler on an untampered-with pepper, cutting it into strips first to make the job easier. 7) Hold a pepper over a gas burner with tongs, turning it to char evenly, then put it in a covered pan.

Covering the peppers after heating them was suggested by several readers, for varying lengths of time, anything from 10 minutes to several hours. I have not myself found it necessary to cover the peppers, since when properly broiled the skin comes off easily.

One suggestion has worked well with the red, mature peppers but less so with the green ones. That is to use a pressure cooker: wait till you see steam, then put on the gauge, bring just to full pressure, and turn off the heat, waiting till the cooker is cool before removing the peppers.

Peppers do vary a great deal, however. Though the broiler method has worked best for me, your peppers may be different; I hope you'll find that one of my correspondents' ideas will help. Just don't give up!

For those who didn't give up, and now find themselves with lovely peeled, sauced, peppers, here are a couple of good ideas for their use, and a recipe for a third. With pasta: either leave the pepper strips whole or chop them into dice, then toss them with hot cooked spaghetti or noodles, adding oil or butter, a good sprinkling of freshly grated Parmesan cheese, and salt and pepper to taste. With cooked leftover rice: make a delicious salad sauced with oil and garlic, and shallots; when you add the peppers, also add some minced parsley, chopped black olives, pine nuts, and what seasonings you fancy after tasting. And here is an excellent sauce to serve with hard-boiled eggs, or boiled fish, potatoes, beef, or chicken, or to use as a dip with cocktail snacks.

Pepper and Anchovy Sauce

For about 1 cup or ¼ L

**About ½ cup (1 dL) sauced green or red
     peppers, page 35**
4 to 6 anchovy fillets
1 or more tsp capers
1 or more cloves garlic, puréed
5 Tb or so fragrant olive oil
Salt and pepper
**Optional: fresh or dried herbs such as parsley,
     thyme, oregano, basil**

This is easy to make in a blender or processor. Put the
peppers in the container of the machine and, if anchovies
are packed in oil, add them as is along with some of their
oil. If they are salted anchovies, wash them off, split and
bone them, and you will probably need no more salt for the
sauce. Add the capers and garlic, and purée for several seconds or until smooth. Then begin adding the oil by dribbles
until the sauce is the consistency you wish it to be—I like
mine quite thick. Taste carefully for seasoning, adding aromatic herbs if you wish them, and parsley for a greenish
tinge, if such is your desire.
❂ Will keep several days, refrigerated in a covered jar.

Butterflied Pork
for a Party

Menu

For 6 people

Celery Root Rémoulade
French Bread

Butterflied Loin of Pork
Butternut Squash in Ginger and Garlic
Collards, Kale, or Turnip Greens

Gâteau Mont-Saint-Michel—
A mound of French crêpes layered with apples and burnt-almond cream

Suggested wines:

A dry white wine on the light side—Sancerre or dry riesling—with the first course; a light red like a Beaujolais or zinfandel with the pork, or a rosé, or even a sturdy white Burgundy or chardonnay; a sweet wine with the dessert, such as Sauternes, or a sparkling wine

Since fresh pork was "only served at family and bourgeois meals," Escoffier wrote in 1903, in his guide for professional cooks, he "would, therefore, give only a few recipes." Twenty years later, Edouard de Pomiane lamented that "pork is considered to be undistinguished, and at grand dinners one never sees a crisp-skinned pork roast or a fragrant *andouille*" (a hearty pork tripe sausage). Poor piggy, when he's so delicious. The tradition is as old as it is foolish; even the Old Testament, in Leviticus and Deuteronomy, calls him unclean and forbids us to eat him. Pigs do wallow in mud to get cool, but they love a fresh bath and they can be housebroken. (I knew of a very polite pet one, named Ointment.) Thoroughly nice, clean, well-conducted, respectable animals, and I side with open-minded de Pomiane, for whom even the humblest of pork dishes, grilled pigs' feet, was *un plat royal*. Quite right; it is.

Snobberies and shibboleths had no place in the happy world of this great teacher of cooking. Unlike Escoffier, de Pomiane was not a professional chef but a nutritionist, who published the book from which I quote, *Le Code de la Bonne Chère*, under the sponsorship of the Scientific Society of Alimentary Hygiene. It is prefaced with an apology to the great chefs. "Indeed," he says, "unlike them I have not catered to thousands of gourmets. For thirty years I have simply been preparing dinner for myself and my family, experiencing in my kitchen the same scientific and artistic delight I feel in my physiology laboratory, before my painting easel, or at my music stand when we play string quartets." Warmly pro-feminist, he found that the newly liberated, well-educated young women of France scorned cooking as too simple-minded, a hodgepodge of unrelated commonplaces to be learned by rote. Therefore, he taught cooking in a structured, theoretical way, in order to interest minds trained in logic. Yet his books are full of poetic descriptions. Vital, enthusiastic, imaginative, de Pomiane called gastronomy "the complete art" because it appeals to all the senses.

I wish I'd known him, and could ask him over to enjoy this party meal at our table. He would consider this dish to be unusual and distinguished, as indeed it is. In fact, it seems to me altogether appropriate for a state banquet. The only reason de Pomiane could find for the unposhness of pork was that it could be so filling as to blunt the diners' appetites for the courses to follow; but on a present-day menu, this argument doesn't apply at all. Certainly butterflying, roasting, and a final quick broil give this pork a sumptuous quality. The lean, even slices have a close grain like velvet, and carving takes only seconds. The herbal marinade accents a certain undertone in the flavor of fine pork, a subtle taste that is often lost if you accompany pork with applesauce or sauerkraut. And butterflied, it cooks in half the time of a bone-in roast. People are mistaken, by the way, if they think pork has to be cooked to bath-towel consistency in order to be safe. *Trichinae*—rarely found nowadays—are destroyed at 137°F/58°C, when the meat is rare. At 160°F/71°C, the meat has lost its pinkness and is an appetizing ivory color, and still full of juices.

The roast is prefaced by an hors d'oeuvre that is commonplace in Europe but less known here. Celery root—alias celeriac, knob celery, turnip-rooted celery, and in French *célerirave*—is simply a variety of celery that is grown for its great bulbous bottom rather than for its stalks. It's said to be easy to grow, and it keeps well through the winter after harvesting in fall. You can braise it in meat stock or chicken stock, or shred it and sauté it slowly in butter, or boil it and mash it with potatoes, or use it in soup for its intense celery flavor, but I think it is at its finest raw, cut into fine strands, and served up in a mustard dressing. (Most restaurants call it a *rémoulade* sauce, so I do; but a real *rémoulade*, a mustardy mayonnaise with capers and chopped pickles, would be too heavy and oily in this case.)

The squash and greens are for beauty as well as flavor. I'm fond of the sturdy greens, with a taste slightly more bitter than spinach, to offset the pork's suavity, and ginger seems to give winter squash more character, besides complementing the pork.

We'll have our apples after, not with, the pork; if the freezer is stocked with crêpes, a plumply layered gâteau is quick to make: a charming dessert, flavored with burnt-almond cream. To caramelize the exterior, I use my nephews' favorite kitchen implement, my indispensable blowtorch. De Pomiane, who learned to cook on a Bunsen burner, would have loved to play too.

Preparations and Marketing

Recommended Equipment:

To julienne the celery root, you really need a machine of some kind because it must be cut very thin. Some processors have disks with holes just the right size to produce strips the thickness of a rawhide shoelace. I find my little French rotary cutter, which comes with several disks, does a perfect job.

Check that you have a broiling pan, or shallow roasting pan, large enough to hold your big flat cut of pork. And if you haven't one already, I urge you to buy an instant, or microwave-type, meat thermometer—you'll have lots of use for it.

A nonstick frying pan with an 8-inch (20-cm) bottom diameter is needed for the crêpes; and be sure the inner surface of your baking-and-serving dish is that size or larger.

Staples to Have on Hand:

Table salt
Coarse or kosher salt
White peppercorns
Dried rosemary leaves
Dried thyme
Powdered allspice
Dijon-type prepared mustard
Pure almond extract
Pure vanilla extract
Olive oil
Optional: salad oil
Flour (preferably Wondra or instant-blending type)
Milk
Optional: light cream
Butter (3 sticks; 12 ounces or 340 g)
Eggs (5 "large")
Fresh parsley and/or chives
Lemons (1 or 2)
Dark Jamaica rum
Orange liqueur or Cognac
Sugar

Specific Ingredients for This Menu:

Sirloin half of a pork loin (about 7 pounds or 3¼ kg), bone in ●

Sour cream

Blanched, toasted, ground almonds (1⅓ cups or 3¼ dL) ●

Celery root (1 with a 3-inch or 8-cm diameter) ●

Optional accompaniment for celery root: green beans, or see Serving Suggestions following the recipe for Celery Root Rémoulade

Collards, kale, or turnip greens (about 3 pounds or 1350g) ●

Yellow butternut squash (about 2 pounds or less than 1 kg)

Large apples (12) ●

Garlic (about 7 large cloves)

1 small fresh ginger root

---

❷ Remarks:

Pork Loin: see the recipe later in the chapter for a picture and a detailed description of the cut you want. You may have to show it to your butcher. With lamb, a "butterfly" means the boned leg, so remind him you don't want leg, you want loin in one piece—the sirloin half of the loin, including the loin strip and tenderloin, the twelfth and thirteenth ribs, and the end of the hipbone. *Almonds*: for blanching, toasting, and grinding, see directions on page 366. Nuts stay freshest when kept in the freezer. *Celery root*: information about choosing and storing in the recipe that follows. I'm not talking about the root of ordinary celery, though the taste is similar. *Greens*: collards, kale, turnip greens, mustard greens, and beet greens—any of which will do—are usually more abundant during cool rather than hot weather. When buying any of them, look for firm, fresh, crisp, tender leaves; take a bite out of a few, to be sure the greens are quite tender and sweet, not old, tough, and bitter. Like spinach, they wilt down as they cook, and you will be using only the leafy parts, not the stems. So if they're leggy, you'll need more. *Apples*: buy Golden Delicious, or another variety that keeps its shape during cooking.

Celery Root Rémoulade

Finely shredded celery root in mustard and sour cream dressing

For 6 people as part of a cold hors d'oeuvre selection

2 to 3 Tb or more Dijon-type prepared mustard
2 to 3 Tb olive oil or salad oil (optional)
4 to 6 Tb or more sour cream
Droplets of milk or thin cream if necessary
Salt and white pepper
1 fine firm celery root about 3 inches (8 cm) in diameter

Equipment:

A medium-sized mixing bowl; a wire whip; a julienne cutter of some sort is really essential

---

A Note on Choosing and Storing Celery Root: Pick celery roots that are firm and hard all over; big ones are just as tasty as small ones as long as they look and feel whole and healthy. The ideal storage place is a cool dark root cellar, where they will keep throughout the winter and early spring. Those of us without such conveniences should wrap each celery root in a dry paper towel and store the celery roots in a perforated plastic bag (for air circulation) in the refrigerator, where they will keep nicely for a week or more.

When peeled, the flesh of a healthy fresh celery root has a strong and vigorous celery aroma; it is crisp and hard. Its color is creamy white with faint wandering lines of pale tan. As it becomes stale, the flesh darkens and softens.

The Sour Cream and Mustard Dressing:

Place 2 tablespoons of mustard in the mixing bowl, then beat in the optional oil and the sour cream; mixture should be quite thick and creamy. If stiff, thin out with droplets of milk or cream. Season well with salt and pepper; sauce should be quite strongly flavored with mustard, since it is the mustard that seems to penetrate and tenderize the celery.

Peeling and shredding the celery root

(Because the celery can discolor, you shred it the moment before saucing it.) Peel the celery root, using a short stout sharp knife and cutting just down into the white flesh all around. When you come to the creased portions at the root, slit down into the celery to remove them. At once cut the root into very fine julienne, and toss in the prepared sauce. (If you are doing several celeries, shred and sauce each as you go along, to prevent discoloration.)

❶ Sauced celery root will keep for 2 to 3 days refrigerated in a covered container.

Serving Suggestions—Celery Rémoulade Garni:

You can, of course, serve the sauced celery root as it is, or simply garnished with lettuce leaves or watercress. But I like to dress it up, as we have in this menu, with lightly colored fresh green beans and sliced tomatoes, seasoned sparingly with oil, lemon, salt, and pepper. However, depending on your menu, you could add quartered hard-boiled eggs and black olives, or even sliced salami or chunks of tuna fish or sardines to make a quite copious first course or main-course luncheon dish.

Pork Talk

Spiced Roast Pork Shoulder:

When I decided to do a menu around pork roast, I thought of a whole shoulder, which I prepared by removing the rind that it came with and slicing off all but a thin layer of fat. Then I put the shoulder in a dry spice marinade for 3 days. It weighed 5½ pounds (2½ kg), so I used 2 tablespoons salt and 1½ teaspoons of my mixed spices (described on page 239), rubbing salt and spices into the pork all over and packing it pretty airtight in a plastic bag. After its marinade I washed and dried it. Then I roasted it to 160°F/71°C in a 425°F/220°C preheated oven for 15 minutes to brown, and I finished it off at 350°F/180°C, which took some 2 hours in all. It was delicious, juicy, and tender. But that marinade was too reminiscent of our preserved goose, and I wanted a change—though I highly recommend it to you for pork chops as well as roasts; it gives pork a particularly succulent character.

Stuffed Pork Loin:

Then I said to myself, why not stuff a loin of pork, thinking it would have flaps like veal or lamb that could enclose a stuffing once the loin had been boned; but it doesn't have that kind of folding flap. Instead I cut crosswise slices from the top almost to the bottom of my boned loin so that each slice would be a serving. I made a delicious mixture of liver pâté, sausage meat, shallots, garlic, thyme, and Cognac, spread it over each slice, tied up the roast, set it in a pan with a sliced carrot and onion, and roasted it 1½ hours to the peak of perfection, as they say in the advertisements. But it didn't taste like pork anymore—it was good, but not porky. And it was tough! Why?

About Pork Quality:

I asked my butcher why my pork was tough, and all he could say was that sometimes pork is tough. It's got to be young enough, he told me, and the color should be pale, almost like veal. Several people I talked to said they'd run into a tough pork chop now and then. So our chief researcher, Marilyn Ambrose, got on the telephone to various authorities, including the National Live Stock and Meat Board people in Chicago. David Stroud, former president of the board, writes that the single most important factor in getting tender pork is the age of the animal—it should be under eight to ten months old; their ideal is to have all pork for the retail trade six months old. The second most crucial factor is the psychological state of the pig at the moment of slaughter: if it is worn out from traveling, or shocked, or scared, its endocrine glands begin working furiously and that alters the texture of the flesh. Now, if you have ever wondered why your pork chop was tough, you can tell for sure it came from an old and/or scared pig. But who knows if you can observe these signs at the meat counter?

After clarifying the toughness question somewhat, I got back to the idea of stuffing a loin, and back to the boning of one. It's easy to bone the sirloin half that contains both the tenderloin and the loin and a bit of the hip. Looking at that fine big boneless flat piece of meat, I said to myself, why even stuff it—why not cook it just like that? All spread out, butterflied, and slathered with a bit of marinade—garlic, rosemary, and oil. We'd done butterflied lamb, so why not pork? And a great idea it is, we found; it cooks in a little over an hour, roasted at first, on the inside side, then turned and browned under the broiler on the fat side. And carving is a breeze: you slice off the tenderloin strip, then slice up the tenderloin and the loin strip, giving you chunks for the tenderloin and neat large slices for the loin. As to flavor, it's some of the best pork I've ever eaten.

Temperature control

As noted, there is no excuse at all for overcooking pork, since *trichinae* are eliminated when the meat is still almost rare. I personally like my pork to be done at around 160°F/71°C, when it is possibly the faintest bit pink but more on the ivory side, and the meat has not lost its juice. The Meat Board recommends 170°F/77°C, as do some other sources. I think it is a question of personal taste, and you should try out various temperatures (over 140°F/60°C!) and make the decision yourself.

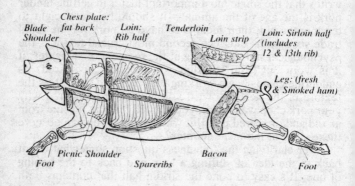

Blade Shoulder

Chest plate: fat back

Loin: Rib half

Tenderloin

Loin strip

Loin: Sirloin half (includes 12 & 13th rib)

Leg: (fresh & Smoked ham)

Foot

Picnic Shoulder

Spareribs

Bacon

Foot

Butterflied Loin of Pork
Roasted with an herb and garlic marinade

For 6 to 8 people, with leftovers

**The sirloin half of a pork loin (about 7 pounds or
     3¼ kg, bone in)
1 or more tsp coarse salt**

For the Marinade:
**2 or 3 large cloves garlic
2 tsp salt
½ tsp each dried rosemary leaves and thyme
⅛ tsp powdered allspice
About 3 Tb olive oil**

Equipment:
**3 skewers about 9 inches (23 cm) long (useful); a
     roasting or broiling pan large enough to hold
     meat easily and, if you wish, the bones too; an
     instant meat thermometer (recommended)**

Butterflying the pork loin (see illustrations on next page)

The full sirloin half of the pork loin includes the twelfth and
thirteenth ribs at the small end, the end of the hipbone at
the large end, the loin strip (the large eye of meat on one
side of the central bone) and the pork tenderloin, the long
conical strip that is small at the rib end and large at the hip
end of the loin (illustrated on page 60). To bone, cut down
the length of the backbone on the the tenderloin side, starting
at the small end, scraping always against the bone and not
against the flesh. The bone is shaped like a T; the flat top
is the fusion of vertebrae that form the backbone, and their
fat prongs go down into the flesh, separating the tenderloin
from the loin strip.

When you come to the large end, you will have to cut
around the hipbone (the only slightly complicated part of the
job); then cut around the fat prongs, going up under the T
and around it, to separate bone from flesh. Spread out the
meat, flesh side up, and cut out any interior fat. Turn it over,
and slice off all but a ¼-inch (¾-cm) layer of fat—or more,
if you wish, but the fat, which will be slashed and salted
near the end of cooking, makes a decorative top.

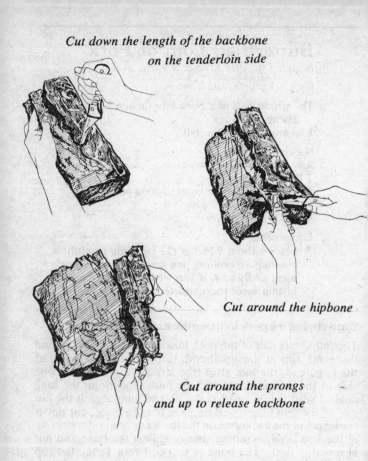

Cut down the length of the backbone
on the tenderloin side

Cut around the hipbone

Cut around the prongs
and up to release backbone

Marinating the pork
30 minutes to 24 hours

Peel the garlic cloves and purée with the salt. Grind the rosemary leaves, using a small mortar and pestle or small bowl and the handle end of a wooden spoon; add the thyme, allspice, and puréed garlic, then stir in the oil.

Spread out the pork, fat side down, and paint the flesh side with the marinade. Skewer the meat flat, if you wish, and place the pork, fat side down, in an oiled roasting pan.

❷ Pork may be prepared to this point a day in advance; wrap and refrigerate.

Preliminary roasting
About 1 hour at 375°F/190°C

Preheat oven in time for roasting, then set meat in upper third level. Roast the pork (and the bones too, if you wish), basting with accumulated juices in pan, for about an hour, or to a meat thermometer reading of 140°F/60°C. Remove from oven. (Bones will need 15 to 20 minutes more.)

❷ Preliminary roasting may be completed an hour before serving; set at room temperature, and cover with an upside-down bowl.

Final browning
About 10 minutes if done immediately

Pork is now to be turned over and browned on its fat side; either place it on another pan or scrape juices out of roasting pan into a saucepan. Turn pork fat side up.

Preheat broiler to very hot. Meanwhile, with a sharp knife cut crosswise slashes ¼ inch (¾ cm) apart down the length of the pork, and sprinkle with a thin layer of coarse salt. Place meat so its surface is 3 inches (8 cm) from heat source, to let it brown nicely and finish cooking. Meat is done (to my taste, at least) at an internal temperature of 160°F/71°C—when it is still juicy. It is a shame to overcook pork! (See notes on that subject earlier in the chapter.)

❷ The pork may be kept warm for half an hour or more in a warming oven at 120°F/49°C.

Carving and serving

To carve, cut off the tenderloin strip, going the length of the loin. Carve it into as many crosswise nuggets as you have guests, and pile at one end of your platter. Then cut the loin strip into crosswise slices. Skim fat off roasting juices, and spoon a little over the meat; pour the rest into a hot sauce bowl and moisten each serving with a spoonful. (The bones make nice finger food for tomorrow's lunch.)

Butternut Squash in Ginger and Garlic

For 6 to 8 servings

A yellow butternut squash (or other winter squash) of about 2 pounds (under 1 kg)
½ tsp salt
2 to 3 Tb butter (optional)
4 or more Tb meat juices (optional)
2 Tb each finely minced fresh ginger and garlic
More salt, and pepper
2 to 3 Tb fresh minced parsley and/or chives

Equipment:

A good vegetable peeler; a stout soup spoon; a vegetable steamer (optional)

Preparing the squash

Cut the squash in half lengthwise; scrape out the seeds and strings, digging in hard and close to the flesh. Remove outer skin with a vegetable peeler, going over the squash several times to expose the deep-yellow flesh. Cut the squash into strips, and the strips into thumbnail-sized dice. You will have about 5 cups (1¼ L).

❂ May be prepared ahead; cover and refrigerate.

Cooking the squash

You may steam the squash, if you wish, simply by putting it into a vegetable steamer set in a covered saucepan over an inch or so (3 to 4 cm) boiling water. Or you may boil it in a covered saucepan—my preferred method—as follows. Pour in enough water almost to cover the squash, add the salt and, if you wish, 1 tablespoon butter; cover and boil slowly for about 10 minutes, or until squash is just tender—do not overcook.

Whether you have steamed or boiled the squash, drain the cooking water into another saucepan and boil it down rapidly with the optional meat juices and, if you wish, 2 more tablespoons butter, plus the finely minced ginger and minced garlic. When well reduced and liquid is almost syrupy, pour it over the squash. Toss with the liquid and correct seasoning.

❷ May be cooked in advance. Reheat the squash (or set over a pan of boiling water to reheat or keep hot). Just before serving, shake and swirl pan by its handle to toss the squash with the herbs.

Variations with Rutabaga and Turnips:

Use the same method with rutabaga or white turnips, which also go beautifully with pork.

Collards, Kale, and Turnip Greens

As well as mustard greens and beet greens—whichever you decide to serve, they all cook the same way

How much to buy?

You'll have to judge by eye, remembering that greens, like spinach, wilt down considerably as they cook, and you will be using only the leafy parts, not the stems. A 10-ounce (285-g) bunch or package of trimmed greens should serve 2 people, but if they are leggy or long stemmed—?

Trimming the greens

So that the greens will cook quickly and retain their bright green color, you should remove all parts of the stems, going up into the leaves, where stems may be tough and woody. Discard any tough or withered leaves. Wash in several changes of cold water, drain in a colander, and if leaves are large, cut into chiffonade (thin strips).

Cooking

Heat a tablespoon or 2 of butter or oil in a large stainless-steel or nonstick frying pan or wok. Put in as many greens as will fit; turn and toss with a long-handled spoon and fork over moderately high heat until the greens begin to wilt (remove and add a second batch if you couldn't fit them all in the first time, then combine to finish cooking). Season lightly with salt and pepper and, if you are using it, toss in a clove of finely minced garlic (for this menu I would dispense with it because we have enough garlic elsewhere). Continue tossing and turning for several minutes until the greens are as tender as you wish them to be—you may have to add a few tablespoons of water, cover the pan, and steam them for a few minutes to complete the cooking; then uncover the pan and let the liquid evaporate. You may wish to toss them with a tablespoon or 2 of butter just before serving.

● Greens may be cooked somewhat in advance; set aside uncovered. Toss for a moment over moderately high heat before serving.

Gâteau Mont-Saint-Michel

A mound of French crêpes layered with apples and burnt-almond cream

Here is a delicious, dramatic, and very easily assembled dessert, once you have your crêpes—which can be waiting for you in your freezer. And you can make a gâteau of as many crêpe layers as you wish. The one suggested here will easily serve 8 people, perhaps more, depending on waistlines and appetites. It calls for a burnt-almond cream. And why is it called burnt *almond? Nobody knows. Why is black butter sauce called black when it is only brown?*

For 8 people

Batter for 8 eight-inch (20-cm) dessert crêpes:

¾ cup (1¾ dL) each milk and water
1 "large" egg
2 egg yolks
1 Tb sugar
⅛ tsp salt
3 Tb orange liqueur, rum, or Cognac
1 cup (¼ L) flour, preferably Wondra or
    instant-blending (measure by dipping dry-
    measure cup into flour container and sweeping
    off excess)
5 Tb melted butter

The Burnt-Almond Cream:

⅔ cup (1½ dL) sugar
1 stick (115 g) unsalted butter, preferably at room
    temperature
2 "large" eggs
1⅓ cups (3¼ dL) ground blanched and
    toasted almonds (directions on page 366)
½ tsp pure almond extract
½ tsp pure vanilla extract
3 Tb dark Jamaica rum
Pinch of salt

The Apples:

**About 12 large fine apples that will keep their
    shape while cooking, such as Golden Delicious
Juice of 1 or 2 lemons
Sugar, as needed
Melted butter, as needed**

Equipment:

**A nonstick frying pan with an 8-inch (20-cm)
    bottom diameter, approximately (for the crêpes);
    a baking-and-serving platter of a size to hold the
    crêpes when mounded; a jelly-roll pan or
    roasting pan for the apples**

The crêpes

Turn to page 132 for illustrated directions on how to cook, stack, and store or freeze crêpes. You will need at least 4, probably 6.

The burnt-almond cream

Beat all ingredients together in a bowl with a whip or beater, or in a food processor. If made ahead, stir over warm water to loosen, for easy spreading, before mounding the crêpes.

The apples

Quarter, core, and peel the apples, and spread in a buttered jelly-roll or roasting pan, tossing with as much lemon juice, sugar, and melted butter as you think appropriate. Bake for 30 minutes or so in a 400°F/205°C oven, tossing up several times, until tender.

❷ Crêpes may be made weeks in advance and stored in the freezer, as may the burnt-almond cream; the apples may be baked a day or 2 in advance, cooled, covered, and stored in the refrigerator.

Assembling the gâteau

Brush the inside of the baking-and-serving platter with a film of butter and lay a crêpe, best side up, in the center. Cover with a layer of apples, then several spoonfuls of almond cream, then a crêpe, pressing down on its center to spread apples out to the edge and to prevent the whole structure from humping in the middle as layers build up. Continue in layers until you have used all but a layer's worth of apples; end with the apples. Sprinkle lightly with melted butter and sugar.

❂ May be assembled even a day in advance; cover and refrigerate.

Baking and serving
About 30 minutes at 375°F/190°C

Bake in middle level of preheated oven until bubbling hot and apple topping has browned nicely. If it has not browned, set it under a moderately hot broiler for a moment, or use the professional pastry chef's blowtorch technique. Serve hot, warm, or tepid.

❂ May be kept warm for an hour or so covered on an electric hot tray, or in a warming oven.

Variation:
Giant Flip-Flop Apple Crêpe:

When you have only 2 or 3 people to serve, make them a giant flip-flop crêpe, which you can flame at the table, if you wish. Make the crêpe batter with just 1 egg, no extra yolks, and half the rest of the ingredients. Dice 2 or 3 apples that you have quartered, peeled, and cored, and sauté with butter, sugar, and a spoonful or 2 of rum or bourbon and perhaps a sprinkling of cinnamon—letting the apples caramelize a little in the pan. Choose a large nonstick pan, brush with butter, and set over high heat. When very hot, pour in a thin layer of batter, let it settle for a moment, then spread on the apples; spoon a layer of batter over the top, and cover the pan. When top of batter has set, in 2 to 3 minutes, it is time to brown it. Either turn by flipping it over in the pan and browning over high heat; or sprinkle lightly with melted butter and sugar, and set pan under the broiler, watching constantly, until crêpe browns lightly, in a minute or 2.

Slide it out onto a hot platter, and if you wish to flame the crêpe at the table, sprinkle with a little more sugar, pour over it several spoonfuls of hot Cognac or bourbon or rum, and ignite with a lighted match. Then spoon the flaming liquid over the crêpe for a few seconds while the flames die down. Serve in wedges.

❂ The cooked crêpe can wait, but it all goes so quickly that I think it best done at the last moment.

❷ Timing

This is what I'd call a mother-in-law dinner: impressive, fresh-tasting, sophisticated food with no last-minute fluster.

In less than 5 minutes, between courses, you can toss the two vegetables in their buttered pots, defat the meat juices, and slice the pork.

Since the pork and the gâteau can safely sit in a warming oven, your only job after the guests arrive is to take the previously arranged hors d'oeuvre platter from refrigerator to table.

Half an hour before serving, brown the pork under the broiler. If you don't have a separate broiler, it's safe to remove the baked gâteau from teh oven while the meat browns; it'll keep warm under an inverted bowl. Give the greens a preliminary cooking.

An hour before serving, set the gâteau in the 375°F/190°C oven, along with the pork, which has already been cooking for half an hour. (This gâteau doesn't mind sharing an oven, though a cake or a soufflé would.)

Several hours before dinner, cook the squash, for re-warming later. Do the squash first, and let its juices reduce while washing and trimming the greens. If you've having green beans and sliced tomatoes with the celery root, blanch the former and peel and slice the latter now, arrange your hors d'oeuvre platter, and refrigerate, covered with plastic wrap. Don't put the celery root on the platter till serving time, since the other vegetables would soak up some of its sauce, and you want contrast.

The day before your party, bone the pork and refrigerate in its marinade. You can assemble the gâteau now, and re-frigerate till baking time. The apples can be baked a day before this, and refrigerated.

Two days ahead, you can shred and sauce the celery root, which actually improves by keeping.

Any time at all, you can make and freeze the crêpes and the burnt-almond cream.

Menu Variations

Celery root: it's unique, and can only be had in the fall or winter months. What would be nice before the pork? Nothing rich like a pâté or quiche. What about the cold beet and cucumber soup, on page 82? Gazpacho, on page 235? A hot consommé sparked with a dash of Port wine, page 109?

Butterflied pork: this, too, is unique. Pork cooked by traditional methods (lots of recipes in *Mastering I*) tastes nothing like it. Butterflied lamb, which we did in *J.C. & Co.*, is delicious, but, again, quite different, and I think I'd want other vegetables with it.

Winter squash: you could use root vegetables as a substitute, like rutabagas or turnips or salsify (oyster plant). Or new potatoes.

Greens: you could use young beet or mustard greens, or chard (save the delicious chard stems for another dish), or spinach, broccoli, or Brussels sprouts.

Gâteau: like King Solomon when he was sick of love, I comfort me with apples all the time; all my books have apple desserts. I wonder how this gâteau would be with pears?

❷ Leftovers

Celery root: since it keeps very well in its mustard sauce, do make extra, and see the recipe for suggested garnishes.

Butterflied pork: it's excellent cold. Rewarmed, I think it's best in a sauce, either diced or ground, or perhaps sliced, but in any case heated *with* the sauce. If you just have scraps, they can be hashed or dropped into a soup (wonderful in a hearty bean or split pea soup).

Vegetables: Fine added to soup.

Gâteau: you can reheat it, or you can serve it cold. If you made extra crêpes, freeze them, and the same for almond cream, which you can use like hard sauce on hot desserts, as stuffing for a *pithiviers*, or in your own improvisations. It's a versatile kitchen staple.

Postscript: Learning to cook

As a penniless student at the Sorbonne, Edouard de Pomiane used to cook his own lunch in the laboratory, presumably over a Bunsen burner. Eventually he was caught in the act by his mentor and professor, who, instead of reprimanding him, appeared the next day with two chops and "a superb *gâteau feuilleté*" and asked de Pomiane to cook for two. De Pomiane describes the event:

"Where did you learn cooking?" he asked me.

"In your physiology course," I replied.

It was the truth. From his lucid teaching, I had learned what meat is. . . . I had heard him speak of the coagulation of albuminoids and the caramelization of sugars. . . .

"Why then," Dastre told me, "Brillat-Savarin was wrong in saying that 'one may become a cook but one has to be born a *rôtisseur*.' Anyone will know how to grill meat if he takes the trouble to think about what's going on during the grilling.'"

Think what you're doing is indeed a golden rule. Think not just about the why but about the how, for you can save a great deal of time by mastering routine processes. I was surprised the other day to find that one of the *J.C. & Co.* team, who has cooked for twenty years, had never really learned to chop parsley. She was holding the knife wrong, and, though the parsley did get chopped, it took ten minutes.

On the other hand, I didn't know until she told me that chopped parsley freezes perfectly. I'd just assumed it didn't, or just hadn't tried it . . . like the butterflied pork in this chapter. Butterflying is for leg of lamb, I thought, and thought no more. *Don't take things for granted*. Keep searching for better techniques, new applications, new ways of combining flavors. *Try things out*. One's imagination can play one false: the only real test is to taste.

Try things twice, and yet once more. "It has worked this way for me" is a valid judgment; you have to trust yourself and your experience. But be willing to test again and again— you may have done something just a shade differently the other time, and a little change in measurements or techniques can sometimes make a real difference. De Pomiane, in his classes, taught cooking as an exact and orderly science, but as an experimental science, too. In a laboratory, in theory if not always in practice, the constant factors can be controlled, so you can get a fair look at the variable; but that's not always true in a kitchen. As an example, it took me 29 trials to solve the mystery of a fresh strawberry soufflé. It worked fine one time, but it was far too fragile. The strawberries too often sank to the bottom of the baking dish, and finally I had to abandon the original recipe altogether and develop a quite different technique for keeping the strawberries suspended where they belonged.

Time yourself. Find out not only how long it takes you to accomplish a whole recipe, but also how much time you need to slice a pound of mushrooms or peel six tomatoes. The result of such self-awareness is order, efficiency, and composure. Some menus, especially those with several last-minute jobs (UFOs in Wine, for instance, on page 1), demand it of you.

Eat out. Drink good wine. It doesn't have to be often, but your palate becomes dulled, if you go too long without stimulus or without quality. That's when an otherwise excellent cook will begin to overseason.

Respect your work. Noncooks think it's silly to invest two hours' work in two minutes' enjoyment; but if cooking is evanescent, well, so is the ballet. As de Pomiane put it, "Gastronomy is an art, because in addressing our senses it refines them, and because it evolves, in turn, as a consequence of their refinement."

A Fast Fish Dinner

Menu

For 6 people

Cold Beet and Cucumber Soup
Fingers of Buttered Pumpernickel Bread

Monkfish Tails en Pipérade—Green and red peppers, onions, herbs, and garlic
Fresh Tomato Fondue (optional)
Sauté of Zucchini & Co.
French Bread

Cream Cheese and Lemon Flan
Cherries, Grapes, Tangerines, or Berries in Season

Suggested wines:

A strong dry white wine with the fish: Burgundy, Côtes du Rhône, chardonnay. You might also serve a sparkling wine or a gewürtztraminer with the dessert.

When a commercial fisherman hauls in his vast nets, all sorts of finny creatures tumble out; of these, many are edible and some, delicious. But only a few kinds ever turn up on ice at the fish store, and it's a shame. Among the missing until fairly recently was monkfish, also called anglerfish, goosefish, allmouth, molligut, and fishing frog; in French it's *lotte* or *baudroie*; in Italian, *rana* or *coda di rospo* (toad's tail); and its Latin name is *Lophius americanus*, for the American species, and *L. piscatorius*, for the European. European cooks consider it a delicacy; because of the great demand, it's expensive there, with much of it imported from our waters. Monkfish is a good resource in these days of inflation and scarcity. What you buy is thick, firm, snowy-white fillets, chunky things you halve or cut into steaks. Monkfish is a cook's delight because it is so adaptable; its firm texture suits it to dishes like bouillabaisse, and its mild flavor can be stepped up with sauces and marinades.

Quickly cooked fish is a shrewd choice for party hosts who will have to be out all day. For this light, attractive meal we chose a cold beet and cucumber soup and a cream cheese and lemon flan, parts of which can be made in advance, and the monkfish is accompanied with a beautiful platter of sliced and quickly sautéed vegetables. The fish is cooked with a *pipérade*, that classic combination of peppers, onions, and garlic; the juices are reduced and added to a fresh tomato sauce (recipe on page 383), making a pretty dish full of flavor. In Europe, monkfish is often mixed with lobster meat, whose flavor and perfume it absorbs, for an effect of vast opulence.

When we decided to cook monkfish for television, we asked our favorite fish purveyor to supply us with a whole one, not an easy trick since fishermen routinely cut off the edible tail (about one fifth of the total weight) and throw the rest of the fish overboard. But if anyone could procure a whole monkfish it would be he, one of the sons of a whole family of fish dealers. My request made him shout with laughter. But he found us the 25-pounder you see here.

Even in France, these fish are considered so terrifying to behold that dealers never display them, only fillets are shown. Nobody in the studio fainted, but everybody screamed when the incredible monster was wheeled in on a cart. Imagine a tadpole almost the size and shape of a baby grand piano, with strangely elbowlike jointed fins on either side, no scales, and skin as loose as a puppy's. Where the piano has keys, the fish has spiny teeth angled inward to form a giant bear trap, and more teeth in patches farther back, and still more under its upward-glaring eyes. The fleshy tongue is as big as your hand; the domed roof of the mouth is as hard as steel plating. Three little wands protrude from the top of the head; the tip of the foremost bears a tiny flap of flesh, the "bait," so called because so used. According to Alan Davidson in *Mediterranean Seafood* (Louisiana State University Press, 1981), the monkfish's "habit is to excavate and settle into a shallow depression on the bottom. By the time sand particles disturbed by this process have drifted down over the angler it is almost invisible...." It waits, motionless except for the "bait" fluttering in the ripples, just above the gaping maw. Any passing fish or diving bird might well think it was a tidbit floating there. Picture the awful scene!

In the stomach of one monkfish, observers found 21 flounders and 1 dogfish, all eaten at one sitting; in another, 7 wild ducks; in another, a sea turtle. Monkfish apparently don't attack swimming humans, but otherwise, as another fish book reports, "nothing edible that strays within reach comes amiss" to this Sidney Greenstreet of the ocean. The enormous mouth makes it possible for the creature to prey on fish almost its own size; one young 26-incher was found to enclose a 23-inch codling.

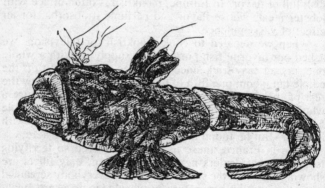

In this ferocious-looking 25-pound monkfish, only the tail is edible and prized.

The book that provides the above riveting facts is a sober-looking, scholarly volume called *Fishes of the Gulf of Maine*, by Henry B. Bigelow and William C. Schroeder (Washington: U.S. Government Printing Office, 1st revision, 1953). My edition is now out of print, but the book has been re-published by Harvard University (Cambridge: Harvard Museum of Comparative Zoology, special publication, 1972). My sources at the museum say there's lots of demand for it. Nothing could be a better sign for American cooks than an increased public interest in fish; it points toward an increased variety at the fishmarket.

Preparations and Marketing

Recommended Equipment:

You can chop the soup vegetables finely by hand, or in a vegetable mill, but a blender or food processor makes it a breeze.

For the fish and its *pipérade*, you need 2 large nonstick frying pans (or 1, if you make the *pipérade* early), and 1 cover of some sort. Another large frying pan, or a wok, is right for the zucchini dish, and a hand-held slicer or *mandoline*—or a very clever knife.

For the flan, I use a flan ring, foil, a baking stone, and a baker's peel or paddle, or a baking sheet, for sliding; but it can be cooked on a baking sheet or even in a pie pan in the usual manner.

Staples to Have on Hand:

Salt
White peppercorns
Sugar
Nutmeg
Italian or Provençal herb mixture
Pure vanilla extract
Horseradish, bottled or grated fresh
Wine vinegar
Olive oil
Chicken broth (1 cup or ¼ L; recipe for
     homemade on page 10)
Fish broth (1 cup or ¼ L), or more chicken broth
Butter
Eggs (4 "large")
Flour
Garlic
Shallots and scallions
Fresh herbs, such as dill, chives, parsley, chervil,
     basil
Yellow onion (1 large)
Carrots (2 or 3 large)
Lemons (2 or more)
Dry white wine or dry white French vermouth

Specific Ingredients for This Menu:

Monkfish fillets (3½ pounds or 1½ kg)
Heavy cream (½ cup or 1 dL)
Sour cream (1 cup or ¼ L, or more)
Cream cheese (8 ounces or 225 g) ●
Young white turnips (2 or more)
Parsnips (2 or 3)
Zucchini (2 or 3)
Cucumbers (1)
Red bell peppers (2 large) ●
Green bell peppers (2 large)
Beets (a 1-pound or 453-g can, or 5 large fresh) ●
Beet juice or bottled borscht (1 cup or ¼ L, or more)
Chopped walnuts (4 to 5 Tb)
Optional: ingredients for Fresh Tomato Fondue (page 239)

---

❶ Remarks:

Cream cheese: try to get the fresh kind, with no additives to glue it up, but plan to use it within a few days because it contains no preservatives. However, it freezes successfully, and the thawed cheese is fine for cooking. *Red bell peppers*: if you can't find them fresh, use canned or bottled pimiento, or tomatoes. *Beets*: if you plan to use fresh ones, please look at the Post-Postscript of this chapter for hints on their preparation.

Cold Beet and Cucumber Soup

With sour cream and dill, and buttered black bread

This is on the idea of a borscht because it is a beet soup. Otherwise it follows no traditions except the taste of its maker. I love fresh beets in season, but am delighted that canned beets have such good flavor and color; I find them excellent here.

For about 6 cups (1½ L)

3 or 4 scallions, or 1 or 2 shallots
1 cucumber, peeled and seeded
A 1-pound (453-g) can of beets, whole, sliced, or julienned, or 2 cups (½ L) cooked fresh beets, including some juice
1 cup (¼ L) or more beet juice or bottled borscht
1 cup (¼ L) or more chicken broth, fresh (see recipe on page 11) or canned
1 tsp or more horseradish, bottled or grated fresh
1 Tb or so wine vinegar
Salt and pepper to taste
For garnish: 1 cup (¼ L) or more sour cream and a handful of fresh dill sprigs (or chives or parsley)

Equipment:

An electric blender or food processor, or vegetable mill, or wooden bowl and chopper

---

With an electric blender or food processor, first chop the scallions, then all the rest of the solid ingredients with just enough of the liquids to blend—do not purée too fine; thin out to desired consistency with beet juice and broth; season to taste. Or, if using a vegetable mill, purée solids into a bowl with enough liquid for their passage (by hand, chop solids fine); blend in liquids and flavorings.

Chill several hours. Carefully taste and correct seasoning again, since it may need more after chilling. Serve in individual bowls, and top each portion with a spoonful of sour cream and a sprinkling of dill, chives, or parsley.

❷ May be made 2 or 3 days in advance of serving; store in a covered container in the refrigerator.

Monkfish Tails en Pipérade

Fish steaks simmered in herbs, wine, and red and green peppers

The firm, close-textured lean flesh of the monkfish needs a little extra cooking time to make it tender, and it wants to simmer with flavorful ingredients because it has no pronounced taste of its own. The hearty Basque combination here does the work it should, besides being wonderfully colorful to look at. Incidentally, this also makes a delicious cold fish dish, as noted at the end of the recipe.

For 6 people

The Pipérade Mixture:

2 large green bell peppers
2 large red bell peppers (if you have none, use tomatoes or pimientos as noted in recipe)
1 large yellow onion
2 Tb or so olive oil
2 or 3 cloves garlic, puréed
1 tsp or so mixed herbs, like Italian or Provençal seasoning
¼ tsp or so salt
Freshly ground pepper

The Fish and Other Ingredients:

3½ pounds (1½ kg) trimmed monkfish fillets
Salt, pepper, and flour
2 Tb or so olive oil
About 1 cup (¼ L) each dry white wine or French vermouth, and fish or chicken broth
Fresh tomato fondue (page 382), optional

Equipment:

1 or 2 large frying pans, nonstick recommended

Preliminary cooking of the pipérade vegetables

Wash, halve, stem, and seed the peppers, and cut into very fine long thin slices. (If you have no red peppers, you may use peeled seeded tomatoes, cut into slices and added when the green peppers go over the fish; or use slices of canned red pimiento.) Peel the onion, halve through the root, and cut into thin lengthwise slices. Film a large frying pan with the oil, add the sliced vegetables, and cook over moderate heat for 4 to 5 minutes while you add the garlic, herbs, and seasoning. Vegetables should be partially cooked; they will finish with the fish.

❷ May be done in advance to this point; let cool uncovered, then transfer to a bowl, cover, and refrigerate.

Preliminary sautéing of the fish

Cut the fish into serving chunks. Just before you are to sauté it, season all sides with a sprinkling of salt and pepper, dredge lightly in flour, and shake off excess. Into a second frying pan (or in the same one, if you have done the vegetables ahead), pour in enough oil to film it and set over moderately high heat. When very hot but not smoking, add the fish in one layer. Sauté for 2 minutes, then turn and sauté for 2 minutes on the other side—not to brown, merely to stiffen slightly. Spread the cooked vegetables over the fish.

❷ May be done several hours in advance to this point; let cool uncovered, then cover and refrigerate.

Final cooking
10 minutes or so

Pour in the wine and broth—enough to come halfway up the fish. Cover and simmer about 10 minutes. Fish is done when it has turned from springy to gently soft—it needs a little more cooking than other fish, but must not overcook and fall apart. Arrange fish and vegetables on a hot platter and cover. Rapidly boil down the juices in frying pan until almost syrupy, then spoon them over the fish, and serve, surrounded by the optional tomato fondue.

❷ Fish can wait, unsauced, 15 minutes or so on its platter; cover and set over a pan of hot water. Boil down the juices separately, drain juices from waiting fish and add to sauce, then spoon sauce over fish just before serving.

Variations on the Sauce—with Cream, or with Aïoli:
Because this menu ends with a cream cheese flan, I did not enrich the cooking juices. Two luscious alternatives, especially if you wish to accompany the fish with plain boiled rice—which goes nicely—are the following:

Cream. When you have boiled down the fish cooking juices until they are almost syrupy, dribble them into a small mixing bowl containing ½ cup (1 dL) heavy cream blended with an egg yolk. Return sauce to the pan and stir over low heat just until thickened lightly but well below the simmer. Pour over the fish and serve.

Aïoli. Another suggestion is to have a mixing bowl ready with 1 cup (¼ L) *aïoli*—thick garlic mayonnaise (page 376). Beat the boiled-down juices by dribbles into the *aïoli*, return to the pan to heat gently for a moment without coming near the simmer, then spoon over the fish and serve.

Monkfish en Pipérade Cold:

This recipe is also very good served cold, but you will need to strengthen the flavors. If you are planning to serve it cold, boil down the juices as described; season them highly with lemon juice, more garlic, salt, pepper, and herbs. Spoon sauce over the warm fish, and then let it cool. Serve with lemon wedges and black olives.

Or beat the juices into an *aïoli* garlic mayonnaise, as described in the preceding variation.

Sauté of Zucchini & Co.

A fast sauté of thinly sliced carrots, turnips, par-snips—and zucchini
Here is a lovely fresh vegetable combination, but while the vegetables may be cut in advance, they can be cooked only at the last moment or they wilt. However, the cooking is a matter of minutes only.

For 6 to 8 people

2 or 3 zucchini
Salt
2 or 3 large carrots
2 or more fine young white turnips
2 or 3 parsnips
2 Tb or more butter
Pepper
Minced fresh green herbs, such as chives, basil,
   chervil, parsley (optional)

Equipment:

A hand-held vegetable slicer is useful here—a food
   processor can't do the work neatly enough; a
   large frying pan or wok

Cut the tips off each end of the zucchini, and scrub but don't peel them; slice very thin crosswise—⅛ inch (½ cm). Toss in a bowl with a good sprinkling of salt, and let drain while preparing the other vegetables. Peel and cut all of them into equally thin rounds.

❷ Vegetables may be prepared several hours in advance; cover and refrigerate.

Just before serving, heat the butter in a frying pan or wok and add the carrots, turnips, and parsnips, tossing them almost continually over high heat. Meanwhile, drain the zucchini and dry in paper towels; when the other vegetables are becoming tender, add the zucchini. Toss for 2 or 3 minutes. Vegetables should retain a lightly crunchy texture. Season to taste, toss with a little fresh butter if you wish, and the optional green herbs. Serve at once.

Forming Tart Shells in a Flan Ring

An open-faced tart or flan encased in just its shell is always chic. The dough is formed in a bottomless ring that sits upon a baking sheet or, in this case, upon a thin sheet of foil placed upon a baker's peel, or rimless cookie sheet, or anything from which you can slide the flan ring and foil onto an oven baking stone.

Always be sure the dough is well rested and chilled, and work as rapidly as possible so that it will not soften and be difficult to handle. If it does soften, refrigerate everything—dough, flan, baking sheet—let chill for 20 minutes, and then take up where you left off.

Butter the inside of the ring and the foil or baking sheet. Roll out the dough to a thickness of 3/16 inch (scant 3/4 cm), and 2 inches (5 cm) larger all around than your flan ring. Here is how to form the dough.

1) Fold the dough in half, and the half in quarters. Set buttered flan ring on buttered foil or baking sheet, and position point of dough in center of ring.

2) Unfold dough and press it lightly against foil or baking sheet, and rest it against edge of ring. Then gently ease and push almost 1/2 inch (1 1/2 cm) of it down side of ring all around, to make its wall thicker.

3) Fold dough outward from side of ring, and roll pin over top of ring to cut off the excess dough.

4) Gently push the dough lining up from the edge all around ring, to make it stand about 3/8 inch (1 cm) above rim.

5) Press a decorative pattern all around top rim of dough with the back of a knife.

6) Prick bottom of dough, going just down through to foil or baking sheet, with a sharp-pronged fork to make tiny holes that will prevent pastry from rising during baking.

Cream Cheese and Lemon Flan

A cheesecake tart

This combination has more texture than a plain custard, and is moister than most cheesecakes I have known. I like it served slightly warm, or at room temperature, although it is good cold, too.

Manufacturing Note:

There is no requirement that you bake the flan on a pizza stone, as illustrated here. Form and bake it in a ring set on a pastry sheet, or in a pie tin, or use a frozen pie shell, or no pastry shell at all—just a baking dish. I developed the pizza stone system because I use one for baking French bread, pizzas, and pita breads; its hot surface gives a crisp brown crust without your having to prebake the shell before you fill it. No soggy bottom!

For a 10-inch (25-cm) flan, serving 10

A 10-inch (25-cm) dough-lined flan ring set on buttered foil (see manufacturing note above, alternatives at end of recipe, and dough formulas on page 370)

The Cream Cheese and Lemon Filling:

About 2½ cups (6 dL)

4 "large" eggs
¼ tsp salt
½ cup (1 dL) heavy cream
The grated rind of 1 lemon
4 Tb fresh lemon juice (or more if you like a very lemony flavor)
8 ounces (225 g) cream cheese, preferably fresh
4 Tb sugar
A pinch of nutmeg
1 tsp pure vanilla extract

For Top Decoration During Baking:
    4 to 5 Tb each sugar and chopped walnuts

Equipment:

**A pizza stone or oven griddle and baker's peel or a
baking sheet; an electric blender or food
processor is useful for the filling, or a vegetable
mill or sieve and wire whip**

Prepare the pastry dough in the flan ring and chill for 20
minutes. Meanwhile, either whisk up all the filling ingredients in a blender or food processor, or purée the cream
cheese through a vegetable mill or sieve, and beat in the rest
of the items with a wire whip.

❷ Both dough-lined ring and filling may be prepared hours
in advance; cover each and refrigerate.

Either Baking on an Oven Stone:
30 to 35 minutes at 425–350°F/ 220–180°C

Set pizza stone or oven griddle on a rack in the middle level
of the oven and preheat oven for 15 to 20 minutes to be sure
stone is really hot. Then slide out oven rack, slide flan and
foil onto stone (1), and pour in the filling to within ⅛ inch
(½ cm) of rim (2). (Do not overfill or you risk spillage during
baking.)

Bake for 10 minutes, or just until filling has set a little;
spread the sugar and walnut mixture over the surface (3).
Bake another 10 minutes, then lower oven temperature to
350°F/180°C. Flan is done when it has puffed and browned
lightly, and when bottom of crust has browned—30 to 35
minutes in all.

Serving

Remove flan from oven, let settle 5 minutes, then with flan
ring still in place, slide off foil onto a rack. Let cool to tepid
before serving. Or serve it cold.

❷ Flan is at its best when freshly cooked, but you may cover
and refrigerate the leftovers, and serve flan cold or rewarmed
the next day.

Or Baking in the Conventional Way:

I do think that if you are cooking a tart, quiche, or flan in a
pie tin or in a ring set on a baking sheet, you are wise to
precook the pastry before filling it. This will prevent the
crust from being uncooked or partially cooked on the bot-

tom. To do so, simply line the pricked raw dough-filled form with lightweight buttered foil, fill with dried beans or rice (which you keep on hand for this purpose), and bake at 400°F/ 205°C for 10 minutes, or until when you lift the foil you see the pastry has set. Then remove foil and beans, prick lightly again, and continue baking for 5 minutes or more until dough is just beginning to color and just starting to shrink from sides of mold. Then pour in the filling, and proceed to bake as in the preceding recipe.

❷ Partially baked pastry shells may be frozen.

❷ Timing

You'll need to be at the stove for about 7 to 8 minutes to cook the sautéed vegetables. If you don't want to spend that much time between courses, leave the root vegetables a bit underdone off heat, while you're having your soup; then add the zucchini and give the mixture a careful 2 to 3 minutes' sauté before serving it. Final cooking of the monkfish takes only 10 minutes, and can be done along with the vegetables or a few minutes earlier, since this dish can wait a little.

Otherwise, you have no problems at all. The soup, the *pipérade*, tomato sauce, and the pastry dough and filling for the flan can be made the day before your party; then you assemble and bake the flan late in the afternoon on the "day of." At that time you would cut the vegetables, while the flan bakes. Or you could make and freeze the *pipérade* and the flan dough far in advance.

In short, if you possess a food processor, this very festive meal can be executed in less than an hour's working time, comfortably broken into short bouts.

Menu Variations

Other cold *soup* recipes are discussed in "Picnic," page 229. There are many possible versions for beet soup and borscht.

Other firm lean white *fish* that can be cut into steaks are conger eel, cusk, and halibut. See also skate wings in black butter and caper sauce, in the Postscript. Tuna (or swordfish, which I much prefer) is good in *pipérade* or braised with lettuce, herbs, and wine (in *J.C.'s Kitchen*), or you could use bluefish. For other ways of cooking monkfish, see farther on.

This would make a wonderful summer meal, but you'd need to suit your *vegetables* to the season—zucchini, carrots, and cucumbers, for instance. The wok sauté of spinach and zucchini in *J.C. & Co.* is a summery thought.

A lemon *dessert* is a natural for a fish dinner. There are other lemon tarts (or flans) in *Mastering I* and *J.C.*'s *Kitchen*; if you want to make this light meal still lighter, what about a sherbet? Or, in between, a lemon soufflé?

And now for more monkfish!

Lotte à l'Américaine

Monfish steaks with wine and tomato sauce

This is a splendid combination, and one that though usually associated with lobsters is also traditional in France with monkfish. Start out in exactly the same way as in the original recipe, seasoning, flouring, and sautéing the fish steaks in oil. When the time is up you may, if you feel flush, pour in ¼ cup (½ dL) Cognac, let it bubble, then ignite it with a lighted match. Flame it away a few seconds, then douse it with the white wine or vermouth. Add the sautéed onion, and garlic, but instead of peppers use tomatoes—spread on and around the fish 2 cups (½ L) fresh tomato pulp and 2 tablespoons tomato paste. Use ½ teaspoon tarragon instead of mixed herbs. Cover and simmer 10 minutes, then remove the fish to a platter, boil down the sauce to thicken it, taste carefully for seasoning, spoon over the fish, decorate with parsley, and serve.

Broiled Monkfish

Since monkfish has no distinctive flavor of its own, I find it needs assistance when it is baked or broiled. I've had good success slicing a large fillet in half horizontally, so it will not be more than about ¾ inch (2 cm) thick. Then I paint it with a mixture of puréed garlic, salt, lemon juice, oil, and thyme, rosemary, oregano, or an herb mixture, and let it marinate for an hour or more before cooking it. I then like to sprinkle the top with a little paprika, broil it close to the heating element for 5 minutes or so, and bake at 400°F/ 205°C for another 10 minutes, basting it with a little white wine or vermouth.

Leftovers

The *soup*, since it keeps for several days refrigerated, is a good recipe to double. I think it loses a bit of its keen flavor if heated, but you might prefer it that way.

The *fish* dish is just as good cold as hot. If you bought extra monkfish, the recipe has variants, and there are two more in Menu Variations. As for *pipérade*, it is a splendid kitchen staple. Here in our recipe it is not fully cooked when it goes over the fish, but while you are at it you could double the amount of vegetables in the pan initially, use half for the fish, and continue cooking the rest until the vegetables are just tender. Then you can bottle and refrigerate or freeze it, and use it, for instance, to garnish an open-faced omelet, or bake it in the egg-and-cheese mixture for a quiche, or serve it as an accompaniment to pasta, hamburgers, steak, broiled fish, or chicken. It's wonderful to have a quick ready-made garnish on hand to dress up otherwise simple dishes.

The *vegetable* sauté is not reheatable, but it's fine in a soup.

Refrigerate the delicious *flan*, which is nice cold, and will keep for several days.

Postscript: Another odd fish

It's odd enough that a squash should behave like spaghetti, but how about a fish? When you eat skate, you don't just cut down through it; you draw your knife horizontally over the flesh, which promptly separates into long juicy white strands, slightly gelatinous and of the most delicate flavor. In Europe, it's tremendously popular, and savvy fish cooks here have always served it, but it should be more widely known. Especially so since skate are profuse in our waters— hideous creatures, cousins to the devilfish and the manta ray. The barn-door skate's flat diamond-shaped body is often 5 feet (1½ meters) long, but you'll rarely see a whole one. Only the wings, or side fins, of skate are eaten, and those generally sold weigh from 1½ pounds (675 g) each untrimmed. Several varieties, all very similar, are marketed here.

A story which keeps turning up in cookbooks is that skate wings are often cut into rounds and sold as scallops, or "mock scallops." It seemed unlikely to me, since scallop flesh is grained vertically, and skate horizontally—moreover, skate meat separates so readily when cooked. But I checked with two experts. George Berkowitz said that in his 30 years' experience in the fish business, he'd never seen it done. Bob Learson, of the National Marine Fisheries laboratory in Gloucester, Massachusetts, pointed out that the way cartilage is distributed in a skate wing would make the process impractical on a commercial scale. Both men dismiss the scallop story as an old wives' tale.

If you go fishing for skate, you'll have fun. They'll bite at any bait and fight like fury.

Having caught a skate or bought a piece of one, you give it special treatment. The skin is covered with a gluey wet film that should smell very fresh, not at all ammoniac, and you remove this by washing the wing in several waters. It should then be refrigerated overnight in water. My favorite way of cooking skate is to be found in a French classic, *La Cuisine de Madame Saint-Ange* (Paris: Larousse, 1958; now out of print, but there is a Swiss edition). Cook the wings of all skate the same way and for the same length of time, as their thickness doesn't vary with their breadth. Cut off the thin, finny, outer-fringe part of the wing with scissors, discard it, and lay the remainder in a high-sided pan like a chicken fryer, cover by at least ½ inch (1½ cm) with cold water, adding 5 tablespoons wine vinegar per quart (or liter), with 1 tablespoon salt, a small onion sliced thin, an imported bay leaf, a pinch of thyme, and 8 to 10 parsley stems. Bring just to the boil, turn down heat, cover, and let poach below the simmer for exactly 25 minutes. Carefully scrape the skin from each piece (it comes off easily), and return to the poaching water until you are ready to serve. I like it best with black butter sauce. For black butter, heat butter until it begins to turn medium brown; remove it from the heat and toss in a spoonful of capers. Sprinkle chopped fresh parsley over the skate, and watch it bubble as you pour over it the hot butter sauce. A wonderful dish.

Post-Postscript: Fresh beets

Fresh beets, with their dusty ruby-purple bulbs and dark green leaves that are ribbed in red, are available every month of the year but appear abundantly in most markets only between May and October. I must admit to quite a passion for fresh beets, with their full-bodied taste and hearty color. I feel I am eating something really worthwhile in the vegetable line, and indeed I am because beets are full of vitamins and minerals as well as flavor. As a matter of fact, plain cooked fresh beets are great food for dieters just because they are so nourishing, and they can be eaten as is, with no butter or oil or cream to fatten your calorie count. Thumbing through my handful of vegetarian cookbooks, by the way, I find among them no interest in beets. Why, when beets have so much going for them in every way?

Anyone who has lived in France remembers the large cooked beets at the vegetable stalls in the markets. You peel them, slice them into a vinaigrette with minced shallots, and surround them with watercress or *mâche* (corn salad, or lamb's lettuce, or *Valerianella olitoria*, which grows wild in this country but is cultivated as a salad plant in Europe). The beets you buy in France have been cooked in an oven, and they are much larger and probably older than ours because they presumably bake for 6 to 8 hours. In an old French book I consulted, I read that one should put the beets on a bed of wet straw, cover them with an upside-down earthenware bowl, and bake them until the skins are shriveled and even charred. The straw and the charring must give French beets their very special taste. (My book doesn't tell me what size of beet, nor what temperature of oven, but I have heard they used to be cooked in bakers' big ovens, after the bread for the day was done. It must, then, have been in a slow oven.)

Fresh beets can be boiled, baked, steamed, or pressure cooked. I like boiling the least because you lose color and, I think, a bit of flavor. Baking takes too long—2½ to 3 hours in a slow oven. Steaming works well, and the beets are done in about 40 to 45 minutes. Pressure cooking is my choice because it takes but 20 minutes, there is little loss of color, and the flavor is fine. I did not, by the way, find that baked beets had better flavor than steamed or pressure-cooked beets, but I had them in a covered casserole at 275°F/135°C along with a sample batch of individual beets wrapped in foil—had no straw on hand!

To prepare beets for cooking

Cut the stems about 1½ inches (4 cm) above the tops of the beets, snip off their tails about ¼ inch (¾ cm) below the bottoms, and be sure the bulbs of the beets are whole and unblemished—a bit of stem and a tight skin will prevent the vivid color and vital juices from escaping too much during cooking. Brush the beets clean under cold water.

Steamed Fresh Beets:
For young beets about 2 inches (5 cm) in diameter

Place prepared beets in a vegetable steamer or on a rack in a saucepan with 1 inch (2½ cm) or so of water, cover tightly, and steam 40 minutes, or until beets feel tender when pierced with a small knife, and peel loosens easily.

Pressure-cooked Beets:
For 2-inch (5-cm) beets

Place beets on rack in pressure cooker with ½ inch (1½ cm) water, and bring to full pressure. Cook for 20 minutes, then release pressure. (Somewhat smaller and somewhat larger beets will take the same amount of time, and slight over-cooking seems to do little harm.)

Some Ideas for Hot Fresh Beets:

Slice off the stem ends, peel the beets, and they are ready to serve in any way you choose. The simplest and one of the best ways is that of quartering or slicing them, then tossing in butter, salt, pepper, and perhaps a sprinkling of minced shallots or scallions, and parsley or chives. Serve them with chops, steaks, hamburgers, broiled fish, or broiled chicken.

Beets Gratinéed with Cheese:

Here is certainly one of the most delicious ways to serve hot beets, and especially recommended if you are having a meatless meal because beets and cheese make a full and almost meaty combination. The only drawback is looks— purply red plus the brown-yellow of the baked cheese—and I don't know how you get around that except to revel in the flavor.

Warm the cooked sliced or quartered beets in butter, salt, pepper, and a sprinkling of minced shallots or scallions, then simmer for 5 minutes or so with spoonfuls of heavy cream (a spoonful per beet would be ample). Arrange in layers in a shallow baking dish with a good sprinkling of cheese, either Parmesan alone or a mixture, and spread grated cheese over the top. Shortly before serving, set under a moderately hot broiler to let slowly heat through until bubbling, and the cheese has browned lightly on top.

These would go nicely with eggs, or broiled meats, fish, or chicken, or could be a separate course.

Some Ideas for Cold Fresh Cooked Beets:

Slice off the stem ends, peel the beets, and slice, quarter, dice, or julienne them. Simply toss them in a vinaigrette dressing (examples are on page 380), decorate with minced parsley and/or chives, and serve them alone, or with watercress or other greens, or with cold string beans, or with potato salad—but do not mix them with other ingredients until the last minute unless you want everything to be stained purple beet color. Serve as a first course, or with hard-boiled eggs, cold fish, or cold cuts.

Or serve them with a sour cream or yogurt dressing— blend into either one prepared mustard and horseradish to taste, season with salt and pepper, and spoon into a serving dish; arrange the beets on top, and decorate with parsley. Serve as a salad course or first course, or to accompany broiled or boiled fish or chicken.

Beet Greens—Beet Leaves:

The fresh leaves from a bunch of young beets make a fine green vegetable. Remove leaves from stems, cut leaves into chiffonade, very thin strips, and sauté in a frying pan or wok, as described on page 66—like kale or collards or turnip greens. I tried blanching beet greens, and found that the green color held up beautifully but the flavor was far less interesting than the plain sauté.

To Get Beet Juice Off Your Hands, Etc.:

Rinse your hands in cold water, then rub table salt over them; wash in cold soap and water, then in warm soap and water. (Salt helps to remove the red color—just as salt on a red wine spill will speed the washing.) Fingernails are another matter—I scrub them, then use cuticle remover solution, and scrub again. Use household bleach on your work surfaces for stubborn beet stains.

Cassoulet for a Crowd

Menu

For 10 to 12 people

Consommé au Porto
Toasted Armenian Cracker Bread

Cassoulet—Beans baked with goose, lamb, and sausages
Pickled Red Cabbage Slaw
Hot French Bread

Sliced Fresh Pineapple—En Boat

Suggested wines:

A hearty red with the cassoulet—Burgundy, Côtes du Rhône, pinot noir, zinfandel

Cassoulet, that best of bean feasts, is everyday fare for a peasant but ambrosia for a gastronome, though its ideal consumer is a 300-pound blocking back who has been splitting firewood nonstop for the last twelve hours on a subzero day in Manitoba. It feeds a lot of people and can be made a day or even two days in advance, with much preparation done even before that, so, when the Child household is expecting a horde of peasants, gastronomes, and blocking backs, cassoulet is what they'll get. Sunrise smiles break out as they come through our door, for the whole house is filled with a full-bodied, earthy fragrance. In every heart the joyous resolution forms: "I am now going to eat myself silly."

It's a mighty dish, with its fragments of rich meats, its golden-brown juice thick with starch from the beans, its top crunchy and flecked with green (and with bits of pork rind, if you decide to use it). But the great thing is the wonderful taste of the beans, which absorb and blend the complex savors of the well-seasoned meats. And there is a mysterious charm in how, by long cooking, a stony little white bean becomes pale amber, redolent, swollen, velvety. Eating one bean at a time, crushing it against the palate, you could make a career of, and some cassoulet buffs apparently do.

Many of us have been privileged to witness the uproarious kangaroo court that all bystanders rush to join whenever one French motorist so much as nudges another. If you can imagine this in full cry for two centuries, you will know what is implied by the Great, Ancient, Passionate, 98 Percent Fact-Free Cassoulet Controversy that still rages unabated. Three neighboring hill towns north of the Pyrenees in Languedoc define this small battleground, but the hullabaloo is audible all over the world. The January 1979 issue of the *International Review of Food and Wine* neatly summarized and simplified the conflicts of the past as follows: "In Castelnaudary, the legend goes, the dish was invented, and therefore a 'pure' version is served. The haricots are cooked with chunks of fresh pork, pork knuckle, ham, pork sausage, and fresh pork rind. In Toulouse the cooks add Toulouse sausage and either *confit d'oie* or *confit de canard* (preserved goose or duck), while in Carcassonne chunks of mutton are added to the Castelnaudary formula, and, during the hunting season, an occasional partridge too." Clear enough, but in the course of their research the authors of this article, William Bayer and Paula Wolfert, soon found that "these regional distinctions are now completely blurred, and that cassoulet, like life itself, is not so simple as it seems."

Mr. Bayer and Ms. Wolfert had traveled to the battlefront for a restaurant tour, with the sensible object of reporting not on the "original" cassoulet or the "definitive" one, both mythical anyway, but simply on the versions they liked best. Their favorite turned out to be a radical-revisionist one using *fresh* beans, favas. I recommend their article to admirers of sound, felicitous food writing as well as to cassoulet fanatics, who will enjoy pondering both the unusual fava formula and another Toulousain type that turned out, after much sampling, to be the authors' favorite of the traditional recipes.

My own current version, the fourth I've developed, is a selection and synthesis of traditional methods and components, but in fact you can use almost anything you have handy in making cassoulet, and I'm sure the cooks of Languedoc have always done likewise. So why fuss? Partly, I think, because the instruments so inspire the imagination that any creative cook is periodically compelled to reorchestrate them. And partly because a fuss is a very French way to have fun.

My efforts have tended toward a progressively lighter and leaner dish, as I see looking back at the recipes in *Mastering I*, *The French Chef Cookbook*, and *J.C.*'s *Kitchen*, which has a quickie version using lentils. Even so, this cassoulet remains hearty indeed. What to eat with it is no problem, since its full flavors need no rounding out or complement. You just want something assertive for contrast and, given the main dish's rather stolid quality, something very light. Nothing sharpens appetites like a perfect, crystalline consommé, and with that I like the crackly crunch of store-bought Armenian flatbread, crisped in the oven. For a juicy crunch, and for an offset to stodge, suavity, and succulence, the cassoulet is accompanied here by pickled red cabbage and hot French bread. Fresh pineapple, honey-sweet but with that haunting acid tang, is an ideal dessert if you can find fruit that were harvested when perfectly ripe. (For clues, and a bit of debunking, see Remarks later in this chapter.)

Some cooks say they serve cassoulet only to joggers and only at midday, so they can run it off before bedtime. I like it any time at all, but especially on the eve of that movable and dire feast (joke) which opens the Season of Nemesis. Hail, Cassoulet! We who are about to diet salute you.

*Cassoulet country centers around Toulouse, Carcassonne,
and Castelnaudary.*

A Note on Beans and Intestinal Motility:

Intestinal motility is polite gobbledegook for flatulence, which
in turn means gas. What about that problem and beans? It
seems, according to scientists at the Western Regional Center in Albany, California, that beans contain the difficult-to-

digest sugars, stachyose and raffinose. The human body does not have the enzymes to break them down, and when these culprits reach the lower intestine of some diners, their resident bacteria react violently, producing gas or, in a word, motility.

The good news, however, is that these same scientists have discovered you can boil 1 cup (¼ L) beans in 10 cups (2½ L) water for 3 minutes, soak them for 10 hours or overnight in the same water, drain and rinse them, and set them to cook in fresh water. This, they assure us, eliminates 80 percent of the trouble.

P.S.: This account came from a newspaper report, but in later correspondence with Alfred Olson, leader of the U.S.D.A.'s bean study group, he writes that he has changed the word "motility"—although he likes the sound of it, he is not sure of its accuracy in this connection, and has regretfully substituted the more prosaic but possibly more safely descriptive "trouble."

Preparations and Marketing

Recommended Equipment:

For clarifying the consommé, you need sieving equipment—cheesecloth for lining an 8- to 10-inch (20- to 25-cm) sieve, a colander to rest the sieve over, and a bowl into which the consommé can drip freely.

For the cassoulet you need a 6-quart (6-L) flameproof baking-serving dish or casserole. You will want an 8-quart (7- to 8-L) pot in which to boil the beans before they go into the casserole.

For preserving the goose you'll need a big bowl or crock in which the cut-up goose pieces may sit during their salting, and something the size of a preserving kettle or stockpot for rendering the fat and then for cooking the goose. If you plan to put the goose down for storage in its own fat, you will want a crock or bowl large enough to hold the cooked goose pieces, and to fit into your refrigerator, plus a rack that will fit in the bottom. A deep-fat-frying thermometer is useful here.

To shred the red cabbage very fine indeed, a shredding or sauerkraut cutter is useful, or a very sharp knife and a practiced hand. The knife is also needed for the pineapples.

Marketing Note: If you are to preserve your own goose for this menu, you will be starting from twenty-four hours to several weeks in advance, so I have marked the items for goose preservation with an asterisk on the lists.

> Staples to Have on Hand:
>
> Salt
> *Optional: coarse or kosher salt or sea salt
> Black peppercorns
> *Special spice mixture (page 381) or ground
>   allspice and thyme
> Mustard seeds
> Juniper berries
> Imported bay leaves
> Optional: dried tarragon
> Tomato sauce (page 382) or tomato paste
> Beef stock or bouillon (at least 3 cups or ¾ L)

Meat or poultry stock, or a mixture of canned
   chicken broth and canned consommé (2 quarts
   or 2 L)
Optional: more stock or consommé (1 cup or ¼ L)
Butter or cooking oil
Yellow onions (3 large)
Dry white wine or dry white French vermouth
Optional: white rum, kirsch, or savarin syrup
   (page 307)
Port wine
Red wine vinegar

Specific Ingredients for This Menu:

* Optional: saltpeter (from a pharmacy)
* "Roaster" goose (10 to 12 pounds or 4½ to
   5½ kg) or preserved goose (3 pounds or
   1350 g) ●
Cooking sausage, like kielbasy, chorizo, or
   sausage meat (1½ to 2 pounds or 675 to 900 g)
Bone-in lamb shoulder (about 4 pounds or 2 kg),
   sawed into stewing chunks
Optional: salt pork, fat-and-lean type, with rind
   (1 pound or 450 g)
* Fresh pork fat and/or lard (about 1 pound or
   450 g)
Dried white beans (2 pounds or 900 g) ●
Red onion (1 large)
Parsley (1 large bunch)
Optional: fresh mint
Garlic (1 large head)
Red cabbage (1 head fresh; about 1½ pounds or
   675 g)
Optional: sweet red bell pepper (1 large)
Optional: small quantities of aromatic vegetables
   like celery, onion, leek, carrot
Tart apples (4)
Pineapples (2 to 4, depending on size) ●
Canned beet juice, or borscht (½ cup or 1 dL)
Egg whites (5)
Nonsweet white French or Italian bread (½ loaf)

❷ Remarks:

Preserved goose (*confit d'oie*), if you don't want to make your own, may be bought in cans at the fancier "gourmet" shops. If you can't get it, don't give up having cassoulet, as several substitutions are possible (see Menu Variations). *The goose*: you will probably have to buy it frozen, and geese freeze well when kept properly, at a constant temperature below −5°F/−20°C for no more than six months. Defrost it either for several days in the refrigerator (in its plastic package), or in a tub of cold water (in its package), where it will take 4 to 5 hours. Plan to use it within a day of its defrosting. *Dry white beans*: I use the medium bean, Great Northern, but small white pea beans will do nicely, too. *Pineapples*: I have learned so much myself, since our encounter with them preparing this dinner, that I think they deserve a special place here. Now, praises be, thanks to modern refrigeration and fast transportation, it is possible to buy field-ripened fresh sweet pineapple anywhere in this country. As a matter of fact, if it was not picked ripe in the first place, it will not ripen at all because of the way the pineapple is built: the fruit gets its nourishment from the stump of the plant on which it grows, and when the starch in the stump turns to sugar, the sugar moves up into the fruit and that is what ripens and sweetens the pineapple. Once it is cut off from its stump, its sugar supply ceases, and it cannot, physically, get any sweeter. It will lose some of its acidity if you keep it for a few days at room temperature, but its sweetness— or lack of it—was predetermined the moment it was picked. Obviously, then, we need good pickers in those pineapple fields, and we want to buy from shippers who know their pickers, and from merchants who are well aware of the whole pineapple syndrome. As usual, it is up to us, the buying public, to heckle our markets into providing us with the fine, ripe, large, sweet pineapples that they can procure for us— and they can, we know it.

But how to tell, when buying a pineapple in a strange place, that it is sweet and ripe? First, you'll have your best luck in full pineapple season, when they are at their peak, from April through June. Color is no indication of ripeness, because a fine sweet specimen can vary from green to greenish yellow to yellow. Pulling a green leaf out of the crown doesn't mean a thing, nor does the sound of the thumping thumb. Probably the best test is the nose test—does it smell sweet like a nice ripe pineapple? Aroma can be difficult to pick up if the pineapple has been chilled, but a faint perfume should exude even so.

Choose the largest fruits you can find—the bigger they are, the more flesh. The whole fruit should look fresh and healthy, with no leaking juices, bleary eyes, or soft spots. The crown of leaves should be freshly green and smartly upstanding. If the pineapple does not seem quite as ripe as it could be, keep it in a shady spot at normal room temperature for a few days, which should help it lose some of its acidity. Then, when it smells ripe (but do not let it soften and spoil), refrigerate it in a plastic bag, and plan to eat it as soon as you can.

By the way, when you have sliced up your pineapple but left the crown intact, you can plant the crown and grow yourself a pineapple plant. Slice off the top ½ inch (1½ cm) with the crown of leaves, says our gardening expert Jim Crockett, and scrape out the flesh. Let the crown dry in the sun for 2 weeks, then plant it in potting soil 2 inches (5 cm) deep and leave in a warm sunny place. Keep it barely moist and it will grow and produce a baby pineapple—presumably even if you have a black rather than a green thumb.

Clear Consommé au Porto

The term "a clear consommé" means a perfectly clear, see-through sparkling dark amber liquid. It is a rare meat stock, bouillon, or canned consommé that can meet these requirements, and if you want them you will have to clarify a soup yourself. It's a quite magical process anyway and a most useful one to know when you need not only a perfect consommé, but aspic to coat a cold fish or a chicken or a poached egg.

For about 2 quarts (2 L)

2 quarts (2 L) meat or poultry stock, or canned chicken broth and canned consommé
Salt and pepper as needed
5 egg whites
Optional for added flavor: 4 Tb each minced celery, onion, leek if available, carrot, parsley stems, and ½ tsp dried tarragon
1 cup (¼ L) dry white wine or dry white French vermouth, or another cup of stock
4 Tb or more Port wine

Equipment:

A large sieve lined with 5 thicknesses of washed cheesecloth, set over a colander set over a bowl (colander must be large enough so its bottom will not rest in the consommé to come); a ladle

Before you begin, be sure that your meat stock, homemade or canned, is thoroughly free of fat or grease, and same for all of your equipment—otherwise your clarification may not succeed.

Bring all but 1 cup of the stock to the simmer in a large saucepan; correct seasoning. Meanwhile, whip the egg whites lightly in a bowl and mix thoroughly with the 1 cup stock, optional flavoring ingredients, and wine. When stock is simmering, dribble 2 cups (½ L) of it slowly into the egg whites, beating all the while. Then beat the egg white mixture into the pan of hot stock. Set over moderate heat and, stirring slowly but reaching everywhere throughout the liquid with a wire whip, bring just to the simmer. Do not stir again. (Stock is constantly stirred so that egg whites will be thoroughly distributed and will draw to themselves all the cloudy particles in the stock, until simmer is reached.) Set saucepan at side of heat and let it almost simmer at one point for 5 minutes; rotate the pan 1/3 turn and let almost simmer another 5 minutes; rotate again, and repeat the process. (This coagulates the egg whites so that they will have enough body to hold themselves back when stock is strained.)

Gently and carefully ladle stock and egg whites into the lined sieve, letting the clear liquid drip through undisturbed. When dripping has ceased, remove straining contraption to another bowl and gently squeeze cheesecloth to extract a little more. If it is perfectly clear, pour it into the rest. Continue, stopping when the slightest suggestion of cloudiness appears.

Pour the Port wine into the clear soup by spoonfuls to taste, and the consommé is ready to serve or to reheat.

❷ May be prepared in advance. When cool, cover and refrigerate or freeze.

Jellied Consommé:

For each 3 cups (¾ L) of consommé desired, soften 1 envelope (1 Tb) plain unflavored gelatin in ¼ cup (½ dL) cold soup or white wine or vermouth. Then heat it with ½ cup (1 dL) or so consommé until completely dissolved; stir into the rest of the consommé. Chill until set, then spoon into chilled consommé cups.

Aspic:

Use the same system as above for making aspics, but with the following proportions. However, always test your aspic consistency before using: pour a little aspic into a saucer, chill until set, then fork up and leave for 10 minutes at normal room temperature to see how it holds. These few minutes of caution may save you from disaster.

For simple aspics
1 envelope (1 Tb) gelatin for each 2 cups (½ L) consommé
For lining a mold
1 envelope (1 Tb) gelatin for each 1½ cups (3½ dL) consommé

Preserved Goose

Confit d'oie

In the old days before anyone had heard of refrigerators and freezers, and even before the invention of canning, you had to preserve meats in some manner to last you through the lean months. For meats, a typical method was first to salt them, then to cook them slowly in fat, and finally to put them down in fat. In French that process was known (and still is) as a *confit*, which comes from the Latin *conficere*, to digest—and that, in a way, is what salt does to meats and sugar to fruits; the fat holds the cooked food in hermetically sealed suspension. A *confit* is a primitive form of canning.

Why bother doing it nowadays, then, when we have modern preserving methods? Well, it has a special character all its own, just as corned beef and sausages have their own special tastes. And, if you don't want to cook a whole goose, you can turn part of it into a ragout, and preserve the rest in a *confit*. Then, for people who love to cook it's fun and interesting to do, and a wonderful resource to have in one's refrigerator, since it is ever ready to furnish forth an unusually fine emergency meal.

Fat Note: This type of preserving sounds as though it would result in very fatty meat, but the contrary is true because the fat renders out of the goose skin as it cooks, and the goose meat, which is lean anyway, does not absorb the rendering fat. You can skin the goose after cooking, and dip each piece into hot broth or even hot water to dissolve and remove all of the clinging preserving fat. Goose fat, however, is a delicious commodity for use in frying potatoes, flavoring vegetables, basting meats, and it keeps for months in your refrigerator—or may be used again and again for preserving more geese, ducks, pork, and so forth and so on.

For Salting the Goose—24 hours:

A 10- to 12-pound (4½- to 5½-kg) "roaster" goose

4 to 5 Tb coarse or kosher salt, sea salt, or regular salt

⅛ tsp saltpeter (from a pharmacy; optional)

½ tsp special spice mixture (page 381) or the following: ⅛ tsp pepper and a big pinch each juniper berries, allspice, thyme, and bay leaf, all finely ground

For Rendering Fat and Cooking Goose:

6 to 8 cups (1½ to 2 L) fat—goose fat and fatty skin, plus fresh pork fat and/or lard (more if needed)
1 cup (¼ L) water

Equipment:

A large crock or heavy plastic bag to hold the goose pieces and something to weight them down during maceration; a large kettle or saucepan for rendering fat and cooking goose; frying thermometer for testing fat useful; a crock or bowl fitted with a rack for storing goose

Cutting up and salting goose
(24 hours)
Remove wings at elbows, and cut goose into drumstick, thigh, wing—lower breast, and breast-with-bone pieces; chop breast into three crosswise pieces. Chop up carcass, neck, and wings, and save for a stock (see page 114) or soup; heart and peeled gizzard can go into the *confit*, or into a stew (gizzard peel into soup); liver can be used like chicken liver.

Mix the salt, optional saltpeter (for preserving rosy color), and spices in a bowl; rub into all sides of goose. Pack goose pieces into crock and weight down with a plate and canned goods or other heavy objects; or pack into a bag, squeeze out air, and tie closed, then weight down in a bowl. Leave for 24 hours.

❷ You may leave it a day or 2 longer—but if you want to keep it for several weeks, triple the salt and spices, and remember to soak the goose pieces overnight in cold water to remove excess salt before using.

Rendering the fat
About 1 hour

Meanwhile, cut fat and fatty skin pieces into rough slices and place in kettle over moderate heat; add the water and cover the kettle to let the fat liquefy and render out slowly—20 to 25 minutes. When it has rendered, skin pieces will begin to brown; watch fat temperature from now on. Fat must remain a clear yellow; temperature should not go over 325°F/165°C. When skin pieces are a light golden brown the fat has rendered; dip them out with a slotted spoon or sieve, and drain fat drippings back into kettle. (Save pieces and turn into cracklings; see end of recipe.)

❷ Fat may be rendered in advance. When cool, cover and refrigerate.

Cooking the goose
About 1½ hours

When you are ready to cook the goose, rub off the salt with paper towels, and liquefy fat if it has cooled and congealed. Place goose in kettle with fat; goose pieces will swell slightly as they cook, and skin will render more fat, but the pieces should be covered by liquid fat at all times. Add lard, if necessary. Start timing when fat begins to bubble, and maintain temperature at 200 to 205°F/95 to 96°C. Goose is done when meat is tender if pierced with a sharp-pronged fork.

To preserve the goose

The goose is delicious, hot and just cooked, as is, or allowed to cool and eaten cold. To preserve, remove goose pieces from fat and arrange them in a crock, wide-mouthed jar, or bowl that has been fitted with a rack—goose pieces should not rest on the bottom because you want liquid fat to surround and protect them. (Dry twigs, bark removed, work perfectly well here instead of a rack.) Bring the cooking fat to the simmer and let cook until it stops spluttering—5 minutes or so—indicating any liquids have evaporated. Pour it through a strainer, lined with several thicknesses of cheesecloth, over the goose pieces. Shake crock gently to allow grease to flow throughout, and when goose is completely covered, let cool and congeal. Pour on more fat if any pieces protrude. Cover with plastic wrap and refrigerate.

❷ The goose will keep at around 37°F/3°C for 3 to 4 months or longer.

Removing pieces of goose

To remove goose pieces, set container in a bowl of hot water until fat has softened, then remove as many pieces as you wish. Cover the rest completely with the fat, and store as before.

Goose Fat:

Goose fat, as previously noted but it bears repeating, will keep for months in a covered jar in the refrigerator. Use it for sautéing potatoes, for basting roasts, for cooking such earthy items as cabbage, dried beans, turnips, or for cooking more *confit*.

Cracklings—Residue from the Rendering of Fat:

You may toss the bits of browned skin, left from fat rendering, in a sprinkling of salt, pepper, and either allspice or special spice mixture (page 381), and serve either as a cocktail snack or along with the cassoulet. Or chop them fine, warm briefly in a frying pan with the seasonings, pack into a jar, and cover with a thin layer of hot goose fat; seal top with plastic wrap and refrigerate—for use as a cocktail cracker spread (known in French as *frittons* or *grattons*).

Goose Stock:

To make a stock out of the chopped-up carcass, wings, neck, and gizzard peelings, place in a large saucepan with a peeled and quartered onion, a carrot, a small leek if you have one, and a celery stalk with leaves. Pour on cold water to cover ingredients by 2 inches (5 cm), salt lightly, and add an herb bouquet (6 parsley sprigs, 1 bay leaf, 1 garlic clove, 4 allspice berries, and ½ tsp thyme). Bring to the simmer, skim off gray scum, which will continue to rise for several minutes, then cover loosely and simmer 2½ hours, adding more water if liquid evaporates below level of ingredients. Strain, let cool, then refrigerate; remove congealed fat from surface when chilled. Use for soups and sauces, or combine with other stock for the consommé earlier in this chapter.

❂ Will keep several days under refrigeration; may be frozen for several months.

Preserved Duck, Turkey, Pork, and Small Game Such as Squirrel and Rabbit:

Treat any of the above as you would goose, cutting the meat into serving pieces before salting it and simmering it in rendered pork fat or lard.

Cassoulet

Beans baked with lamb, goose, and sausages

For a 6-quart (3-L) casserole, serving 10 to 12 people

For the Beans:

To make 3½ quarts or 3¼ L cooked beans

5 cups (2 pounds or 900 g) dry white beans—Great
    Northern or small white
4½ quarts (4 L) water
1 pound (450 g) fat-and-lean salt pork with rind
    (optional)
1 large yellow onion, peeled and sliced
1 large herb bouquet (8 parsley sprigs, 4 cloves
    garlic, ½ tsp thyme, and 2 imported bay
    leaves, all tied in washed cheesecloth)
Salt as needed

For the Lamb:

About 4 pounds (2 kg) bone-in lamb shoulder,
    sawed into stewing chunks
Rendered goose fat, or cooking oil
2 large onions, sliced
4 or 5 large cloves garlic, minced
½ cup (1 dL) tomato sauce (page 382), or 4 or 5
    Tb tomato paste
½ tsp thyme
2 imported bay leaves
2 cups (½ L) dry white wine or dry white
    French vermouth
3 cups (¾ L) or more beef stock or bouillon
Salt and pepper

Other Ingredients:

About ½ the preserved goose in the preceding
    recipe, and the cracklings
1½ to 2 pounds (675 to 900 g) cooking sausage
    such as kielbasy or chorizo, or sausage meat
    formed into cakes
3 Tb or more rendered goose fat or melted butter

2 cups (½ L) moderately pressed down, fresh
    white crumbs from crustless nonsweet French or
    Italian bread
½ cup (1 dL) moderately pressed down minced
    fresh parsley

Equipment:

**An 8-quart (7- to 8-L) kettle or pressure cooker for
the beans; a medium-sized casserole or chicken
fryer for the lamb; a 6-quart (6-L) flameproof
casserole for baking the cassoulet**

The beans

Pick over the beans to be sure there are no stones or other
debris among them, wash and drain them, and place in a
large kettle or in the bottom of a large pressure cooker. Add
the water, cover, and bring to the boil. Boil uncovered for
exactly 2 minutes. Cover and let sit for exactly 1 hour. (This
takes the place of the old-fashioned overnight soak.) Meanwhile, if you are using salt pork, remove the rind, and cut
the pork into slices ½ inch (1½ cm) thick; simmer rind and
pork in 3 quarts (3 L) water for 15 minutes to remove excess
salt; rinse in cold water, drain, and set aside.

As soon as the beans have had their soak, bring to the
simmer again, adding the optional pork and rind, the onion,
the herb package, and 1 tablespoon salt if you have not used
salt pork—½ tablespoon if you have. Either simmer slowly,
partially covered, for about 1½ hours or until the beans are
just tender (add boiling water if needed, to keep beans covered at all times, and salt to taste near end of cooking). Or
pressure cook as follows: cover and bring to full pressure
for exactly 2 minutes; remove from heat and let pressure go
down by itself for 15 minutes, then remove pressure knob;
taste, and add salt as necessary.

❹ The beans may be cooked 2 or 3 days in advance; when
cool, cover and refrigerate. Bring just to the simmer before
proceeding with the cassoulet.

The lamb—braised shoulder of lamb

Dry the lamb pieces. Film casserole or chicken fryer with
fat or oil, heat to very hot but not smoking, and brown the
lamb pieces, a few at a time, removing those that are browned

to a side dish. Pour out excess fat, and brown the onions lightly. Then return all lamb to casserole, add the garlic, tomato, herbs, and wine or vermouth, and enough stock or bouillon just to cover the lamb. Salt lightly to taste, cover, and simmer slowly for about 1½ hours, or until lamb is tender. Carefully correct seasoning; when cool, remove and discard bones from lamb.

❷ May be cooked several days in advance; when cold, cover and refrigerate the lamb in its cooking liquid. Discard congealed surface fat before using.

Assembling the cassoulet

Remove bones from preserved goose and, if you wish, the skin; cut goose into serving chunks about the same size as your lamb pieces. If you are using salt pork, cut it into thin slices. If you are using sausage such as kielbasy, cut in half lengthwise, then into chunks, and brown slightly in a frying pan with goose fat or oil. If you are using sausage meat, form into cakes about 1½ inches (4 cm) across, and brown in fat or oil.

With a slotted spoon, dip beans from their liquid (be sure to save it) and arrange about ⅓ of them in the bottom of the casserole you have chosen for the cassoulet. Cover with a layer of lamb, goose, sausage, a handful of goose cracklings and, if you are using it, half the salt pork. Repeat with a layer of beans and of meat; end with a layer of beans, coming to within about ¼ inch (¾ cm) of the rim of the casserole. Ladle on the lamb-cooking liquid plus as much bean-cooking liquid as needed just to cover the beans.

❷ May be assembled a day or even 2 days in advance, but if the beans and lamb have not been freshly cooked, be sure to bring them to the simmer for several minutes before assembling, to prevent any possibility of spoilage. When cool, cover and refrigerate.

Just before proceeding to cook, spread bread crumbs and parsley over the top—if they go onto a warm cassoulet and the dish is then covered and set aside the crumbs could sour. Baste with a spoonful or so of goose fat or melted butter.

Warning on refrigerated cassoulets

The assembled cassoulet nneeds a good hour of baking so that all elements can combine deliciously together, thus the contents of the casserole must be decongealed and simmering before the actual baking effect can begin. Heating on top of the stove can be risky because you may scorch the bottom of the beans. I suggest, then, that the casserole be covered and set in a 325°F/165°C oven for an hour or so until its contents are bubbling; test center with a thermometer if you have any doubts—it should read 212°F/100°C. Then proceed with the baking in the next step. (I have had my troubles in this category, thinking that, because things were bubbling in the oven, the cassoulet was baking properly when it was just cooking around the edges but had not really heated through.)

Baking
About 1 hour

Preheat oven to 400°F/205°C. Bring casserole to simmer on top of the stove (or see preceding paragraph if casserole has been refrigerated), then set in oven. Bake for 20 to 30 minutes, until bread crumb topping has crusted and browned lightly; break the crust into the beans with the back of a spoon, and return the casserole to the oven. Lower thermostat to 350°F/180°C, and continue baking for another 15 minutes or so, until a second crust has formed itself on top. Break it, in turn, into the beans, and if cooking liquid seems too thick or the beans dry, add a spoonful or so of bean-cooking liquid from your pot. When the crust forms again, leave it as is; the beans are ready to serve.

❶ The beans will stay warm in a turned-off oven, door ajar, for a good half hour, or you may keep them warm on an electric hot tray. They will gradually dry out if kept too warm for too long a time.

Pickled Red Cabbage Slaw

*You can't treat red cabbage like green cabbage, I
have found, at least if you want to serve it raw. It
needs to be very finely shredded and wants a maceration of a day or 2 in a solution of salt and
vinegar to tenderize it; being a red vegetable, it must
have some acid with it anyway to keep its color.
The following is, I think, a refreshing way to serve
it, being neither too sharp nor too picklelike, and a
fine accompaniment to the likes of a cassoulet.*

For about 2 quarts (2 L)

**A good fresh red cabbage weighing about 1½
pounds (675 g)**
A large red onion
A large sweet red bell pepper (optional)
2 to 3 cloves garlic, minced
4 imported bay leaves
1 tsp mustard seeds
½ tsp juniper berries
½ cup (1 dL) canned beet juice, or borscht
1 cup (¼ L) red wine vinegar (more if needed)
2 cups (½ L) water (more if needed)
2 Tb salt (more if needed)
1 Tb sugar
4 tart apples
4 handfuls minced fresh parsley

Equipment:

**A cabbage shredder, such as a mail-order
sauerkraut cutter, or other device, or an expert
person with a very sharp stainless-steel knife
(carbon steel can turn the cabbage blue)**

Discard wilted outer leaves, halve and quarter the cabbage,
and cut out the core. Cut cabbage into shreds as thin and
fine as possible—¹⁄₁₆ inch (¼ cm); do the same with the
onion and optional pepper. The finer and thinner you cut
the vegetables, the more efficiently the flavors can penetrate
and tenderize the cabbage and the more successful your

relish. Toss in a bowl with the garlic, bay, mustard, juniper, and beet juice or borscht. Bring the vinegar and water to the simmer with the salt and sugar, pour over the cabbage, and toss to mix well. Pack into a 2-quart (2-L) jar. Liquid should just cover ingredients by a finger width—add more vinegar and water in the proportions of 1 part vinegar to 2 parts water if necessary. Cover and refrigerate, turning jar upside down several times for the first 2 days; taste, and add a little more salt if you feel it necessary. The relish should marinate for 2 days at least.

When ready to serve, dip out as much of the relish as you think you will need, and for every 2 cups (½ L), blend in 1 minced apple and a handful of parsley.

❹ The cabbage will keep for at least several weeks under refrigeration, and the pickling juice may be used over and over again—just add more seasoning if you think it is needed.

Sliced Fresh Pineapple—En Boat

In its shell

For 10 to 12 people

2 of the largest, ripest, sweetest, and finest pineapples available (or 3 or even 4 smaller pineapples)
Sprigs of fresh mint, if available
White rum or kirsch, or savarin syrup, page 309 (optional)

Equipment:

A very sharp, long heavy knife for slicing the whole pineapple; a smaller very sharp flexible knife for other cutting; a platter upon which to serve the pineapple

---

Cutting and Slicing Note:

While trying things out for the television show depicting this dinner, all of us cooks had a hand in cutting pineapples. We used the coring gadget. We tried a long knife. We shaved off the peel all around and spiraled the eyes out of a pineapple. And we even butchered another pineapple trying a half-remembered system of somebody's grandmother, who, it was said, cut diamond wedges around each eye, slanting into the pineapple so each wedge could be pulled out individually—the pineapple collapsed halfway through. We all preferred the following.

Cut the pineapple in half, being very careful when you come to the crown to keep it attached to the fruit—for decoration later. Then cut the halves into lengthwise halves or thirds. Cut out the hard core at the top of each wedge; with a sharp flexible knife, cut close against the skin to free the wedge of flesh. Then, if the wedge seems a bit wide, cut it in half lengthwise before cutting it crosswise into wedge-shaped slices. Replace the slices on the skin—or boat—and arrange attractively on a platter with, if you wish, sprigs of fresh mint.

❷ If not to be served promptly, cover closely with plastic wrap and refrigerate.

As you serve the pineapple at the table, and particularly if it is not as sweet as you could wish, you might drizzle a few drops of rum or kirsch, or savarin liqueur-flavored syrup, over each wedge.

❷ Timing

Last-minute planning won't work for a cassoulet party, obviously, but the nice thing is that there are practically no last-minute *jobs* with this menu.

Half an hour before sitting down, put the cracker bread in the oven to crisp for 5 minutes (careful it doesn't scorch), set the consommé on the stove ready to heat, and check the cassoulet. If it is done, turn off the oven.

Whether it should be 1½ hours or 3 hours before you intend to serve the cassoulet that you put it in the oven depends on whether or not it was made ahead and refrigerated. Since how long it simmers is crucial to its final flavor, please see the discussion of that important matter in the recipe itself, page 117.

Sometime in the afternoon, or even that morning, cut and refrigerate the pineapple, closely covered with plastic wrap.

The day before your party, or even the day before that, assemble the cassoulet. That same day, buy the pineapples, and maybe some parsley to garnish the red cabbage.

The day before *that*, in other words up to three days before your party, cook the lamb and the beans, and make and cook the sausage if you're doing your own. (There's a good recipe for homemade sausage meat in *J.C. & Co.*) You could preserve the goose now, if you had thought to buy and defrost your bird 2 or 3 days beforehand; then you could cook the *confit* while you were braising the lamb—the goose needs a 24-hour salting before it cooks, however. But you can cook a *confit* months ahead and "put it down"—that's the point of it anyway, to have something marvelous and waiting.

As much as 2 weeks beforehand, you can pickle the red cabbage, but it does need its jar tipped once or twice for the first 2 days.

Clarify the consommé any time at all, and keep it in the freezer.

Menu Variations

If you weren't having a fruit dessert, you could move your pineapples up front and, rather than consommé, serve them sliced with prosciutto, or use some other fruit for your *first course*. I love a plain chilled half grapefruit or melon—a perfect specimen. Just be sure you have something light before cassoulet; shellfish seem to me too bland and too meaty, somehow. You want piquancy.

The *cassoulet* can be infinitely varied. Bearing in mind that the dish was not conceived in a fancy restaurant with bought-to-order ingredients, do experiment with whatever you have on hand. Some of your combinations will, of course, be better than others, and some you may decide never to try again. You can use sausages only, or roast or braised pork instead of lamb, or duck or turkey instead of (or along with) goose, or ham hocks or veal shanks, or such small game as squirrel or rabbit. You can use other kinds of dry beans, or lentils, or even fresh beans. I've never tried limas or Kentucky Wonders, but you might. One item you must have, however, is a good cooking stock of some sort to pour over the beans and give them real flavor during their final baking. As for a vegetarian cassoulet, how about lots and lots of garlic, onions, tomatoes, herbs, and perhaps the sautéed eggplant on page 189?

Not too many accompaniments occur to me as good substitutes for the *pickled red cabbage*. Sauerkraut is a possibility, or coleslaw, or you might like a chiffonade salad—lettuce with sliced cooked (preferably pickled) beets and a light sieving of hard-boiled egg, for that sweet-sour taste. Or you could try sliced cucumbers, lightly wilted with salt, then drained well, tossed in a little lemon juice with a few grains of sugar and some finely chopped red onion, and sprinkled with parsley.

For *dessert*, pineapple does seem ideal to me; but you could serve ice-cold very ripe persimmons, Persian or honeydew melon, or sliced oranges, plain or with blueberries, as on page 17, or perhaps glazed, as in *Mastering I*, or perhaps a sherbet. If you had a first course of fruit, a coffee granita (the large-crystal sherbet) might be nice. Here's a last-minute trick we tried and liked after one cassoulet dinner: if you have a food processor, use the steel blade and

dump in frozen sliced peaches cut in chunks plus ⅓ their
volume of Champagne and drops of lemon juice; process,
sugar to taste, and process again. The whole thing takes two
minutes and gives you a sherbet of perfect ready-to-eat consistency.

❹ Leftovers

A fully cooked *cassoulet* can be reheated and is very good,
but usually not quite as good as after its first baking. Be sure
it is moist enough; add a little stock if it's not. Or you can
turn the remains into a soup: mince the meats (slicing the
sausage) and add them to the beans, puréed in stock.

When you have made your own *preserved goose*, you
have a splendid kitchen staple on hand, in fact several. The
fat can be re-used many times, if you don't overheat it, and
is delicious for preserving other meats, or for frying. The
goose stock, like any stock, can become a consommé or can
go into soups, sauces, and stews, and can of course be frozen. If you have *cracklings* to spare, you can treat them as
suggested earlier in the chapter and use as a cocktail cracker
spread. The preserved meat is delicious cold: dip the pieces
in boiling stock or even boiling water to remove fat, and you
may also wish to discard the skin. Season lightly and roll in
a mixture of finely chopped parsley and shallots. Serve with
potato salad, watercress, or curly endive with a garlic and
bacon dressing, or with a hearty mixed vegetable salad. If
you're having a pot of beans, lentils, sauerkraut, braised
cabbage, or the like, you can bury the goose pieces in the
beans or cabbage and let them warm up for 8 to 10 minutes
before serving. Or you can add pieces of preserved goose
to a boiled dinner or *pot-au-feu*, giving them 4 to 5 minutes
to simmer with the meats, just before serving. (They do get
stringy if overcooked, so be careful.) Or you can roll the
goose pieces in seasoned bread crumbs, baste with droplets
of goose fat, and let warm under a slow broiler for 4 to 5
minutes on each side, or until hot through and tender. Serve
with a purée of turnips, potatoes, parsnips, dried beans or
lentils, or braised onions, celery, or leeks, or with sauerkraut
or braised cabbage, or with Brussels sprouts or broccoli.

The *pickled cabbage* will keep for weeks in the refrigerator, and may be used hot as well as cold; wouldn't it be

nice in a sizzling Reuben sandwich? And you can re-use the pickling juice when you run out of cabbage.

Pineapple doesn't keep long. You can serve leftover bits the next day with other cut-up fruit (strawberries especially), or use it instead of crackers with cream cheese and guava jelly or Bar-le-Duc preserve. With slices of prosciutto, it makes a sublime first course, and dieters, as we all know, mix it with their penitential low-fat cottage cheese. But don't try freezing it or putting it in an aspic: no go.

Postscript: They're funny that way

Cassoulet de Castelnaudary, Cassoulet de Toulouse, Cassoulet de Carcassonne...they're all good, and so's the cassoulet I've just described. So too are any number of variants. For most of us, which cassoulet we make or concoct depends on what looks good in the market. For the peasant cooks who probably thought up the dish in the first place, it most certainly depended on what was available. Fresh meat would have been used if an animal had just been slaughtered; otherwise, before the invention of refrigeration, every Mrs. French Peasant had to rely on what she had preserved. If she raised geese for a cash crop of *foie gras*, using only the livers, then *confit d'oie* would take care of the liverless gaggle. At hog-killing time, salting and the making of "summer" (keeping) sausage would preserve any meat not eaten fresh. From *confit d'oie*, she could progress to *confit de canard* if she raised ducks. Dry beans keep and they, like other legumes good for cassoulet, can be grown almost anywhere.

Certainly cassoulet's earthy simplicity, its lack of expensive or exotic ingredients, its nourishing heartiness suggest a peasant origin. Because an oven was something of a luxury in the poorer farmhouses of France, country women always used to carry their pots to the village baker, to be placed in his still-hot oven when the morning's last batch of bread was done.

Only history locates cassoulet in Languedoc, since the ingredients are easily produced almost anywhere in France. But that doesn't prevent French gastronomes from endlessly rehashing often unsubstantiated legends about the veritable cassoulet, and quarreling fervently over which of three towns—all quite close by—produced the truest and best, the one and only, cassoulet.

And yet I wonder: why *are* the French so passionate, not just about food itself or about naming dishes for their authentic region of origin (like potatoes *à la dauphinoise*, or our New England baked beans)—but for naming them after tiny, insignificant localities? We Americans have a few dishes named for big cities, and the English have a few named for counties (Devonshire cream, Cornish pasties, Yorkshire pudding, etc.), but nothing like this intense particularity. Doesn't the brouhaha over names and attributions arise from an almost amorous sense of place, a lover's appreciation of the special character of every corner of the land? For it's not just cassoulet the French are geographically potty about, it's bouillabaisse and pâté and all kinds of things to eat. Why they and not other great cooks like the Chinese?

There is, though, another nation of great cooks, the Italians, who are similarly inclined, with their myriad dishes *alla* somewhere-*ese*. The scholar Mario Pei has said that's because Italy was broken up until so recently into tiny city-states, each with its own cuisine. Not so true of France.

But almost every little place in both France and Italy makes its own particular wine, and it is part of wine's magic to speak with eloquence and precision of the very earth it came from. Grow the same grapes by similar methods in vineyards yards apart, and you often get unlike wines. How natural, then, for the children of wine-making cultures to be so sensitive to the special personality of every field and hill. How natural for them to name a garnish of peas for Clamart, an otherwise dull place that grows fine peas, or one of spinach for little Viroflay, or to name variants, as with cassoulet, for the places where they are supposed to have been invented.

For a Frenchman, a mental map of France must look like a vast hexagonal buffet. Even for me, some dishes powerfully evoke a beloved region. When I taste an apple tart *à la normande*, all fresh and creamy, my mind's eye dwells on the drowsy cattle and the scented orchards Paul and I drove past en route to Paris from the war-shattered docks of Cherbourg, on my first day in France thirty-odd years ago. And where is my mind's eye now, as I taste this excellent cassoulet? Why, on the busy kitchen behind the *J.C. & Co.* set, where we of the cooking team developed our own version. Above us looms not the sunny sky of fabled Languedoc, but a frightful mess of pipes and lights and rubber-covered cables. Nevertheless, this too is a beloved place. Ought we, perhaps, to name our dish in the classic fashion *Cassoulet des Coulisses de J.C. et Cie*, or J.C. & Co.'s Backstage Cassoulet?

Old-fashioned Chicken Dinner

Menu

For 6 people

Long Fresh Asparagus Spears, with Oil and Lemon
French Bread

Hen Bonne Femme—A sprightly stuffed fowl poached whole,
and served with onions, mushrooms, and Sauce Ivoire
Steamed Rice

Tossed Green Salad
Melba Toast or French Bread

Bombe aux Trois Chocolats—A chocolate mousse hidden
under a mold of chocolate fudge cake, topped with chocolate
sauce and a sprinkling of walnuts

Suggested wines:

Although some worthy wine wallahs abstain from wine with
asparagus, I like a light dry riesling or Sancerre; a full
dry white would go with the chicken, like a Burgundy or
chardonnay, or you could present a light red Bordeaux or
cabernet; sweet Champagne or a sweet but still wine would
go with the chocolate dessert—a Sauternes, Vouvray, or
gewürztraminer.

When a hen's too old to lay, she still is useful for something—good eating! Her great egg-producing days are over, and it doesn't pay the poultry man to keep on feeding her. So we feed *on* her, and well, for the great thing about this beldame is her wonderful flavor. Mass produced (battery raised, as some call it), with no exercise and standardized rations, young chickens today don't have the rich taste they used to when they ran around snacking on anything they fancied in the hen yard; but with age and, I presume, experience, they acquire flavor as people do character. Matronly hens taste the way all chicken used to and ought to.

My market says there's not much demand for stewing chickens nowadays, because a lot of customers don't know how to cook them. They treat them like roasters, end up with rubber chicken, and come back to the store mad. But, though you may have to special-order your stewing chicken (or fowl, to be technical), it is available. The demand comes from commercial food processors, and from hotels and restaurants, which use fowl by preference for salads and sandwiches. It's not just because of the fowl's rich taste: hens, not *old* but of a certain age, have an excellent, tender texture when cooked right. The key is long simmering—but not too long, for just after the point of perfection is reached, utter disintegration sets in and the meat falls flaccidly from the bone. It's curious: the fowl stays obdurately tough for the longest time, then its consistency changes quite quickly; you really have to keep testing.

A "boiled fowl" (gross phrase!) is so useful a resource to have on hand that more households—particularly where everybody goes out to work—should make it a staple. The next step is so quick and easy, whether you opt for chicken stew, pie, salad, or sandwiches, and the golden broth makes sauce or soup. But don't use a capon or a young chicken or a middle-aged roaster for the purpose. They don't have enough flavor, and long cooking practically dissolves them. (Best moist-cooking method for roasters, in my experience, is the casserole poach, where there is little liquid and the bird steams in a covered pot in the oven, as described in *Mastering I* and *The French Chef Cookbook*.) With a fine fowl (see page 133 for standards of quality), I use a stuffing to bring out the grand flavor, and the broth for sauce (the rest for soup later), and carve before serving. For the price of 3 lamb chops, one can serve from 6 to 8 people, or get at least 3 well-varied dinners for a couple.

Practicality, of course, is something a party should possess but certainly not proclaim! Don't think there is anything humdrum about our "elegant fowl" (as the Owl was addressed by the Pussycat). This is the finest of party food. The full, super-chickeny taste marries so well with a good wine, and platter looks handsome: smooth-grained meat, ivory satin sauce, and a pretty array of vegetables. It's an easy dish to serve. And to eat, which can be a consideration. (I remember a very young niece, returning from her first dinner dance in pink tulle—and red wrath. "I'm starved!" she howled. "All the kids are! It was *squab*!" If you have young guests all gussied up in their first party clothes, do feed them something manageable.)

The choice of a first course before chicken is no problem at any time, but in joyful springtime asparagus, for me, is the ideal thing. Is there anything it doesn't complement? (Scallops, maybe—too much too sweet—or a very spicy "made dish" like lasagne . . .) Anyway, the clear fresh green of it and the soft flavor—sweet in the stalk and subtle, vaguely mushroomy, in the tip—are bliss before the sturdy yet delicate chicken. Why before and not with? With is fine, I concede, but consider the sumptuousness, the sheer all-outness, of a whole plateful of nothing but asparagus!—peeled, of course, so the pure green is streaked with ivory. And perfectly drained, and cooked just to the pivot-point between crunchy and soft, and very, very cold—or very, very hot. Rapture . . .

With a bread crumb stuffing and a rich dessert, you don't need bread or rice for starch; but for texture they are nice— fresh French loaf for contrast, the rice (recipe on page 380) for a sauce sopper-up. The salad, with a vinaigrette dressing, is just a hyphen, a refresher.

The dessert on this menu is called Bombe aux Trois Chocolats because it looks like a floating mine and the threat is triple: chocolate mousse encased in chocolate cake, and then, forsooth, coated with more chocolate. (But a little lightly whipped cream, passed separately, softens the chocolate onslaught.) Anybody who comes to this dinner will gaze upon the dark and lustrous dome and know he's at—A Party.

Preparations and Marketing

Recommended Equipment:

Start with one big pot. It's essential that the one for your chicken be deep enough so that the liquid level can be 4 inches (10 cm) above the chicken; stainless steel or enamel is best for cooking with wine, and the pot has to be covered. For asparagus, a large oval casserole or roaster is ideal. For lots of asparagus, a rack fitting the pot (as in a fish steamer) is a nice convenience for lifting out and draining. To truss the chicken, you need plenty of soft white string.

A covered, heavy-bottomed saucepan is a help with rice, and you need 2, preferably 3, more saucepans for sauce, onions, and mushrooms. Onions can, if you like, be precooked and reheated with the mushrooms when you do them.

For the dessert, you need a jelly-roll pan to bake the fudge cake, and a homemade paper pattern or template (which you can file and re-use) as a guide to cutting it. To form the bombe, use a 6-cup (1½-L) bowl, or smooth-sided mold, or even a flowerpot.

Staples to Have on Hand:

Salt
White peppercorns
Granulated sugar
Confectioners sugar
Dried sage
Imported bay leaves
Dried thyme
Whole cloves
Pure vanilla extract
Optional: chicken stock
Gelatin
Butter (3 sticks; 12 ounces or 340 g)
Swiss cheese (2 ounces or 60 g)
Day-old nonsweet white French- or Italian-type
    bread (½ loaf)
Flour
Garlic (2 or more cloves)
Optional: leeks (1 or 2)
Celery (3 stalks)

Carrots (2 medium)
Lemons (1)
Cognac, dark Jamaica rum, or bourbon whiskey

Specific Ingredients for This Menu:

Stewing chicken (5 to 6 pounds or 2¼ to 2¾ kg) ●
Best-quality semisweet chocolate (16 ounces or 450 g)
Unsweetened chocolate (6 ounces or 180 g)
Walnuts (2 Tb, chopped)
Heavy cream (3¼ cups or 7 dL)
Eggs (7 "large" plus 2 whites)
Parsley (1 good-sized bunch)
Yellow onions (4 or 5 large)
Small white onions (18 to 24)
Mushrooms (1 quart or 1 L), preferably small
Asparagus (36 to 48 spears) ●
Optional: dry white wine (1 bottle)
Optional: dry white French vermouth (2 cups or ½ L), or use more dry white wine

---

● Remarks:

Chicken: a good stewing chicken, or fowl, or stewing hen, is just on the shady side of middle age. An "old hen" is great for soup, but too tough to eat. What you want is a bird from 14 to 16 months old, weighing between 4 and 6½ pounds (1¾ and 3 kg), in general—but buy one on the big side to feed 6 amply. She should be plump and chunky-looking; her skin should be white—not yellow; her breast is reasonably full, and her breastbone, if you feel it down to the tip, is not cartilage but solid bone—that shows she's at least a year old. See the introduction to this chapter for more details on this somewhat-neglected—but highly meritorious—type of bird. Since you may have to special-order your fowl, it's worth knowing what to ask for and what you can expect.
Asparagus: fresh asparagus is sold nowadays from February to June. For information about buying, storing, and preparing, see the following.

Fresh Asparagus

Buying

Fat asparagus is just as tender, in my opinion, as thin asparagus, but I do think you should choose spears all of the same diameter to be sure of even cooking. Pick them spear by spear if you can, choosing firm stalks with closely clinging leaves at the bud ends; the peel from end to end should be tight, bright, and fresh with no creased or withered areas. The butt ends should look moist, and if your grocery store is really serious about asparagus, they will have it standing upright in a tray with an inch of water. Asparagus spears are like flowers: they wilt without moisture.

Storing

When you bring your asparagus home, unwrap it at once, cut a finger width off the butts to reach the moist ends, and it is a good idea to let the asparagus lie for half an hour in warm water, which will refresh it. Then stand the spears upright in a bowl, their butts in 2 inches (5 cm) of cold water, cover loosely with plastic wrap or a plastic bag, and store in the refrigerator. Treated this way, fresh asparagus will stay fresh for 2 or 3 days.

Peeling

There is no doubt at all in anyone's mind who has compared peeled asparagus with unpeeled asparagus—they are two different vegetables. Peeled asparagus cooks evenly from tip to butt in half the time, remains greener, and has a far better texture than unpeeled asparagus. (The same is true of peeled versus unpeeled broccoli.) To peel the spears, you want to take the tough outer skin from the butt end up to near the tip, where the skin is tender. I use a small knife, and lop off a finger width of the butt—or if necessary, I make the cut where the green begins. Then, starting at the butt end, and holding the spear butt up, I start the peel, cutting down to the tender flesh and making the cut more shallow as I reach the tender area near the tip. Using a knife, you can direct the depth of the peel, and it is also good practice in control of the knife. However, you can use a vegetable peeler: hold the spear on your work surface, its butt away from you, and go round and round until you get down to the tender flesh—

but be careful holding and turning it, so as not to break the spear.

If you bend an asparagus spear to where it breaks, you are losing a lot of asparagus, whereas a properly peeled spear can be eaten from butt to tip.

Plain Boiled Asparagus

For 6 people, with 6 to 8 spears per person

36 to 48 fine fresh asparagus spears all the same diameter, peeled
4 to 5 quarts or liters rapidly boiling water
1½ tsp salt per quart or liter water

Equipment:

A large oval casserole or roaster; 2 wide spatulas for lifting asparagus out of water; a tray, or rack over tray, lined with a clean towel if asparagus is to be served cold; a platter lined with a double-damask or linen napkin if asparagus is to be served hot

---

With a small amount of asparagus, there is no need to tie it in bundles for cooking if you have an oval casserole or roaster that will hold it comfortably so that it does not tumble about as it boils.

Bring the water to the rapid boil with the salt, lay in the asparagus, and cover the casserole just until the water begins to boil again—the sooner it reaches the boil, the greener the asparagus; but the casserole must be uncovered while the asparagus is actually boiling—again to keep it green.

Boil slowly, uncovered, for 4 to 5 minutes, or just until asparagus spears start to bend a little when lifted. Remove a spear; cut and eat a piece from the butt end to make sure. Asparagus should be just cooked through, with a slight crunch. Immediately remove the asparagus from the water.

To serve cold

Arrange in one layer on the towel-lined tray or rack, and cool near an open window if possible. Serve with lemon wedges and a pitcher of good olive oil, or with vinaigrette or one of its variations, or with mayonnaise—recipes for which are on page 376.

To serve hot

Arrange on napkin-lined platter and pass lemon wedges and melted butter, or lemon butter, or hollandaise, page 301, or one of the butter sauces on page 369. Another method, which I always remember delighting in at my grandmother's house, was to arrange the hot asparagus on a rather deep rectangular platter, season it with salt and pepper, pour lots of melted butter over it, and stand small triangles of white toast all around the edge of the platter.

Whole Stuffed and Poached Stewing Chicken

"Boiled Fowl"

For 6 to 8 people

Herb and Bread Crumb Stuffing:

1 cup (¼ L) minced onions
3 Tb butter
The gizzard, heart, and liver of the chicken
  (optional)
2 or more cloves garlic, minced
1 celery stalk, minced
1 "large" egg
2½ cups (6 dL) lightly pressed down crumbs
  from crustless day-old French- or Italian-type
  nonsweet white bread
½ cup (1 dL), lightly pressed down, fresh
  minced parsley
½ tsp dried sage
Salt and pepper
½ cup (1 dL) coarsely grated Swiss cheese

For Stewing the Chicken:

A 5- to 6-pound (2¼- to 2¾-kg) fine plump
  white-skinned stewing chicken, ready to cook
About 6 quarts (6 L) liquid: 1 bottle dry white
  wine, plus half-and-half water and chicken
  stock; or chicken stock and water; or water only
Salt to taste (1 tsp per quart or liter if using only
  water)
2 large celery stalks
2 medium carrots
1 large peeled onion stuck with 2 cloves
1 or 2 washed leeks, or another large onion
1 large herb bouquet (8 parsley sprigs, 2 imported
  bay leaves, and 1 tsp dried thyme, tied together
  in washed cheesecloth)

Equipment:

Either a trussing needle and white string, or a lacing pin (for neck skin) and 4 feet (120 cm) of soft white string (butcher's corned-beef twine recommended); a stew pot just tall enough to hold the chicken submerged plus 4 inches (10 cm) of extra room (make it stainless steel or enamel if you are cooking with wine; aluminum can discolor both the wine and the chicken)

Herb and bread crumb stuffing

Cook the onions slowly in the butter until tender and translucent. Meanwhile, peel and mince the gizzard, and add to the onions; then mince the heart, and add to the onions; and finally, when onions are almost tender, mince the liver. Stir it in and cook a minute or 2, just to stiffen. Scrape into a mixing bowl, stir in the rest of the ingredients, and season carefully to taste.

Preparing and stuffing the chicken

Pull any clinging fat out from the chicken's cavity, and make sure the cavity is free of other extraneous bits. For easier carving, remove the wishbone: open skin flap at neck and feel the fork of the bone with your finger, running from top of breast down each side; cut around the 2 tines of the fork and the top, then cut down to detach fork ends at each side. Cut off wing nubbins at elbows. If you wish an automatic basting system and there is enough chicken fat to do so, place fat between 2 sheets of wax paper and pound to a thickness of about ⅛ inch (½ cm). Slip your fingers between skin and flesh over the breast on both sides, to detach skin, and slide in the fat over the breast meat. Secure the neck skin, as illustrated, against the back of the chicken and fold wings akimbo.

Just before cooking it, salt the cavity of the chicken lightly, spoon in the stuffing (picture 1, on page 139), and truss the chicken.

Trussing a Chicken with String:
(Illustrated on pp. 140–141)

Sew or skewer the neck skin against the neck end of the backbone, to hold it in place. Provide yourself with a piece of soft white string (butcher's corned-beef twine recommended) 4 feet (120 cm) long and proceed as follows:

2) Set chicken on its back, its tail toward you. Fold the string in half, and place its center under the chicken's tail piece.

3) Cross the string over the top of the tail piece.

4) Bring one end of the string from its side of the tail piece *under* the end of its opposite drumstick, then up over it, and down toward the side of the tail piece from which it came. Repeat the same movement from the other side.

5) To close the vent and bring the drumstick ends together, pull the 2 ends of string away from the sides of the chicken.

Turn the chicken on its side.

6) Fold the wings akimbo, wing ends tucked against the back of the neck. Bring the end of string nearest you along the side of the chicken and on top of the folded wing on the same side, then under the wing, coming out at the back again from under the armpit. Repeat with the string on the other side—along side of chicken, over top of wing, under it, and back again under armpit.

7) Pull both string ends tight across back to hold the chicken in form, and by doing so you will make the wings stand out akimbo to brace the chicken when you turn it breast up. Tie the string ends together at one side of the backbone.

Note: You may have to sew or skewer the vent opening closed if you have a loose stuffing, but the string truss is often sufficient to hold everything in place.

❷ Chicken should be stuffed only just before cooking, since stuffing may start to spoil (especially because it contains bread crumbs), and that will spoil the whole chicken, resulting in a nasty case of food poisoning for all who dine upon it.

Poaching the chicken
2½ to 3 hours

Place the chicken in the pot and pour on enough liquid to cover it by 3 inches (8 cm). Add the specified amount of salt, cover loosely, and bring rapidly to the simmer. Skim off gray scum that will continue to rise for 5 minutes or more, then add the vegetables and herb bouquet. Maintain at the slow simmer, partially covered, for 2 hours. (A hard simmer or boil will break the flesh apart.) Add water if liquid evaporates to expose ingredients.

Chicken is not done until a sharp-pronged fork will pierce the large end of the drumstick easily. For 2 hours or more, flesh will be rubbery; then, suddenly, it will become tender, and it should be tested frequently, at 7-minute intervals, when the time might be close. Drumstick meat will just begin to fall from bone when chicken is done; white breast meat will hold, but be tender. Do not overcook.

❷ Chicken will stay warm in its pot for 2 hours or more, partially covered, and may be gently reheated if it cools too much. Chicken should stay in its poaching liquid until serving time; the meat dries out otherwise.

Warning about Covered Pots: Always allow for air circulation, especially when the chicken is not simmering. Cooking liquid and chicken can easily spoil in a nonsimmering covered pot, due to some chemical or bacterial relation between closed containers and warm chicken.

Serving suggestions

The chicken is now ready to be eaten. To serve it cold, let it cool in its cooking liquid and it is ready for salads and sandwiches.

Here is one way to serve it hot:

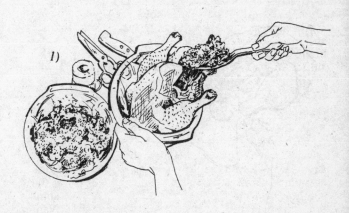

1)

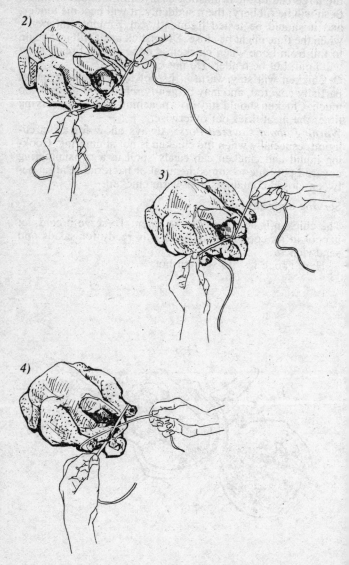

2)

3)

4)

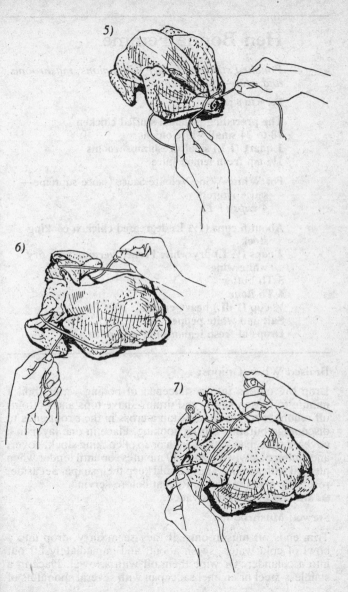

5)

6)

7)

Hen Bonne Femme

Poached stewing chicken with onions, mushrooms, and white-wine sauce

For 6 to 8 people

The preceding poached stuffed chicken
18 to 24 small white onions
1 quart (1 L) small fresh mushrooms
1½ tsp fresh lemon juice

For White-Wine Velouté Sauce (sauce suprême—
    sauce ivoire):
    4 cups (1 L)

About 6 cups (1½ L) degreased chicken cooking
    stock
2 cups (½ L) dry white French vermouth or dry
    white wine
5 Tb butter
6 Tb flour
½ cup (1 dL) heavy cream
Salt and white pepper
Drops of fresh lemon juice as needed

Braised White Onions:

Drop the onions into a saucepan of boiling water, boil 1 minute to loosen skins, and drain. Shave tops and bottoms off onions, peel them, and stab a cross in their root ends to discourage bursting during cooking. Place in one layer in a covered saucepan with an inch or so of cooking stock, cover, and simmer slowly for 20 to 30 minutes, or until tender when pierced with a knife. They should keep their shape. Set aside, reserving cooking liquid. Reheat before serving.
❷ May be cooked in advance.

Stewed Mushrooms:

Trim ends off mushrooms. If they seem dirty, drop into a bowl of cold water, swish about, and immediately lift out into a colander. Or wipe them off with a towel. Place in a stainless-steel or enamel saucepan with several spoonfuls of chicken cooking liquid and 1½ teaspoons lemon juice. Toss mushrooms with the liquid. Cover pan and simmer 3 to 4 minutes, until just tender. Set aside, reserving cooking liquid. Reheat just before serving.

❷ Best not cooked much more than half an hour in advance so the mushrooms will not darken, although you may prepare them for cooking several hours before and refrigerate in dry paper towels and a plastic bag.

The White-Wine Velouté Sauce:

Boil the chicken stock and wine slowly in a stainless-steel or enamel saucepan until reduced to about 4 cups or 1 liter. Melt the butter in a separate enamel or stainless-steel saucepan, blend in the flour, and stir over moderately low heat until butter and flour foam and froth together for 2 minutes without turning more than a buttery yellow. Remove from heat, and when this *roux* has stopped bubbling, pour in a ladleful of the hot chicken stock and vigorously beat to blend liquid and *roux*; blend in another ladleful, and when smooth pour in all but a ladleful. Beat in all but a spoonful or so of the onion and mushroom cooking liquids. Bring sauce to the simmer, stirring, over moderately high heat and simmer 2 to 3 minutes—if you have time, let sauce simmer half an hour or so, stirring frequently; longer cooking will only improve its flavor. Stir in the heavy cream and simmer a few minutes longer; carefully correct seasoning with salt and pepper, adding lemon juice to taste. (Sauce should be just thick enough to coat a wooden spoon nicely, meaning it will just coat the chicken; thin out with chicken stock or cream if necessary. To thicken, boil slowly, stirring, to concentrate it.)

❷ May be made an hour or so in advance—add the mushroom juices before serving in this case. To prevent a skin from forming on the surface, lay plastic wrap right on top of the sauce, leaving air space at 2 or 3 places around the edge of the pan.

Serving the chicken

At serving time, remove the chicken from the pot to a carving board with a curved edge—to catch juices. Cut off trussing string, and remove the leg-thigh assembly from one side—it should fall off easily. Peel off and discard the skin and remove the meat—which will be so tender you can probably use a spoon and fork—and arrange on a hot serving platter.

Peel skin off breast, and slice breast meat off the now legless side—breast meat may also be so tender it will come off with a fork and spoon. Arrange breast meat at the other side of the platter, and repeat on the second side of the chicken. Spoon out the stuffing and arrange down the middle of the platter, as shown. Arrange the onions and mushrooms around the meat, and spoon some of the sauce over the meat. Serve rest of sauce separately, in a warmed bowl.

Chicken should be sauced and served as soon as it is arranged on the platter, to prevent meat from drying out.

The Cooking Stock:

You will still have a good amount of fine chicken stock to use in soups and sauces. Simmer the chicken carcass and scraps in it for half an hour or so, strain and degrease it. Store in the refrigerator in a covered container when it is cold, and boil it up every several days, or freeze it.

Variations on the Sauce:

You can have no sauce at all, if you are counting calories: instead, boil down a good quantity of the degreased cooking liquid until its flavor is full and fine, and spoon some of that over the chicken and vegetables, ending with a generous sprinkling of parsley over the chicken itself; pass the rest of the liquid in a warm sauceboat. Or you can be far richer and creamier with your sauce: boil down 4 cups (1 L) degreased cooking liquid with half that amount of dry white wine or dry French vermouth until reduced by half or less, and then boil down with 2 to 3 cups (½ to ¾ L) heavy cream until sauce has thickened lightly; season to taste, adding lemon juice if needed; pour some over the chicken and pass the rest in a warm bowl.

Variations on the Vegetables:

Rather than onions and mushrooms, you might use the kind of vegetables you'd have with the usual boiled dinner—carrots, turnips, cabbage wedges, onions, and potatoes—all boiled or steamed separately in some of the chicken cooking liquid.

Variations on the Chicken Cooking Method:

Rather than poaching the chicken whole, cut it into serving pieces and place the carcass remains, gizzard, and neck in the bottom of a casserole, topped by the dark meat, and ending with the breast and wings; add the same vegetables to the casserole, and enough liquid to cover the ingredients; cooking time may be a little shorter. By the way, I tried out the oven-steaming method in a covered casserole with a stuffed stewing hen, liquid coming up to mid thigh, wax paper on, and an oven heat of 275—300°F/135–150°C; the breast, wings, and thighs were fine, but the drumsticks dry and strange; the chicken took about 3¾ hours to cook tender. Perhaps the whole bird needed draping in a sheet of pork fat? I have not yet gone into the pressure cooker or slow cooker—they will have to wait for another hen party.

Chicken Pot Pie:

Using the chicken and its sauce and vegetables, turn them into a chicken pie: arrange in a pie dish or casserole, cover with the buttermilk and herb biscuit dough described for the rabbit pie (page 37), and bake in the same way. Or use the pâté dough (page 245). Baking time is about 30 minutes in a 400°F/205°C oven.

Bombe aux Trois Chocolats

A chocolate mousse hidden under a chocolate-covered fudge cake dome

This is a dessert for true chocolate lovers, and one that's beautiful to look at and fun as well—though not difficult to make. It consists of a chocolate fudge cake, a kind of brownie mixture, that bakes in a jelly-roll pan. When that is cool, you cut it so that it will line a bowl—or a soufflé mold, if you wish—you fill the lined bowl with chocolate mousse and chill it for 6 hours or overnight. Then unmold (it unmolds easily because first you have lined your bowl with plastic wrap), spoon a little melted chocolate on top, sprinkle on a pinch of chopped nuts for decoration, and you have an incomparable combination of three chocolates: the taste of brittle chocolate topping, the crunch of fudge cake, and the smooth velvet of the mousse.

Our cooking team worked on this for weeks. I had for some time been developing a rich dark mousse, trying to duplicate one I had found remarkable at André Surmain's restaurant in Mougins, in the south of France. But we all thought the mousse cake idea was what we were after, so we set our two chefs, Marian and Sara, to work on developing the perfect combination of cake, mousse, and molding technique. They made more than a dozen, which we solemnly tasted, one by one, and voted upon, narrowing the field to 3. Ultimately, this one really took the cake—and it was the cake indeed that made all the difference, because we wanted the contrast in texture vis-à-vis mousse that the solid fudge cake gave us.

Manufacturing and Timing Note:

I find it best to make the mousse first, so it can set a little bit, yet be soft enough to spoon into the lined mold. While the fudge cake is baking and cooling, you can cut out the template, or pattern, that will guide you in lining your bowl or mold with the cake. (Once I got my first template made, I kept it on file so I wouldn't have to go through that fussy fitting of things again.) The recipe here is for a 6-cup (1½-L) bowl of about 8 inches (20 cm) top diameter, which fortunately just works out for the standard rectangular jelly-roll pan that is about 11 by 17 inches (28 by 43 cm). A charlotte mold or even a flowerpot could be used, of course, and either is fine because they are both tall enough for drama.

For the Mousse—Chocolate Mougins

For 4½ cups, serving 8 people

12 ounces (340 g) best-quality semisweet chocolate
1½ ounces (45 g) unsweetened chocolate
2½ tsp plain unflavored gelatin
3 Tb dark Jamaica rum, Cognac, or bourbon whiskey
3 "large" eggs
2 egg whites (4 Tb)
1½ cups (3½ dL) heavy cream
1½ Tb pure vanilla extract
Large pinch of salt
3 Tb sugar

Equipment:

A small covered saucepan for melting the chocolate and a larger pan with water to set it in; a 2-quart (2-L) stainless-steel saucepan for the custard sauce; a very clean bowl and beater for egg whites, which can also serve for chilling the mousse

Flavor Note: This is a very strong, rich, dark, very chocolaty mousse, on the bittersweet side. It consists only of melted chocolate that is folded into a rich custard sauce, and is lightened by beaten egg whites, yet given body with a little gelatin.

Melting the chocolate

Break up the two chocolates and set in the small covered saucepan. Bring 2 inches (5 cm) of water to boil in a larger pan; remove from heat. Cover chocolate pan and set in the hot water. Chocolate will melt while you proceed with the rest of the recipe. Renew hot water if necessary; chocolate should be smoothly melted and darkly glistening.

The gelatin

Measure gelatin into a bowl or cup, pour on the rum or other liquid, and let soften.

Custard Sauce—Crème Anglaise:

Separate the eggs, dropping the whites, plus the extra whites, into the beating bowl, and the yolks into the stainless-steel saucepan. Set whites aside for later. Beat the yolks for a minute with a wire whip, or until thick and sticky; then blend in the cream. Stir rather slowly over low heat with a wooden spatula or spoon, reaching all over bottom of pan, as liquid slowly heats. (Watch it carefully, and do not let it come to the simmer.) Bubbles will begin to appear on the surface, and in a few minutes the bubbles will start to subside. Then watch for a whiff of steam rising—this indicates that the sauce is thickening. Continue for a few seconds until the sauce clings in a slight layer to the back of your spatula or spoon. Immediately remove from heat, and stir for a minute or so to stop cooking.

Combining custard, gelatin, and chocolate

At once stir the softened gelatin mixture into the hot custard, stirring until the gelatin has dissolved completely. Stir in the vanilla, then the melted chocolate.

Finishing the dessert

Set the egg white beating bowl over the hot water that melted the chocolate, and stir for a moment to take off the chill (egg whites mount faster and more voluminously when slightly warmed). Beat at slow speed until they are foamy, beat in the salt, and then gradually increase speed to fast until egg whites form soft peaks. Sprinkle in the sugar, and beat until egg whites form stiff shining peaks. Fold them into the chocolate, then return the whole mixture to the egg white bowl, cover, and chill. Mousse should be somewhat set, not runny, when it goes into the cake-lined mold.

❶ If made and chilled in advance, leave out at room temperature until it has softened. Mousse will keep several days under refrigeration or may be frozen.

Note: This makes a delicious chocolate mousse just as it is. Turn the mousse into an attractive dish or individual pots, and serve with bowls of chocolate sauce (page 370) and of whipped cream.

Kate's Great Chocolate Fudge Cake

Note: This recipe was developed by our Chef Marian's daughter, Kate Morash, when she was only twelve years old, and makes a most superior brownie as well as perfect cake to surround a mousse—it is crunchy-chewy, yet soft enough to blend to the contours of a bowl.

For a jelly-roll pan about 11 by 17 inches (28 by 43 cm)

Butter and flour for baking pan
1 stick (4 ounces or 115 g) unsalted butter
4 ounces (115 g) unsweetened chocolate
1 more stick (4 ounces or 115 g) unsalted butter, cut into 8 pieces
2 cups (380 to 400 g) sugar
3 "large" eggs
1 tsp pure vanilla extract
½ tsp salt
1 cup (140 g) all-purpose flour (measure by scooping dry-measure cup into flour container and sweeping off excess)

Equipment:

A jelly-roll pan and wax paper; a saucepan for melting chocolate and butter, and another saucepan in which to set the first; an electric mixer, or a food processor; a flour sifter; a cake rack

Preliminaries

Preheat oven to 350°F/180°C. Butter the jelly-roll pan (so the paper will stick to it), cut a sheet of wax paper to fit it with 2 inches (5 cm) of overhang at each end, and press into pan. Butter and flour the paper, knocking out excess flour. Measure out all your ingredients.

Melting the chocolate

Set the first stick of butter and the chocolate in their melting pan, and place in the other pan with 2 to 3 inches of water; bring near the simmer and let the chocolate and butter melt together while you continue with the next step.

Hand-made or mixer-made batter

Cream second stick of butter with the sugar until light and fluffy. Beat in the eggs one by one, and the vanilla and salt. Stir in the warm melted chocolate mixture, then gradually sift and fold in the flour. Spread the batter evenly into the pan, and bake at once in middle level of preheated oven, setting timer for 25 minutes.

Food-processor-made batter

Or—cream butter and sugar in processor fitted with steel blade; add eggs one by one, then vanilla, salt, and chocolate. Pour in flour by thirds, blending with 2 or 3 on-off flicks. Spread evenly into pan, and set in middle level of preheated oven.

Baking and cooling

Bake about 25 minutes, until set but top is still spongy. A toothpick inserted into the cake should come out with a few specks of chocolate on it. It should be chewy when cool, and you want it to bend a little so that you can mold it into the bowl; do not let it overcook.

Remove from oven and let cool in pan for 10 minutes. Then turn pan upside down over a cake rack and unmold the cake, gently pulling off wax paper. Cool 10 minutes more. ❷ May be baked in advance. When cool, cover with wax paper, reverse back into baking pan, and cover airtight; store in the refrigerator for a day or 2, or freeze.

Brownies

When cool, cut the cake into 3- by 1½-inch (8- by 4-cm) rectangles. Serve as is, or you may glaze them with the chocolate and nuts suggested at the end of the bombe recipe.

Assembling the Bombe aux Trois Chocolats

The preceding recipes for chocolate mousse and chocolate fudge cake

4 ounces (115 g) best-quality semisweet chocolate

½ ounce (15 g) unsweetened chocolate

2 Tb chopped walnuts

A bowl of lightly whipped cream sweetened with confectioners sugar and flavored with vanilla

Equipment:

A chilled serving platter and, if you wish, a paper doily

The template—or cut-out pattern

Whatever you have chosen as a container for molding the dessert, you will need a pattern of cut-outs to guide you in fitting the cake into the container. This is the system we use for our round bowl: a small cake circle for the bottom of the bowl; 7 wedges of cake to rest on the circle and touch the top of the bowl all around with a little space between each wedge, allowing the mousse to peek through its encircling walls of fudge cake. We also have a large circle to cap the mousse, and all scraps of fudge cake go into the center, giving the bombe a little extra sturdiness for its life out of the mold.

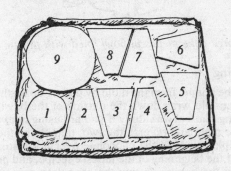

Keep your paper pattern for your next bombe

Molding the bombe

Before cutting the fudge cake, slice off a ½-inch (1½-cm) border all around the rectangle, since the edges tend to be brittle—these cut-offs make nice little cookie bits to serve another time. Then cut around the pattern.

Line the bowl with plastic wrap (for easy unmolding), and arrange the cake pieces in the bowl, pressing gently in place with the best side out. Pile half the mousse into the bowl, cover with scraps of the cake (leftovers from cutting patterns). Fill with the remaining mousse and place the large circle on top, pressing it down to force the mousse into the bowl and around the cake. Cover and chill at least 6 hours or overnight.

❶ Bombe may be refrigerated for several days. It may be frozen, and thawed before serving—several hours at room temperature, or a day or more in the refrigerator.

Arrange cake pieces in bowl lined with plastic wrap

Unmolding

Loosen the bombe from the mold by pulling up on the plastic wrap, then fold wrap down the outside of the bowl. Center the serving platter (with doily if you are using one) over the top of the mold and reverse the two, unmolding the bombe onto the platter. Melt the chocolate over hot water, as described at the beginning of the mousse recipe, and pour over the top of the bombe, letting the chocolate drip lazily and unevenly down the sides. Top chocolate, while still warm, with a sprinkling of the chopped nuts.

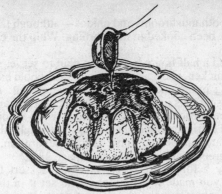

Let the chocolate drip lazily and unevenly down the sides

Serving

Cut into wedges, like a round cake, and let each guest help himself to the whipped cream.

❶ Timing

This easy dinner allows you lots of flexibility. If guests are late or want to linger over their cocktails, no harm is done. Your first course of asparagus can be either hot or cold, and that is up to you. If cold, you have nothing to do at the last minute, your chicken and vegetables can wait, and you can go in to dinner whenever you wish. (I shall assume that you are serving cold asparagus in what follows.)

Just before the guests arrive, warm the chicken sauce, the onions and mushrooms together, and the rice—use the restaurant trick of having a roasting pan of simmering water on the stove, big enough to hold those three saucepans, each loosely covered. Have the salad in its bowl, covered and refrigerated, undressed but with dressing ready. Warm the bread if it needs freshening.

About an hour before that, test the chicken for doneness; once tender it can sit in its pot for 2 hours or more, just keeping itself warm. Ladle off the broth you'll need from the pot for cooking the mushrooms, onions, and sauce; if you expose the chicken, drape it in washed cheesecloth and baste with broth—cheesecloth should extend down into the broth on all sides and will draw it up like a wick, thus continuously basting the chicken. Make the sauce now, and you can cook both mushrooms and onions—although the onions could have been cooked in the morning. Whip the cream for the dessert.

Four and a half hours before you plan to serve, stuff and truss the chicken, and start it cooking—you could have made the stuffing in advance and have refrigerated it. Peel and cook the asparagus too, and make its vinaigrette sauce. Prepare the mushrooms for cooking now; wrap in dry paper towels and refrigerate in a plastic bag. You might also sauce the chocolate bombe and finish its final decoration, prepare the salad greens, and cook the rice (page 380).

The day before your party, take the dessert from the freezer, if you made it beforehand, and set it in the refrigerator to thaw. Or make the dessert now—or assemble it from its thawed, prefrozen components. Just be sure it has 6 hours or more to sit, in the refrigerator.

Menu Variations

Out of *asparagus* season, what would be a fitting preface for boiled fowl? Artichokes vinaigrette would be my choice, or a salad of sliced artichoke hearts with bits of crab or shrimp or lobster. Young string beans, tossed with butter, lemon, and parsley—another attractive idea, or a salad of cold fresh string beans dressed with onion rings and tomatoes. Still another suggestion, and a nicely old-fashioned one, is clear chicken broth made from your fine pot of chicken-cooking stock.

The chicken: rather than stewing it whole, see the suggestions at the end of the recipe. Or add other meats to simmer with it, like beef, pork, sausages, for a super boiled dinner. Or use turkey instead of chicken. Or serve the braised beef, on page 336.

The sauce: in some families melted butter with parsley and lemon is traditional for boiled chicken, as is hollandaise sauce, recipe, page 301. Some like tomato sauce, and some prefer sour cream with mustard and horseradish, much like the sour cream sauce served with the terrine in the "Picnic," page 243.

The vegetables: rather than onions and mushrooms, you could serve boiled or mashed potatoes, or braised topinambours, and something green like Brussels sprouts or broccoli or peas. You could arrange the chicken over a bed of buttered noodles, surrounding it with a green vegetable or with broiled tomatoes.

The *dessert*: the chocolate bombe is indeed a rich and now, because of the price of chocolate, an expensive dessert. You could have the pretty filled meringue cases, or *vacherins* (page 43), or the apple-filled burnt-almond-and-rum-layered gâteau of crêpes on page 67. Other chocolate cakes in other books are the Victoire in *J.C. & Co.*, and the always popular Reine de Saba chocolate-almond cake in *Mastering I* and in *The French Chef Cookbook*.

Leftovers

Asparagus leftovers will be rare, if you have bought 6 to 8 spears per person; they can be used in a salad the next day, or in the vegetable and crêpe gâteau, on page 192.

Any leftover *chicken*, *mushrooms*, and *onions* can be arranged in a buttered baking dish along with leftover *sauce* and perhaps a sprinkling of cheese from your frozen and grated hoard; bake in a hot oven until bubbling and nicely browned on top, and you have another splendid meal. Or put them into a chicken pot pie, as suggested at the end of the recipe. Ground *chicken* can be added to a stuffing for braised cabbage or stuffed vegetables, or can go into the makings of a meat loaf. Salads and sandwiches are obvious choices for *chicken*—great club sandwich possibilities are there, and it's always handy to have a little chicken to garnish a chef's salad or as an inspiration to make the handsome Cobb Salad on page 172. The *mushrooms* and *onions* can be reheated in leftover sauce and served another day; or put them into a chicken soup.

There is never any problem with leftover *rice*, since it can be reheated (see page 380), or turned into a salad, or stirred into a soup.

Simmer all *chicken bones* and scraps in the cooking broth to enrich that already delicious brew, and plan to use it for chicken soup or as a general sauce base.

That good old hen is a good provider!

There will be leftovers of *cake*, thank heavens, because it is so rich you won't be serving it in great hunks. You might make more fudge cake, and then you could trim the leftover dessert cleverly, press decorative pieces of fudge cake onto it, and perhaps pass it off as a brand new *bombe*. It's worth a try, anyway, because it keeps nicely for several days in the refrigerator, or can be frozen.

Postscript: De gustibus nil nisi bonum

I translate this as: somebody likes it, so don't knock it.

Now and then our team throws itself a party, complete with spouses, paramours, and other affiliates; but the other night we threw a plebiscite. We wanted to hear the voice of the people, on the merits of our three competing recipes for a triple chocolate bombe. After butterflied lamb, scalloped potatoes, and a great vat of vegetable salad, the three candidates, each bearing a numbered banner, were paraded forth and tasted. Comment sheets were pinned up on which everyone wrote his or her opinion of each cake.

The cake that appears in this chapter was by far the popular choice. "Excellent," wrote Dick Graff, a visiting vintner, "good contrast in texture (brownielike cake), luscious chocolate." "Clearly, the only serious choice," proclaimed Russ Morash—unswayed, I feel sure, by the fact that his daughter Kate had developed the fudge cake recipe. Nevertheless, the two other candidates won a share of support, though it was of an ambiguous kind. The same cake Herb Pratt called "nice and wet" Dick Graff perceived as "light and spongy"; and the third seemed to me "a bit soft," though a noncook found it "robust," and added, "Grand bouquet, elegant nose." Winetaster's terms, but the word "nose" does apply in a way. The nose anyone follows in designing a recipe is, ultimately, his own; it has to be. Follow a recipe precisely the first time is my advice. But then, if you don't quite like it, don't lump it. Change it, and suit yourself.

Soup for Supper

Menu

For 6 people

French Onion Soup Gratinée—With bowls of grated cheese and a large basket of toasted French bread rounds

Cobb Salad—A mixture of fresh greens with Roquefort cheese, avocado, eggs, herbs, chicken, and other delicacies

Vesuvial Bananas—A flambéed extravaganza

Suggested wines:

A moderately hearty red wine, like a Beaujolais or zin-fandel; and a sweet wine, sparkling wine, or Champagne with the dessert

It could be said that the onion has done a lot more for France than Napoleon, and deserves its own Arch of Triumph, whose design might include bas-reliefs of grateful peasants holding soup tureens over their hearts, in salute to onion soup and the comfort and sense of luxury that it has brought over centuries to France's thrifty farmers. All it takes is onions from the kitchen garden, broth from Sunday's boiled dinner (maybe the week's only meat, so its juices provide a welcome memory), cheese and wine very likely made at home, and yesterday's hard bread: not a crumb wasted, and its staleness treated as a virtue. So far as I know, the French haven't built it a monument, but they do honor their national dish by calling it *soupe à l'oignon*, in the singlar not the plural; otherwise they say *soupe aux pois*, *aux carottes*, etc.: not onions, in other words, but The Onion.

No other soup can compare in flavor with the rich, mahogany-colored brew of slowly caramelized onions simmered in a meaty broth; and it can be expanded into a hearty one-dish meal, La Gratinée Lyonnaise, by alternately layering the tureen with toasted rounds of French bread and cheese, right up to the top, pouring in soup to fill every cranny, and slowly baking to produce a fragrant onion and cheese pudding. This is described farther on as a variation of the classic recipe, along with other ways of using this excellent soup.

It's excellent at any time of day, too. In our youthful Paris years, we had it to top off a night on the town at one of the all-night cafés in Les Halles, the central market that no longer exists. At the same time, onion soup was eaten for breakfast by the farmers who'd just carted in their produce and by the *titis parisiens* and the *forts des Halles*, the blue-smocked workmen and porters, who took their soup with a *p'tit coup* of red wine and a *p'tit coup de fouet*, a whiplash of bitter coffee: guaranteed to grow hair on the chest—or depilate it, I suspect, if applied externally. On cold evenings nowadays when we come home in need of a quick restorative, we've even been known to heat up canned onion soup, pour a bit of wine into it, slice and toast some of the homemade French bread we frequently have on hand, and float it on the soup with plenty of grated cheese from the freezer. And it makes a fine lunch for unexpected guests: a meal in itself if you wind it up with a basket of crisp, chilled apples. We find both canned and dehydrated onion soup extremely good;

homemade is just that much better, simply because it tastes homemade. (A warning, however: you don't gain anything by slicing and cooking your own onions if you then simmer them in canned broth—the result will taste as though all of it came out of a can.)

Homemade stock couldn't be easier. Plan to make it some day when you'll be at home, starting it after breakfast and letting it simmer practically unattended until dinnertime. Its presence in the freezer makes homemade onion soup an easy possibility when you're planning a company menu. For anything but a formal dinner, a hearty soup can certainly be the centerpiece of a meal, and you can't beat onion for popularity, especially when you dress it up with Cognac and top it with a beautiful gratin of mixed cheeses. Then, for more drama at the table, just before serving tweak up a corner of the puffy, bubbling, fragrant gratin and stir in egg yolks whisked with Port wine. It imparts a smooth texture, the flavor booms out like a gong, and there's something warm and hospitable about this final gesture. When our nieces and nephews were little, we'd sometimes give them purses or wallets for Christmas, and Paul always slipped in a shiny dime before wrapping them; the feeling is a bit like that.

If it's an informal supper party, you might well prefer the statelier pace, and of course the variety, of a three-course menu, simple though it may be, with a pretty, light dessert and a fairly substantial salad. The one I am suggesting here was born in California, certainly the cradle of salads in this country. I am not, by the way, offering anything like the one I shall always remember at a ladies' luncheon (of non-Californians) some years ago; it was composed of chopped marshmallows and bottled mayonnaise molded with pineapple gelatin into the shape of a peeled banana and posed upright on one piece of pale iceberg lettuce far too small for the cleverest of diners to hide anything under. No. I am proposing a famous salad served for the first time at the Hollywood Brown Derby, not the original restaurant designed by Wilson Mizener in the shape of a hat on Wilshire Boulevard, but the Brown Derby at Hollywood and Vine.

It was invented there in 1936 by Robert Cobb, president of the restaurant group, who apparently improvised the dish from leftovers in the refrigerator, just as any cook will serve a few savory scraps on lettuce and call it a chef's salad. But Cobb's leftovers included good Roquefort cheese, chicken, avocado, bacon, hard-boiled eggs, herbs, tomatoes, and a variety of salad greens; he diced them fine, the greens too, and tossed them all together. An epicure's inspiration. He was bragging about his invention one day when Syd Grauman came to the restaurant. Grauman wanted one, and he found it so good he told all his friends about Cobb's marvelous salad. Friends told friends, and so forth... And no wonder. Each mouthful rewards you with a whole spectrum of delicious flavors, and of textures ranging from rich and suave to downright crunchy.

You present Cobb Salad beautifully arranged in strips or segments, and then you have the fun of tossing it into confetti, a savage joy rather like jumbling up a completed jigsaw puzzle before passing it on to your little brother. A more sophisticated pleasure, if you enjoy tabletop cookery, is the concoction of Vesuvial Bananas in a chafing dish. It takes a good 5 minutes for the sauce to boil down to a syrup while the bananas cook through, and when I'm all alone on the stage or the TV screen, I have to have some trifle ready to fill the silence like "Life in California in the Golden Age of Cobb (or of Caesar, he of that other salad)" or even "Big Bananas I Have Known." But at home, you don't need talk or stunts. The bananas are spectacle enough, from the appetizing sizzles of their buttery beginning, through the expanding fragrances of their liquorous cooking, right on to the climactic fiery cloudlet of their final moment. Certainly, good points about this menu are its relative ease of preparation and its quite reasonable expense—take or leave a few dollops of wine and spirits along the way—and, except for a rapid change of plates between courses, you can be in the dining room with your guests the whole way through.

Preparations and Marketing

Recommended Equipment:

To serve the soup, you'll need either a 3-quart (3-L) oven-proof tureen, or else individual ovenproof bowls. For slicing onions, you can use (in order of expense and splendor): a sharp knife; an efficient small slicer, The Feemster, made by the M. E. Heuk Company, Cincinnati, Ohio 45223; a cabbage shredder often shown in country store catalogues; the chic and intricate *mandoline* manufactured in France by the Bron people (and maybe other companies); or a food processor.

To serve Cobb Salad, a wide bowl is desirable, so that you can present it, before tossing, with each colorful ingredient mounded separately on the greens.

Although you can do the Vesuvial Bananas in an electric skillet at the table, a chafing dish setup is far more attractive. You do not need the intense heat provided by the fluid-alcohol flame in our professional burner, but it must be strong enough to cook the orange syrup in a reasonable amount of time. I've found it perfectly satisfactory to take a can of Sterno and either remove the lid and use the can itself as a container, or scoop the material into a small metal bowl with a top diameter of about 4 inches (10 cm). What you need is a large burning surface that you can rig to fit your chafing dish contraption. I also find it a good idea to set the chafing dish apparatus on a tray to catch spills, hold utensils, etc.

Staples to Have on Hand:

Table salt
Optional: coarse or kosher salt
Peppercorns
Sugar
Imported bay leaves
Dried thyme
Whole cloves or allspice berries
Olive oil and/or fresh peanut oil
Flour
Eggs (3 to 5)
Unsalted butter (less than 2 sticks)
Garlic

Optional: Port or Madeira wine

Orange liqueur

White rum, dark Jamaica rum, or bourbon
   whiskey

Optional: Cognac

Specific Ingredients for This Menu:

Meaty soup bones (2 or more quarts, or 2 L; see
   recipe, plus suggestions for a boiled dinner in
   Manufacturing Note preceding recipe)

Boneless chicken breast halves (2)

Bacon (6 slices)

Roquefort or best-quality blue cheese (2 ounces
   or 60 g)

Firm Swiss cheese, of several kinds, if possible—
   such as Gruyère, Emmenthal, Fribourg, Sbrinz
   (9 ounces or 250 g)

Salad greens: 1 green crisp head iceberg lettuce;
   1 smallish head chicory; 1 smallish head
   romaine; 1 medium-to-large bunch
   watercress •

Parsley •

Shallots •, scallions, or chives

Celery (1 head)

Optional: 1 leek

Yellow onions (about 3½ pounds or 1½ kg)

Carrots (2 large)

Tomatoes (2; see recipe)

Avocado (1)

Lemons (2)

Oranges (2)

Bananas (6) •

An accompaniment for the bananas: fresh
   strawberries (2 pints or 900 g)

Dry white wine or dry white French vermouth
   (2½ cups or about ½ L)

Bread for French Onion Soup

❶ Remarks:

Salad greens: surround with slightly dampened paper towels, and store in plastic bags in the refrigerator. Wash watercress, shake or spin fairly dry, wrap in paper towels, and refrigerate in a plastic bag—cress is perishable and will keep only about 2 days before beginning to turn yellow. *Parsley* is more sturdy: prepare like watercress, but it will keep several days longer. *Shallots*: shallots will keep in a cool, dry place for a number of weeks, but if you happen to have more than you need, you can freeze them whole, in a plastic bag or container. They soften up as soon as they thaw, so peel and mince them almost as soon as you take them from the freezer; they are then fine for cooking, though too limp for salads. *Bananas*: for cooking, they should be just barely ripe—all yellow, but without any soft spots. Store at room temperature. *Bread for French onion soup*: you want white bread with body here; if it is soft and fluffy and squashy to begin with, it will become a miserable disintegration of white slime when baked in the soup. Ideally you would use old-fashioned French bread, from the regular long loaf cut into crosswise slices less than ½ inch (1 cm) thick. But if your French bread is soft and limp, you will be better off with a firm loaf of nonsweet sliced sandwich bread, cut into rounds about 3 inches (7 to 8 cm) in diameter. If you have any doubts, toast a slice of bread and simmer it to see what happens. Your own homemade French bread would, of course, be ideal.

French Onion Soup

Entirely homemade onion soup base

Manufacturing Note:

As long as you are making a beef stock, you may also want to include the ingredients for a boiled dinner, such as a piece of stewing beef or pork, or a chicken, or a fresh beef tongue. Tie it up and attach a long end of its string to the handle of your kettle; then you can pull it up for checking, and remove it when it's done. If you want vegetables with this boiled dinner, tie in a piece of washed cheesecloth, and they are easy to remove, too, when their time is up.

Plain Brown Beef Stock—Fonds Brun Simple:
For about 2 quarts or 2 L, serving 4 to 6 people

For the Beef Stock:

> 2 or more quarts (2 L) sawed beef bones, including knuckles and some meaty scraps attached; plus veal and poultry bones, raw and/or cooked
> 2 large carrots, scrubbed and roughly sliced
> 3 large onions, peeled and roughly chopped
> Sufficient cold water to cover all ingredients
> 1 large leek, washed (optional)
> 3 celery ribs with leaves, washed
> 1 Tb coarse or kosher salt (or table salt)
> 1 large herb bouquet tied in washed cheesecloth (8 parsley sprigs, 1 large imported bay leaf, 1 tsp dried thyme, 4 whole cloves or allspice berries, 3 large cloves garlic, unpeeled)

Spread the bones and meat scraps (except for poultry) and the carrots and onions in a roomy enough roasting pan; set in the upper middle level of a 450°F/230°C oven and roast for 40 or more minutes, turning and basting ingredients several times with accumulated fat until nicely browned. Transfer to a large soup kettle, leaving fat in pan. Discard fat and deglaze pan—pour in a cup or so (¼ L) of water and set over heat, scraping coagulated roasting juices into the liquid.

Pour into the kettle, and add enough cold water to cover ingredients by 2 inches (5 cm). Bring to the simmer, skim off gray scum that will rise to the surface for several minutes, then add rest of ingredients. Cover partially and simmer slowly 4 to 5 hours at least, adding more water if needed to cover ingredients. Strain into a large bowl, chill, peel coagulated fat off surface, and your stock is finished.

● Stock may be refrigerated in a covered bowl, but needs boiling up every 2 or 3 days to prevent spoilage; or it may be frozen for several months. If your stock lacks savor, boil it down in a large kettle (after degreasing) to concentrate it.

Meat Glaze—Glace de Viande:

You can concentrate your stock even further, almost to the consistency of a bouillon cube, actually. Keep on boiling it down until the stock thickens into a syrup (be careful near the end since it burns easily); pour into a jar, and cover it. Meat glaze will keep for months in the refrigerator, ready at all times to enrich a soup or a sauce, or to become a bouillon. A real kitchen treasure to have on hand, and it doesn't take up much space, either.

For the Onion Soup:

3 Tb butter
1 Tb olive oil or cooking oil
6 cups (1½ L) quite thinly sliced yellow onions (about 1½ pounds or ¾ kg)
½ tsp sugar (which helps the onions to brown)
1 tsp salt
2 Tb flour
2 quarts (2 L) homemade stock, heated (the preceding recipe)
2 cups (½ L) dry white wine or dry white French vermouth
Salt and pepper as needed

Melt the butter with the oil in a heavy-bottomed 4-quart (3¾-L) pan; stir in the sliced onions. Cover the pan and cook slowly for 15 to 20 minutes (or cook them in a 350°F/180°C oven), stirring up occasionally, until onions are tender and translucent. Raise heat to moderately high, stir in the sugar and salt, and cook 20 to 30 minutes more, stirring frequently, until onions have turned a fine deep caramel brown.

Lower heat to moderate, blend in the flour, and cook, stirring, for 2 to 3 minutes. Remove from heat, and blend in 2 ladlefuls hot stock. Stir in the rest, and the wine. Season lightly to taste, bring to the boil, then simmer slowly, partially covered, for 30 minutes. Carefully correct seasoning. ❷ May be cooked several days in advance. When cold, cover and refrigerate, or freeze.

Serve as is, with a bowl of grated cheese and toasted French bread, or make onion soup gratinée as follows:

French Onion Soup Gratinée—The Classic Version

There are a number of opinions on the very best recipe for gratinéed onion soup. My French colleague Simca has her excellent version in Volume I of *Mastering*, and I did it also for *The French Chef* black-and-white TV series: it has a little grated raw onion and some slivers of cheese in the soup before its toast and cheese topping go on, and it finishes with a *de luxe* enrichment of Worcestershire sauce, egg yolk, and Cognac that is slipped under the brown crust just before serving. A trip through other French sources confirms a spirited egg-yolk finish, and also reveals conflicting information on what can cut down on the length of the cheese strings that drip from the spooon as you consume your soup—although certainly to some enthusiasts those dangling ropes of cheese are a large part of the soup's authentic character.

Stringy cheese solutions

1) Rather than grating the cheese, either cut it into small dice or very thin slices. 2) Use two or three kinds of cheese rather than just one. 3) Beat egg yolks into the soup before gratinéing, and bake it in a pan of boiling water. 4) White wine can de-string cheese—as suggested by Jim Beard and confirmed by the French—and it does indeed work for a

cheese sauce. Well, I've tried all but method number 3, and my soup-cheese does string somewhat, though not excessively. However, I think one should select pieces of cheese that are on the rather hard and dry side, and I do use a good bit of spirits.

For a 3-quart or 3-L ovenproof tureen or casserole, serving 4 to 6 people

A loaf or 2 of firm, full-textured French bread
2 Tb or more butter
3 ounces (85 g) firm Swiss cheese in a piece, cut into very thin slices
Freshly ground pepper—2 to 3 turns of the pepper mill
2 quarts (2 L) or so simmering onion soup
4 to 5 Tb Cognac (optional)
1¼ cups (3 dL) lightly packed, coarsely grated mixed Swiss cheeses
2 egg yolks, beaten with 4 to 5 Tb Port or Madeira wine (optional)

Equipment:

An ovenproof tureen or casserole; a serving spoon and fork for the crust; a ladle for serving the soup; and a platter on which to set the tureen. A small decorative pitcher for the optional egg yolk and wine mixture

---

Toasted French Bread Rounds:

Preheat oven to 425°F/220°C. Cut bread into slices less than ½ inch (1 cm) thick, place in one layer on a baking sheet or sheets, and dry out in upper third (or middle and upper third) level of oven, watching and turning frequently until bread is a fairly even lightly toasted brown. (You may want extra bread rounds to pass with the soup; do them now, too, and/or do extras, since they freeze nicely for several weeks.)

Filling and baking the tureen
About 45 minutes

Preheat oven to 425°F/220°C. Smear a tablespoon of butter in bottom of tureen and arrange over it a closely packed layer of toasted bread; spread over bread layer the sliced cheese, grind on pepper, ladle in the boiling soup, and pour in the optional Cognac. Float a closely packed layer of toast on the top of the soup, and spread over it the grated cheese with a few grinds of pepper; sprinkle over that a tablespoon or 2 melted butter. Set tureen in middle level of oven and bake for about half an hour, or until soup is bubbling hot and top has browned nicely.

❷ Plan to serve the soup fairly soon, for fear the crust might sink down into it. Until then, keep it hot, almost at the simmer.

At the table, and just before serving, lift a side of the crust with a serving fork, pour into the soup the optional egg yolk—wine mixture, and stir gently under crust with your ladle. Serve, giving each guest some of the top crust along with the soup.

Individual Servings of French Onion Soup Gratinée:

Use the same system as that outlined above, but make individual servings in ovenproof earthenware bowls set on a sturdy baking sheet; they will take about 20 minutes in the oven.

Thick French Onion Soup—La Gratinée Lyonnaise:

Proceed in exactly the same way as in the master recipe, but fill the tureen with layer upon layer of toasted bread rounds, each topped with a mixture of grated cheese and sliced cheese. (You will need probably 1½ times more cheese and soup than the amounts specified.) Pour the soup in to cover the bread and bake for 30 minutes or until soup is absorbed and cheese has browned on top; then pour in more soup and bake another 5 to 10 minutes. Stir in the optional egg yolk and wine mixture at the table. The bread and soup will have combined and transformed themselves into a richly flavored, soft, melting cheese-and-onion dumpling in your bowl—a very special Old World dish.

Cobb Salad

Ingredients for 6 to 8 people

½ head firm fine green iceberg lettuce
1 small head chicory (frizzy lettuce)
½ medium head romaine
1 medium bunch watercress—to make a cup or so
    (¼ L) or leaves and tender stems
2 poached chicken breast halves (see directions at
    end of this recipe)
Salt
Freshly ground pepper
1 lemon
Olive oil or fresh peanut oil
6 slices crisply cooked bacon
3 hard-boiled eggs
2 Tb minced fresh chives (or the white part and
    some of the tender green of scallions, or a
    mixture of shallots and fresh parsley)
2 ounces (60 g) real Roquefort cheese or best-
    quality blue cheese
2 medium-sized ripe red firm tomatoes (out of
    season, mix tomatoes with drained, seeded,
    Italian plum tomatoes and/or canned red
    pimiento)
About 1 cup (¼ L) plain vinaigrette dressing
    (page 380)
1 fine ripe firm avocado

Preliminaries
(To be done several hours in advance if necessary)

Separate the leaves of the salad greens, discard tough or
wilted parts, wash leaves and spin dry; wrap loosely and
refrigerate in a clean towel. Pull off leaves and tender stems
from watercress (discard tough bits); wash, wrap in a damp
paper towel, and refrigerate in a plastic bag. Cut the chicken
breasts into fine dice (by first cutting into thin slices, the
slices into strips, and the strips laid lengthwise then cut
crosswise into dice); toss in a small bowl with a sprinkling
of salt and pepper, a few drops of lemon juice and of oil;

cover and refrigerate. Mince the cooked bacon and set aside in another bowl; chop or sieve the eggs (an egg slicer comes in handy for this. Simply slice egg as usual, turn egg, slice again. Repeat for a total of three times until the egg is in a fine dice.) and toss in another small bowl with a sprinkling of salt and pepper. Mince the chives or scallions fine, and put them in the bowl with the eggs, and do the same with the Roquefort or blue cheese (dicing in the same fashion as you did either the chicken or the eggs; you should have about ½ cup or 1 dL diced). Drop the tomatoes for exactly 10 seconds in boiling water, and set aside (to loosen their skins for later peeling). Prepare the vinaigrette.

Half an hour or so before serving
(Items that wilt if done too soon)

Choose a fine big salad bowl. With a large, very sharp knife, cut the salad greens into very fine dice, ³⁄₁₆ inch or ½ cm. The easiest method, I think, is to lay 3 or 4 leaves flat, cut them into fine julienne shreds, pile the shreds together lengthwise, and cut across them—as for the chicken. The object here is to make clean nonbruising cuts. Place the greens in the bowl, mince the watercress also, and add to the greens. Peel, seed, and juice the tomatoes (cut out stem, peel, halve horizontally—not through stem—squeeze each half gently and poke out seeds), dice fine, and set aside on your chopping board with a sprinkling of salt and pepper. Halve the avocado peel and dice it, and scoop into a sieve, then swish in a bowl of cold water for a moment and drain (water bath helps prevent avocado from discoloring); turn into a small bowl and fold with a sprinkling of salt and a few drops of lemon juice and of oil.

Just before serving

Beat up the vinaigrette and toss about ⅓ of it with the minced greens, taste for seasoning, adding a little more dressing, salt, and pepper, etc., if necessary; arrange greens in a shallow mound. Arrange the rest of the ingredients attractively over the greens. Present at once to the table for general admiration, then toss the salad and serve it forth.

Note: If you wish to arrange the salad somewhat in advance, do not season the various ingredients, or they will lose their freshness; arrange the salad, cover with plastic and refrigerate, then toss with the dressing at the table.

Variations:

Arrange the salad in individual bowls, and each guest may then toss his own—or not—as he desires. You may substitute fresh mushrooms for chicken, or shrimp, crab, ham, or lobster; capers are also permitted when accompanying anchovies.

Poached Chicken Breasts:

Lay boned chicken breast halves in a lightly buttered saucepan just large enough to hold them in one layer. Pour in ½ cup (1 dL) dry white wine or dry white French vermouth, enough cold water just to cover the breasts, and add a bay leaf, a finely minced shallot or scallion, 3 parsley springs, 4 peppercorns, and ½ teaspoon of salt. Bring just to the simmer, cover, and cook at the barest simmer for 8 to 10 minutes, until the meat is springy to the touch. Let cool for 30 minutes in the cooking broth, then drain, let cool, wrap, and refrigerate. (Save cooking broth and add to your store of chicken stock, or use in soups and sauces.)

Vesuvial Bananas

Bananas simmered in orange butter and flamed in rum

Almost everyone loves bananas, and they make a most delectable flaming dessert when you want a chafing dish finish. Desserts done at the table demand the drama of flaming and, besides, that burning evaporates the alcohol—what we want with our bananas is the flavor of those spirits, not the kick! Although you may serve them just as they are, I think you'll find they most definitely need something to dress them up, such as a mound of sherbet or ice cream that they might surround, or a sprinkling of cinnamon or shaved chocolate. My solution is strawberries sliced and spread over the banana midriffs and placed whole at their either ends, then a basting of all elements with the buttery cooking juices.

For 6 people
Note: Because of timing restrictions on our television program, I did only 4 bananas, but our dinner here is for 6 people and so is the following recipe.

2 oranges
½ cup (1 dL) sugar
¾ stick (3 ounces or 85 g) unsalted butter
5 Tb orange liqueur
5 Tb white rum, dark Jamaica rum, or bourbon
  whiskey
1 lemon
1 pint (½ L) fresh strawberries, halved or
  quartered lengthwise
1 pint (½ L) fresh strawberries, whole, stems
  removed
6 bananas

Equipment:

A chafing dish large enough to hold the bananas easily; a burner with a reasonably strong heat source (or an electric frying pan); a tray to set the cooking apparatus upon; a long-handled spoon and fork for the bananas; a table fork for the lemon; a platter and/or dessert plates

Preliminaries in the kitchen

Arrange the dining room accessories on the tray. Just before dinner, so it will not lose its freshness, grate the peel of 1 orange onto a decorative plate, with the sugar and butter. Squeeze the juice out of 1½ of the oranges and pour into a pitcher; refrigerate, along with the butter and sugar plate. Set out the bottles of orange liqueur and rum, and halve the lemon. Ready your strawberries and place in decorative bowls. Peel the bananas, removing any strings clinging to their flesh, only the moment before cooking, either in the kitchen or at the table.

The cooking

Set the chafing dish on the lighted burner and add the butter. Let it bubble up, then stir in the sugar and grated orange peel. Pour in the orange juice and, with drama, pierce the cut side of a lemon half with your fork as you squeeze in the juice from on high, repeating with the second lemon half. Pour in the orange liqueur—from the bottle, if you can judge the amount of approximately 5 tablespoons. Let the liquid bubble up, then arrange the bananas in the pan. Baste them with the liquid almost continuously as it cooks and bubbles and gradually turns into a thick syrup, almost a caramel. This will take some 5 minutes of basting and animated conversation. However, do not cook the bananas too much or they will be too limp to transfer from chafing dish to platter or plates.

The flaming finish, and serving

As soon as you conclude the bananas are done and the syrup is thick enough, pour in the rum or whiskey, let bubble up, then either tip the pan into the flame, or ignite with a lighted match. Spoon the flaming liquid over the bananas until the flames subside. Arrange them either on a platter and decorate with strawberries as illustrated, or serve onto individual plates. Baste bananas and strawberries with the syrup.

❶ Timing

Long before you ever thought of this party, you might—just as a matter of good kitchen routine—have stocked your freezer with home-grated cheese, hard-toasted French bread rounds, and good brown stock. Perhaps you've been fooling the family dog all along by freezing any leftover bones, though you'd want to add a couple of good fresh meaty ones before boiling up your hoard. It does take from 6 to 7 hours to make a meat stock, but you can set it to boil whenever you wish and stop and start it at will. Homemade onion soup is never a last-minute decision, then, but since so much can be prepared beforehand, including the onions (several days), it's not a last-minute job either.

The day before you serve Cobb Salad, you can poach and chill the chicken breasts, then dice them, as well as cooking and dicing the bacon and the eggs. You can also wash, dry, and refrigerate the greens.

In the late afternoon, organize your chafing dish tray, but keep the butter, orange peel, and juice refrigerated. Peel the tomatoes, make the vinaigrette, and prepare the cheese for the onion soup.

An hour before your guests come, prepare the tureen or bowls for the onion soup, except for the topping. Finish the topping and slip the tureen into the oven 45 minutes (20 to 25 for individual bowls) before supper. Then dice your salad greens, tomatoes, and avocado.

Just before dinner, arrange the salad bowl and prepare the egg yolk and wine mixture for the tabletop finish of your gratin. Peel bananas just before you cook them.

Menu Variations

The recipe gives you three ways of serving *onion soup*, whether homemade or canned; and some other hearty soups are mentioned in the section on Menu Alternatives.

Cobb Salad, if you beef it up as suggested in the recipe, can be almost a supper in itself—a lunch, certainly. Other sturdy salads might well follow onion soup: a beef salad *à la parisienne*; a turkey salad; chicken salad; fish and shellfish salads; lentil and dried bean salads; *salade niçoise* with tuna, oil-cured black olives, egg, and anchovy. Other composed salads, like a *salade à la d'Argenson* of rice and beets, or a vegetable salad of the season, might need some additions, like fish, meat, poultry, cheese, or chick-peas. You might arrange a pretty Greek salad, with zucchini and porphyry-purple Calamata olives snowed with feta cheese. If you enjoy the speckled, sparkly look of Cobb Salad but want something lighter, try dicing colorful raw vegetables for an old-fashioned Calico Salad. An amusing variant, nice with cold ham, is blanched chopped carrots with blanched shredded red cabbage, cooled and marinated in a sweet-sour vinaigrette or sour cream dressing.

For other chafing dish *desserts*, there are always sweet omelets, and crêpes Suzette, and ice cream bathed in hot blazing fruits or flaming sauces, such as the mincemeat in rum on page 196.

Leftovers

French *onion soup* has as many cheerful consequences as saying "I do." That meat you might have removed when just tender from your possibly meaty soup bones could in itself become a small boiled dinner, or could make a fine hash. But beef stock aside, you can do a lot with leftover onion soup. You can add cooked rice or potatoes to it, with some cream, and process the whole lot for a soubise soup. If you strain out the onions, you have a delicious, freezable broth to add to other soups, or to sauces or stews (if not already oniony); and you might even clarify it and reduce it to make an aspic coating for the likes of chicken livers or duck. The beef broth, if you made extra, is of course a kitchen fundamental, as acknowledged in the French term *fonds de cuisine*. The toast rounds can be frozen or refrozen, as can the grated cheese; and the cooked cheese topping can be puréed, to be added as thickening to the same soup, or to another soup another day.

You can't keep a finished, tossed *Cobb Salad*, but you could simmer its remains in those of an onion soup for a sort of "Robert Cobb minestrone." If you diced but did not dress more ingredients than you needed after all, they can be put to excellent use. The lettuce and greens can be tossed into a *potage santé* or a vegetable broth (the French heal-all for a cold or an upset stomach). You dice a turnip, an onion, two carrots, a large potato, and very little parsley, add lettuce if you have it, and simmer in water for 20 minutes, then strain. It's pallid but pleasant, and it does stay down. Extra avocado can be run through the processor with a scallion or small onion, lemon juice, salt and red pepper to taste, and a little cream cheese, if you like, for thickening; this gives you a version of guacamole, or try the avocado *brandade* spread on page 330. It also stuffs cherry tomatoes, as does a mixture of minced hard-boiled egg, bacon, and chives, bound with mayonnaise. That same mixture, without the mayonnaise but with browned buttery crumbs, makes a nice garnish for cooked broccoli or spinach. Extra diced tomatoes can be simmered briefly in oil or butter and herbs for a delicious sauce.

If you have extra bananas and don't want to take them straight, you could process them with cream, lemon, rum, and sugar, then chill for a mousse or freeze for a sort of ice cream. Or use them in a fruit cup or, if they've ripened a bit, make banana bread. Finally, mine eyes have actually seen sandwiches of peanut butter and bananas—but this is more a dare than a suggestion!

Postscript: Una furtiva lagrima

Often before the piano, as French chefs call their stoves, I shed a furtive tear—not because I'm lovelorn like the poor tenor in *L'Elisir d'Amore*, but because I have onions to cut. So I took up the topic in my column in *McCall's* magazine, hoping my friendly correspondents would have some helpful ideas. I've learned a lot over the years from their letters. This time I got no fewer than 19 suggestions, every one guaranteed surefire. Space prevents my quoting them all, but here are a few.

Hold your breath while slicing, so that you don't breathe in the vapors. Slice by candlelight, and the vapors will be burned off by the flame. Hold a match between your teeth, flint end sticking out. Stand with a fan behind you and an open window in front of you. Keep your mouth open. Keep your mouth closed.

I've tried them all, to not much effect; but onions are worth a tear or two and, besides, one of these days I'll make my way to a sporting-goods store, to equip myself for a final experiment. One writer says she just puts on a diving mask or swimming goggles. "It looks funny," she says, "but it really works." I bet it does.

P.S.: A late bulletin—
Since the first printing of this book, Dr. Eric Block, a scientist at the University of Missouri, has discovered that onions contain a chemical called propanethial S-oxide which, when it comes in contact with the moisture in the eyes, produces sulfuric acid. Even just a little bit of that is so irritating that the eyes try to protect themselves by producing an avalanche of tears. Fortunately S-oxide is soluble in water and is slowed down by cold. Therefore, peel onions in a basin of water or, if you are also to chop them, chill them first and work fast.

A Vegetarian Caper

Menu

For 6 people

Spaghetti Squash Tossed with Eggplant Persillade

Gâteau of Crêpes—Layered with vegetables and cheese

Mixed Green Salad
Hot French Bread

Ice Cream and a Rum and Meatless Mincemeat Sauce

Suggested wines:

A light red wine like a Bordeaux, Beaujolais, or merlot; or a rosé; or a dry riesling or Chablis

"That was *so* good!" a friend exclaimed the other day. "Maybe I'll change my ways, too!" It took me a minute to catch on: she thought Paul and I had become vegetarians because we'd just served a dinner without meat, fish, or fowl. (And why not? There's no law . . .) No, we're not about to change our ways, which are omnivorous; but our pace, certainly. Any time. And this was one of those mild late-winter days when melting snow trills in the gutters and you hear birds and smell the earth again. Suddenly we craved light food and fresh flavors, and this menu hit the spot.

We serve it to carnivores, but it was, I admit, designed originally for vegetarian friends who happen to be of the moderate, or ovo-lacto, persuasion, meaning that they use eggs and milk and cheese. On the whole, I think the soft full flavors of dairy items are the ideal enrichment for good fresh produce; indeed, this sort of cooking is a stimulus to me. I would, though, find it a bit dull to work for long within the restrictions set by purist vegetarians.

Marcella Hazan, that queen of Italian cookery, presented me with my first spaghetti squash a few years ago, and it turns out that they are easily grown almost everywhere. We're seeing more and more of them in the markets, and a fine thing that is. You steam your great golden whopper whole, halve it and seed it, and then, heaven knows why, the flesh turns into spaghetti right under the spoon as you scoop it onto the platter: fine, long, bright gold strands with a crunchy juicy texture. Like spaghetti, its flavor is bland so that it takes beautifully to sauces and garnishes: all the exuberance of pasta without the concomitant calories! For this menu, and a hearty main dish to come, we use eggplant tossed with parsley and garlic (in itself a good dish); in the recipe I've suggested a nice variant as well, using sesame seeds. (If this meal weren't so strong in protein—I calculate that it affords one almost a full day's supply—sesame seeds would be a good way to boost it. Like mushrooms, they're prized by vegetarians for this reason. I like them simply because they are delicious.)

A stratum of practicality underlies the charm and the festive air of concerned hosts, and the same could be said of our main dish. Not only can it be largely prepared in advance, but it's good hot or cold, and is so compact and easily served that we often take it along (in its mold, of course) on fork picnics. You can use any combination of vegetables to fill the crêpe-walled compartments. As for crêpes themselves, they're one of the most versatile elements in cookery, one of the first things a beginning cook should master. Only their name poses a problem.

For the tomato sauce recipe, don't look in this chapter but in the Q & A section in the back of this book, where I've grouped a few basics. This is a sauce I use to add piquant flavor and brilliant color to all kinds of dishes: it has accompanied a boiled dinner, lasagne, and a baked fish with equal success, which gives you an idea of its versatility; you might also like to try it with an omelet sometime, or with a soufflé. The gâteau doesn't need a sauce, having plenty of flavor on its own, but enhancement is the name of the game in cooking an all-veg meal, and I like the look of the stratified slice in a sparkling red puddle. (In general, I prefer the old-fashioned custom of saucing around, not over, food.)

One recipe I am sorry *not* to supply here is one for homemade French bread. I've given it twice before, in *Mastering II* and in *J. C.'s Kitchen*, and it just takes too much space. It's not that a long recipe means a long job; with practice, most cooks find it takes about 15 minutes' working time per batch. The quality is seraphic, and I hope you'll want to try it. As for green salad, look in Q & A again for a basic vinaigrette dressing, vary it to your taste, and choose the freshest greens in the grocery.

Marvelously inquisitive and resourceful, the really good cooks among my vegetarian friends have steered me toward many good things to eat. I have vast respect for their imagination and care in cooking, and for the way they seek out the ultimate in fresh, exquisite produce. And for their realism and, well, sense of proportion. In America we still eat needless, indeed preposterous, quantities of animal protein, but I think the time is coming when we'll have to join with the rest of the world.

❶ Preparations and Marketing

Recommended Equipment:

If you don't have a big kettle or covered roaster, and a steaming rack, you can bake the spaghetti squash in the oven.

The gâteau recipe precisely fills a 2-quart (2-L) dish. I use the French charlotte mold 3½ inches (9 cm) deep, the one I like for soufflés, since it produces a dramatically tall Hadrian's Tomb-type cylinder; but any straight-sided, deep, ovenproof dish will do. When it's done, the gâteau will let you know by puffing up and becoming divinely fragrant, but you can make a more precise test by using an instant, microwave type of thermometer, a gadget you'll use for meats, poultry, and all kinds of other dishes as well.

For crêpes, while it's nice to have the classic French pan, a shallow iron one about 6 inches (15 cm) in diameter, with an angled handle for easy flipping will do; I also like an American-made one of thick cast aluminum with a nonstick lining. Because crêpe batter is very runny, you must have a pan the size you want your crêpe to be. That rules out pancake griddles and big frying pans, but not those amusing patented devices that make crêpes upside down or right side up.

Staples to Have on Hand:

Salt
Peppercorns
Nutmeg
Optional: fresh or fragrant dried dill weed
Optional: saffron threads
Optional: dried orange peel
Imported bay leaves
Italian or Provençal herb mixture
Olive oil ●
Butter
Optional: fresh sesame or peanut oil
Flour: Wondra or instant-blending type
    preferred ●
Milk
Optional: heavy cream (1 cup or ¼ L)
Garlic

Shallots or scallions
Lemons (1)
Optional: canned Italian plum tomatoes
Dark Jamaica rum or bourbon whiskey

Specific Ingredients for This Menu:

Swiss cheese (½ pound or 225 g)
Cream cheese (½ pound or 225 g) ●
Eggs (9 "large")
Optional: Parmesan cheese (½ pound or 225 g)
Salad greens
Parsley
Onions (2 medium)
Broccoli (1 bunch) ●
Carrots (1 pound or 450 g) ●
Eggplant (1 large) ●
Spaghetti squash (1 large) ●
Tomatoes (9 or 10 large) ●
Mushrooms (1 pound or 450 g) ●
French bread
Vanilla ice cream (1½ quarts or 1½ L)
Meatless mincemeat (1 jar)

---

❷ Remarks:

Staples to have on hand

Olive oil: if you want the best quality and are willing to pay for it, see that it is labeled "virgin olive oil," which means that this was the first pressing of the olives and that they were pressed cold. Olives are pressed not once but several times, and in later batches, in order to extract more oil, they are usually warmed. Be sure in any case that the label reads "pure olive oil," since otherwise it may contain adulterants. On keeping olive oil, there are many and fervent controversies—whether to decant it, whether it should breathe, etc.—but I have never had any trouble keeping an opened half-gallon of olive oil, covered and stored in a cool dark closet. *Flour*: Wondra, or other instant-blending type, is good for crêpes, since it mixes smoothly and almost instantly in cold liquid, and you don't have to let your batter rest an hour or two before using it, as you would with regular flour.

Specific ingredients for this menu

(With special thanks to *Crockett's Victory Garden* and to *Wyman's Gardening Encyclopedia*)

Cream cheese: best of all is the fresh kind, without gluey additives and preservatives, but it will keep only 3 days or so in the refrigerator. *Broccoli*: it's passé if the florets have begun to open. Ideal stalk length, below where the stem branches, is from 4 to 6 inches (10 to 15 cm); if the base of the stem is hollow, cut that part off, since it will be tough. *Carrots*: buy firm crisp carrots, refrigerate them in a plastic bag, and use them soon. *Eggplant*: take pains; you can turn people off this lovely vegetable for life by serving a bad one. Buy shiny, firm, taut-skinned ones, use them within 2 or 3 days, and do not keep them too cold. Soft spots and the slightest sign of wrinkle or shrivel or flab are all bad news. Although they are picked when the seeds are still sparse, soft, and immature, eggplants vary greatly in shape and in size—from 6-inch (15-cm) midgets to foot-long monsters. Most of those in your market will be the deep purple variety, but ivory, green, and mottled purple types exist and are similarly cooked. *Mushrooms*: the cultivated ones are best when the caps are curled tight to the stem, so that you can't see the gills. Refrigerate in a plastic bag and use as soon as you can, before they darken or soften. For field mushrooms, pick none you can't positively identify as edible. Dr. Wyman recomends Alexander H. Smith's *The Mushroom Hunter's Field Guide* (Ann Arbor: University of Michigan Press, revised edition, 1969). A standard field guide used by many mycologists I know is *One Thousand American Fungi*, by Charles McIlvaine and Robert K. Macadam (New York: Dover Publications, 1973), and one of my favorites for recipes is Jane Grigson's *The Mushroom Feast* (New York: Alfred A. Knopf, 1975). *Spaghetti squash*: use the fingernail test to be sure the rind is soft; if hard, the squash was picked when too mature. Here's a puzzle: the grower I consulted says its botanical name is *Cucurbita ficifolia*, and that it is a gourd of tropical origin. All the ones I've seen are bright gold, but a delightful old book by Cora, Rose, and Bob Brown, *The Vegetable Cook Book: From Trowel to Table* (Philadelphia: J. B. Lippincott, 1939), says it's cream-white like a honeydew melon. You can tell at a glance that it's a cucurbit, like cucumbers, squash, gourds, pumpkins, and some melons; but the great horticultural authority Dr. Wyman gives the name *C. ficifolia* to a white, *in*edible fruit (or vegetable) grown in the tropics and commonly called Malabar gourd. His encyclopedia doesn't describe anything like my big beauty. *Tomatoes*: the U.S. Department of Agriculture says so, county agents say so, any farmer who knows a hoe from a harrow says so, and I'm so sick of saying so that now I sing it instead. In my sleep. But the markets still plod along with their thumbs in their ears and their minds in neutral. What do we tomato lovers have to do, for pity's sake? Well, again: in the summertime, you can buy locally grown tomatoes that are ripe or that will ripen. However, no tomato at any season will ever ripen if it has been kept at a temperature of less than 40°F/4.5°C for any length of time; it may eventually turn red, but its flavor-developing facilities have been killed. In fact, any temperature less than 50°F/10°C is bad news for the tomato. Even a picked green tomato that is old enough to have developed the normal amount of seeds and jelly in its interstices will ripen in a few days at room temperature—in a week or so if kept around 60°F/16°C—if it was never abused by a low temperature. Tomatoes should never ever be refrigerated unless they are so ripe they will spoil! Any market that stores an unripened tomato in a refrigerated case has no sense of decency, no respect for tomatoes, and certainly no knowledge at all about them—or concern for us, the tomato-buying public. (End of tomato discussion—for this book, anyway.)

Spaghetti Squash Tossed with Eggplant Persillade

Serving 6 people

1 spaghetti squash about 10 by 7 inches (25 by 18 cm)
1 eggplant about 9 by 5 inches (23 by 13 cm)
Salt and pepper
4 or more Tb olive oil
2 or more large cloves garlic, minced
5 to 6 Tb minced fresh parsley (a small bunch)
2 to 3 Tb butter (optional)
1 cup (¼ L) freshly grated Parmesan cheese (optional)

Equipment:

A kettle large enough to hold the squash, and a vegetable steaming rack (or you may boil or bake the squash); 1 or 2 large frying pans, nonstick recommended; a long-handled spoon and fork for table tossing

Preliminary cooking of spaghetti squash

To cook the squash, you may bake it for 1½ hours in a 350°F/180°C oven, or boil it for 20 to 30 minutes, or steam it. I opt for steaming, as the easiest method. Place a rack or colander in the bottom of a large kettle or roaster with a tight-fitting lid, add 1½ inches (4 cm) water, lay in the squash, and bring to the boil. (Weight down the lid if necessary, so the steam can do its work.) Steam for 25 to 30 minutes, or just until the outside of the squash will cede to the pressure of your fingers. Cut the squash open lengthwise, and scrape out the thick yellowish threads and big seeds from the center, going crosswise with a big spoon—careful here or you will mix these nonspaghetti threads with the real meat of the squash. Then scrape down the squash lengthwise, and the meat will separate itself into strands.

❶ May be cooked and scraped even a day in advance; cover the spaghetti and refrigerate.

The Eggplant Persillade—Eggplant with Garlic and Parsley:

Having chosen a fine, firm, shiny eggplant, cut off the green cap, and remove the skin with a vegetable peeler. Cut into ½-inch (1½-cm) slices, cut the slices into ½-inch strips, and the strips into ½-inch dice. Toss in a colander with ½ teaspoon salt, and let drain for at least 20 minutes, then dry in a towel. Film a large frying pan (preferably a nonstick one) with ⅛ inch (½ cm) olive oil, and sauté the eggplant over moderately high heat for 4 to 5 minutes, tossing frequently, until tender—test by tasting a piece. Add the garlic and toss for a minute to cook it, then toss with the parsley only at the last moment. Incidently, this is a good dish all by itself, either hot or cold.

❶ The eggplant may be cooked several hours in advance and set aside in a bowl, but do not add the parsley or reheat until the last moment.

Final assembly and serving

Heat several tablespoons of oil and/or butter in a large frying pan, add the spaghetti squash strands, tossing and turning over moderately high heat for several minutes to cook the squash a little more—or to your taste. Toss with salt and pepper, then turn out onto a hot platter. Spoon the hot eggplant in the center, and bring to the table. Then toss the spaghetti and eggplant together with, if you like, spoonfuls of cheese, and pass more cheese separately for those who wish it.

Variation:

Here is another squash and eggplant combination we like very much.

For the squash

Steam and shred the spaghetti squash as usual. Heat several tablespoons of oil in a large frying pan and swirl in 2 or 3 cloves of garlic, minced, cooking them gently for a minute or two. Then toss in the spaghetti squash and fold with the garlic, and salt and pepper to taste, adding more oil (or butter, if you wish) and cooking to the degree you prefer. Then toss with spoonfuls of Parmesan cheese, turn onto a hot platter, and garnish with the following eggplant. Serve the spaghetti squash with a piece or two of the eggplant—but do not toss them together.

Sesame baked eggplant

For one fine, firm, shiny eggplant about 9 inches long and 4 inches in diameter (23 by 10 cm). Cut the green top off the eggplant, and slice the eggplant into lengthwise quarters (or sixths), and each quarter (or sixth) into halves. Salt the flesh sides lightly and let stand 10 to 15 minutes, then pat dry with paper towels. Brush lightly on all sides with olive oil, and arrange skin side down in a shallow baking dish or jelly-roll pan. Bake in the upper third of a 425°F/220°C oven for about 15 minutes, or until the eggplant is soft. Meanwhile, toss ½ cup (1 dL) sesame seeds in a frying pan over moderate heat, shaking pan continuously until nicely toasted (they burn easily). Roll the cooked eggplant in the sesame seeds just before serving.

Gâteau of Crêpes

Molded mountain of crêpes layered with vegetables and cheese

Here is a handsome dish indeed, layers of fresh vegetables bound with a cheese custard, baked in a mold lined with crêpes—those multipurpose thin French pancakes. Serve it hot as a first course, a luncheon dish, or as the main course for a vegetarian meal, and any leftovers are good cold.

Serving 6 to 8 people

For the Crêpe Batter:
For 18 to 20 crêpes 5½ inches (14 cm) in diameter

1 cup (140 g) flour (Wondra or instant-blending preferred
⅔ cup (1½ dL) each milk and water
3 "large" eggs
¼ tsp salt
3 Tb melted butter, or sesame or peanut oil

Vegetables and Cheese for Filling:

1 pound (450 g) carrots
6 to 8 Tb butter
Salt and pepper
½ tsp or so fresh or dried dill weed (optional)
1 pound (450 g) fresh mushrooms
4 Tb minced shallots or scallions
1 bunch (18 to 20 ounces or 500 to 550g) fresh broccoli
2 cups (½ L) coarsely grated Swiss cheese

Custard Mixture for Filling:

1 cup (½ pound or 225 g) cream cheese
6 "large" eggs
1 cup (¼ L) milk and/or heavy cream
Salt and pepper
A pinch of nutmeg, to taste

Optional Sauce for the Gâteau:

**2½ to 3 cups (about ¾ L) fresh tomato sauce
(page 383; optional)**

Equipment:

**A heavy cast-iron or cast-aluminum (nonstick
recommended) frying pan with 5½-inch (14-
cm) bottom diameter, for the crêpes; an 8-cup
(2-L) baking dish, such as a metal charlotte
mold, 4 inches (10 cm) deep; an instant
(microwave) meat thermometer is recommended.**

The crêpes—batter

Scoop dry-measure cup into flour container until cup is overflowing; sweep off excess with the straight edge of a knife,
and pour flour into a pitcher or bowl. Blend the milk and
water into the flour, beating with a whip until smooth (easy
with Wondra or instant-blending flour), then beat in the eggs,
salt, and butter or oil. Let rest for 10 minutes (an hour or 2
if you are using regular flour) so that flour granules can
absorb the liquid—making a tender crêpe.

The crêpes—cooking

To cook the crêpes, heat frying pan or pans until drops of
water sizzle on the surface. Brush lightly with a little butter
(usually only necessary for the first crêpe), and pour 2 to 3
tablespoons or so of the batter into the center of the pan,
turning the pan in all directions as you do so to spread the
batter over the bottom surface. (If you have poured in too
much, pour excess back into your batter bowl.) Cook for 30
seconds or so, until you see, when you lift an edge, that it
is nicely browned. Turn and cook for 10 to 15 seconds more—
this second side never cooks evenly and is kept as the non-
public or bottom side of the crêpe. Arrange crêpes, as they
are made, on a cake rack so they will cool and dry off for 5
minutes or so. When dry (but not brittle!), stack together,
wrap in foil and place in a plastic bag.

❶ Crêpes will keep for 2 to 3 days in the refrigerator. To
freeze, it is best to package them in stacks of 6 or 8; either
thaw at room temperature or unpackage and heat in a covered dish in a moderate oven for 5 minutes or until they
separate easily.

Note: I used to stack my cooked crêpes between sheets of wax paper or foil, but now that I have learned the cool-and-dry system, I have not found it necessary, even for freezing.

Preparing the vegetables

Trim and peel the carrots, and cut into julienne matchsticks. Sauté in 1½ tablespoons butter in a large frying pan, swirling and tossing frequently until carrots are nicely tender and being careful not to brown them. Season well with salt, pepper, and optional dill; set aside in a bowl.

Trim and wash the mushrooms, and cut into fine mince (a food processor is useful here); a handful at a time, twist the mushrooms in the corner of a clean towel to extract as much of their juice as possible. Sauté in the same large frying pan in 1½ tablespoons butter with the shallots or scallions, until the mushroom pieces begin to separate from each other. Season to taste with salt and pepper, and set aside in a separate bowl. This is now officially a mushroom *duxelles*.

Trim and wash the broccoli. Cut bud ends off stalks, to make them about 2 inches (5 cm) long. Starting at the cut ends, peel as much skin off as you easily can; peel skin off stalks, cutting down to expose tender whitish flesh, then cut into pieces half the length of your little finger—all this for quick and even cooking. Drop the peeled broccoli into 4 quarts (4 L) rapidly boiling salted water and boil uncovered for 3 to 5 minutes, or until just barely tender. Drain immediately; chop into pieces about ¼ inch (¾ cm) in size. Toss briefly in 2 tablespoons hot butter, and salt and pepper to taste. Set aside.

❷ Carrots may be cooked a day ahead, and so may the broccoli; cover and refrigerate. Mushrooms may be cooked weeks ahead and stored in the freezer; be sure to defrost before using.

The custard mixture

To blend the cream cheese with the rest of the custard ingredients, either force it through a sieve with the eggs into a bowl and beat thoroughly, adding the rest of the ingredients, or mix everything together smoothly in a blender or food processor.

Assembling

Preheat oven to 350°F/180°C. Smear some butter over inside of baking dish and line bottom of dish with buttered wax paper. Fit 1 crêpe, good side down, in the bottom of the dish, and space 4 around the sides (the good sides against dish); cover with a second layer of 4 more overlapping crêpes, as shown.

Spread ¼ of the grated Swiss cheese in the bottom of the dish, cover with the carrots, pressing them well in place, and top with ⅓ of the remaining cheese. Ladle in enough custard mixture to come just to the level of the carrots and cheese. Arrange 1 crêpe on top, and spread over it the mushrooms and another ladleful of custard. Arrange 1 more crêpe over the mushrooms and spread on ½ of the remaining cheese, then the broccoli, and the final bit of cheese. Pour on the last of the custard mixture and fold the first layer of overhanging crêpes up over the filling; cover with a crêpe, fold the outside layer of overhang up over it, and cover with 1 or more crêpes (depending on their size and the top of your dish). Place a round of buttered wax paper over the dish, and cover with a sheet of foil.

❷ I think it best to bake almost immediately, in case the custard leaks against the sides and bottom of the dish, sticking the crêpes to it and making a mess later when you attempt to unmold.

Baking
About 1¾ hours

Bake on lower middle rack in preheated oven, placing a pizza pan or something on the rack below to catch possible dribbles. In about 1 hour, when the gâteau has started to rise, turn oven up to 400°F/205°C. It will eventually rise an inch or more (2½ to 3 cm) and is done when a meat thermometer, its point at the center, reads 160°F/71°C. Remove from oven and let rest at room temperature for 10 to 15 minutes, allowing the custard to set and settle. Then run a thin-bladed knife carefully around inside of dish, and unmold onto a hot platter. Surround the gâteau, if you wish, with fresh tomato sauce. To serve, cut into wedges, as though it were a cake, and spoon sauce around.

❷ May be baked in advance; unmold the gâteau after its wait, and keep it warm in the turned-off oven, covered with an upside-down bowl. In any case, do not let the baked gâteau sit in its baking dish in a hot turned-off oven—as I did (but you did not see!) on our TV show. The cooking liquids leaked into the bottom of the baking dish, evidently, and the hot oven then glued the crêpes to the dish. Fortunately we had a standby gâteau safely loosened from its mold, which replaced my messy unmolding caper on the serving dish. There is indeed nothing like experience as a teacher!

To serve cold

This makes a delicious cold dish for a luncheon or to take on a picnic. Accompany with a tomato or cucumber salad and, if you wish, a sour cream dressing or the same tomato sauce, which also is good cold.

Ice Cream and a Rum and Meatless Mincemeat Sauce

Serving 6 people

Following the general line of quick and easy but good desserts, here is an idea for using a jar of mincemeat, which is so good it should be eaten more often than just on Thanksgiving. You need no recipe for this, only 1½ quarts (1½ L) or so best-quality vanilla ice cream and half a jar or so of good mincemeat. Place the ice cream in a serving bowl, and heat the mincemeat with several spoonfuls of dark Jamaica rum, or even bourbon whiskey, which is a fine substitute. Spoon the hot mincemeat sauce over each serving (you may wish to heat and flame it at the table), and you may also wish to pass some attractive sugar cookies along with the dessert.

❶ Timing

You have little to do at the last minute to serve this meal, and more than half the work is already done if you make it a habit to freeze and stock such staple items as loaves of French bread, stacks of crêpes, grated Swiss cheese, mushroom duxelles, and fresh tomato sauce. Even if you must prepare these things specially for your party, you can do so 2 or 3 days beforehand, freeze the French bread, and store the other items in the refrigerator.

You can steam the spaghetti squash and prepare and cook the carrots and broccoli on the day before your party.

That morning, wash, dry, and refrigerate your salad greens, mix the vinaigrette dressing, compose (and refrigerate) the custard sauce for the gâteau, and cook the eggplant.

Two and a half hours before dinner, assemble the gâteau and start baking it.

Half an hour before serving it, test the gâteau for doneness. At this time you could start warming the mincemeat in a pan of water over low heat. Just before you sit down, unmold the gâteau, and move the ice cream from freezer to refrigerator, to soften, and reheat the eggplant and spaghetti squash and the tomato sauce. Toss your salad just before you serve it.

Menu Variations

All kinds of garnishes are nice with spaghetti squash—or you might use real spaghetti with the eggplant garnish for a main dish, instead of the gâteau. You can vary the gâteau itself by substituting other vegetables in the layers. Or you can make one of the filled crêpe recipes in *Mastering I*, assembling the entire dish in the morning and heating it just before dinner. The fillings can be infinitely varied—try cooked minced chicken sometime, for omnivores, or creamed shellfish—and the crêpes are served beautifully sauced in their baking dish. *J.C. & Co.* has other good toppings for store bought ice cream, and it's easy to think up your own.

J.C.'s Kitchen contains several good recipes for dried legumes, which make hearty main dishes for all vegetarians, including the strictest; if your guests, like ours, will eat eggs and cheese, that opens up a world of soufflés, omelets, and gratins. If, however, your guests are coming not just for a meal but for several days, you may want to look at a specialized vegetarian cookbook. Frances Moore Lappé's *Diet for a Small Planet* (New York: Ballantine Books, rev. ed. 1975) analyzes nonanimal proteins and shows how to boost protein values by combining complementary foods. It contains a lot of recipes, and even more may be found in its companion volume, *Recipes for a Small Planet*, by Ellen Buchman Ewald (New York: Ballantine Books, 1975). Martha Rose Shulman's *The Vegetarian Feast* (New York: Harper & Row, 1978) is concerned with fancier vegetarian cooking and helps out the amateur with a wide choice of menus. Finally, Anna Thomas's two volumes, *The Vegetarian Epicure* (New York: Alfred A. Knopf and Vintage Books, 1972 and 1978), have such delicious and well-considered dishes that they belong on the shelf of any blissfully greedy cook of any persuasion including Red Fang.

Leftovers

If you have last-minute no-shows, go ahead and cook all your eggplant, but put some aside before the addition of parsley and garlic. It's the foundation of several splendid dishes (see *Mastering II* and *J.C.'s Kitchen*), some of which you can eat cold. Two versions of eggplant caviar (a puréed spread or dip), one containing walnuts and the other sesame seed paste, are special treats for vegetarians.

With extra cooked vegetables, custard sauce, and cheese, you have the makings of a nice gratin or the filling for a quiche, and of course cooked or uncooked vegetable scraps are a natural for soup. I have no great suggestions for leftover salad. But extra French bread begs to be sliced and toasted for *croûtes* that you can store in the freezer until it's onion soup time again (see page 169); or blend or process them into crumbs—a jar of them, kept in the freezer, is a handy resource for any cook.

Leftover mincemeat, of course, makes splendid tarts, pies, and turnovers; since it keeps a long time in the refrigerator, once opened, you need be in no hurry to use it up.

Postscript: R & D in cooking

Certainly, one of the pleasures of cooking is thinking up new ways to present familiar ingredients. You will note that I have borrowed an engineering term rather than using the word "invent" because "invention," to me, means something like producing the very first mayonnaise, or puff pastry, or ice cream. Few cooks achieve such distinction, or have such happy accidents or discoveries. (Who would have known in advance that egg yolks would emulsify, or that flour and fat would separate in the oven into towering, airy layers?) But hardly any of us who cook has not put something together in an unusual, original, or different way, drawing from general knowledge, experience, and imagination.

I think our crêpe and vegetable gâteau could be called a creation, using the term loosely in its meaning of "investing something with a new form." Anyway, the recipe grew out of the combined activities of us cooks on the *J. C. & Co.* team, and we are very pleased with ourselves. I might mention that in our first experiments we baked the gâteau in a bain-marie (pan of water) in a 350°F/180°C oven; it came out beautifully—ideally, rather—but *3 hours* is a very long time, so for the recipe and for television we threw out the water and stepped up the heat. As noted, other cooks might like to fill the layers with other ingredients, keeping our *R* (Research) but continuing with their own *D* (Development). What we're offering you is an attractive idea, not a sacrosanct monument.

Lobster Soufflé
for Lunch

Menu

For 6 people

Lobster Soufflé—on a Platter
Salade Mimosa
Pumpernickel Melba

Les Délices aux Poires—A pear dessert

Suggested wines:

A fine white Burgundy, Graves, or chardonnay with the lobster, and a sweet white wine or Champagne with the pears

Even in the days when lobsters were common as pea gravel, they were prized like rubies by great chefs, who joyfully elaborated on their intense flavor and azalea coloring to create sophisticated dishes for the most elegant occasions. And family cooks loved to call out, "Have another, anybody?" over big red clattering piles of lobsters simply boiled in the shell. Recent experiments in commercial lobster farming give us hope that those days will return, but for the moment lobsters are mighty scarce. In natural conditions, only one in one thousand infant lobsters will survive the predators of its critical first three weeks, during which time it lives near the sea's surface and is frequently in molt; thereafter it takes six years (in northern waters) to attain a weight of one pound. So it will be a while before we can make up for a century of overfishing. Consequently, we think twice nowadays about serving lobster: *whether* to as well as *how* to. Luckily—as happens so often in cookery—the second question can be turned around karate-wise to resolve the first.

While it's expensive indeed to offer guests a lobster apiece, let alone seconds, you *can* offer a richly lobstery dish, affordably, elegantly, and without waste—though "stretching a lobster" sounds like the oddest, if not neatest, trick of the week. These crustaceans have more —s (I'm in need of a word like "ergs" or "amps" here, for units of flavor) per milligram than almost any other foodstuff: the —s are lodged in the shells themselves and in every cranny thereof. So take advantage of those shells, by chopping, then sautéing them until they yield their all to a lovely sauce (well, not quite all; after that the shells can still go into the stockpot and produce a fine lobster broth—that's how flavorful they are). Use every morsel but the small stomach sac (which enfolds the tiny, crowned, blue-robed "lady"); amplify the flavor with butter, aromatics, wine, spirits, and flame; enhance the rich texture with crisp croutons and a savory soufflé blanket, and you will find that the meat of two or three small lobsters, or one middle-sized, easily serves six.

The model for this idea is a classic dish, which was not devised in the first place for reasons of economy. It originated at the Plaza-Athénée Hotel in Paris, which in the old days was reputed to have the most exquisite cuisine-for-the-happy-few imaginable. Its base is the famous lobster *à l'américaine*, whose name is a pedant's delight. Chauvinists among French gastronomes say that nothing so delicious could possibly be American; the word, they claim, is a corruption of *armoricaine*, derived from *Armorique*, the romantic old name for Brittany, whose cold seas certainly do produce good lobster. Not so, retort the anti-*armoricaines*, the dish contains tomatoes and Brittany is not tomato country. It was surely invented in Paris, they affirm, probably by a tomato-loving chef with a Mediterranean background, and it was named for an American client, or for the Americas from which tomatoes came. The argument will continue, and we shall never know the truth. But back to those lobsters.

Mounding a soufflé over the lobster meat was the Plaza-Athénée's contribution to elegance. But why not bake it on a platter, rather than in a soufflé dish? It makes for a splendidly dramatic presentation, for easy serving, and for a rather sturdier party offering. While the soufflé doesn't rise as high as if baked in a dish, it doesn't have as far to fall. Though it takes a bit of doing, you can prepare most of it the day before. And, once you add this wonderful concoction to your repertoire, you have added the possibility of a grand array of easy variants.

The flavor is robust as well as subtle, and, especially at lunch, I like something simple and delicate to follow. Salade Mimosa, gold and pale green, soothes the excited palate; Melba toast makes an even crisper contrast if you do it with pumpernickel. A poached pear has a lovely cool suavity; you can dress it up and enhance its fragrance with a chocolate base—perhaps tucking in a wine-soaked macaroon as a buffer—and add a satiny caramel sauce at the last moment. Its smoothness, the pear's velvet grain, and the friable chocolate combine incomparably.

Chocolate cups may strike you as old hat, and, moreover, tricky to make. Well, I haven't seen one since the thirties. Is that old hat or is that classic? And in working out the recipe through many trials and experiments, our cooking team found that the cups are quite easy to form if you use chocolate bits, with their slight extra viscosity, and then chill them well before peeling off the paper cases that serve as molds. With its pretty serrated edge and finely fluted sides, the choclate case looks as airy as a dry autumn leaf. But it's not riskily fragile. The pear squats on it with all the confidence of Queen Victoria, who never looked around for a chair but just lowered away, calmly relying on the alertness of her equerries. This royal reference is no accident, for here is a lunch befitting any palace.

Preparations and Marketing

Recommended Equipment:

To cook the lobsters, a casserole or kettle; to get at the meat, lobster shears, page 212, are useful; to bake and serve the soufflé, a large ovenproof platter, oval preferred, or a shallow baking dish.

Paper baking cups (cupcake size) are ideal molds for the chocolate cases; for added stability, they may be set in flat-bottomed custard cups, shells, small bowls, or large muffin tins. We flattened out our paper cups a trifle, to accommodate our fine big pears.

Macaroons are heavy work without a food processor.

Staples to Have on Hand:

Salt
White peppercorns
Hot pepper sauce
Dried tarragon
Optional: dried oregano, thyme, or herb mixture
Garlic
Cream of tartar
Stick cinnamon or powdered cinnamon
Prepared mustard
Pure almond extract
Tomato paste or tomato sauce
Olive oil or fresh peanut oil
Flour
Unsalted butter
Milk

Specific Ingredients for This Menu:

Lobster, boiled or steamed: one 2 to 2½ pounds (1 to 1¼ kg) or two or three 1-pounders (450 g) ●
Lobster stock, fish stock, or chicken broth (1 cup or ¼ L)
Beef stock or bouillon (½ cup or 1 dL)
Swiss cheese (a 6-ounce or 180-g piece)
Parmesan or mixed hard cheeses (see recipe; 2 ounces or 60 g)

Pumpernickel or rye bread, unsliced
Nonsweet homemade-type white bread
Eggs (9 or 10 "large")
Heavy cream (1 cup or ¼ L)
Chocolate bits or morsels (12 ounces or 340 g, or
    2 cups or ½ L)
Almond paste (see recipe; 8 ounces or 225 g)
Sugar (3½ cups or 8 dL; 700 g)
Fresh green herbs: such as parsley, basil, chives,
    tarragon
Lettuce: Boston, butter, or romaine (1 or 2 heads,
    depending on size)
Good-sized ripe unblemished pears: Anjou,
    Comice, or Bartlett (6)
Ripe red tomatoes (6 to 8 medium)
Carrots (1 medium)
Onions (1 medium)
Lemons (1)
Dry white wine or dry white French vermouth
    (4 cups or 1 L)
Optional: rum or bourbon whiskey
Cognac (⅓ cup or ¾ dL)

---

❷ Remarks:

Lobster: many fish markets carry ready-cooked lobsters. To boil or steam your own, which is usually more satisfactory, see recipe. Hen (female) lobsters are more desirable, since they contain coral (roe), to give your sauce extra red color. In buying live lobsters, choose the most active specimens; in buying ready-cooked ones, be sure that the tail is tightly curled and snaps back when pulled straight. Live lobsters can be kept for a day or 2 in the refrigerator, in paper bags pierced with a pencil for air.

Lobster Soufflé—on a Platter

A Plaza-Athénée-like soufflé accompanied by the famous lobster sauce à l'américaine

Manufacturing Note:

Although the classic recipe for lobster *à l'américaine* calls for it being cut up raw, sautéed, then simmered in its sauce, I have found that boiled lobster meat is a perfectly satisfactory alternative in this recipe, where the meat is seasoned with sauce made from the shells before the soufflé is mounded upon it. Boil the lobster, pick out its meat, make the sauce—all the day before—and you'll have only the actual soufflé mixture to complete before you pop the dish into the oven. Baking takes only 15 to 18 minutes, unsupervised.

Serving 6 people

The Lobster and Its Sauce Américaine:

**Either one 2- to 2½-pound (1- to 1¼-kg)
    boiled lobster, or two or three 1-pound (450-g)
    lobsters (see directions at end of recipe)**
4 Tb soft butter
2 to 3 Tb olive oil or fresh peanut oil
1 medium carrot, diced
1 medium onion, diced
⅓ cup (¾ dL) Cognac
**1 cup (¼ L) lobster stock, fish stock, or chicken
    broth**
½ cup (1 dL) beef stock or bouillon
**1 cup (¼ L) dry white wine or dry white French
    vermouth**
**1½ cups (3½ dL) peeled, halved, and juiced
    tomatoes, chopped**
2 to 4 Tb tomato paste or tomato sauce
1 tsp fragrant dried tarragon leaves
1 clove garlic, minced or puréed
Salt, pepper, and drops of hot pepper sauce
Beurre manié: 1½ Tb each flour and butter

Equipment:

A kettle, covered roaster, or steamer for cooking the lobsters; lobster shears are useful; a heavy large saucepan or casserole for simmering the shells

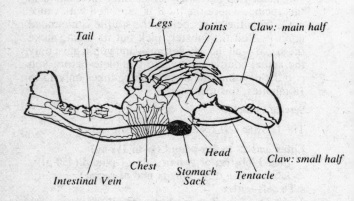

Legs   Joints   Claw: main half

Tail

Head

Claw: small half

Chest   Stomach   Tentacle
Sack

Intestinal Vein

Because you will want the end section of the tail, the front part of the chest, and the claws for shell decoration, remove the lobster meat from the shells so as not to damage these parts. Discard sand sack and intestinal vein; scoop tomalley (green matter) and coral into a sieve set over a bowl. Rub through the sieve with the butter, scrape all residue off bottom of sieve into bowl, cover, and refrigerate, for enriching the finished sauce later. (Swish sieve into the sauce when it is boiling, to gather into the sauce all extra flavors.) Cut lobster meat into smallish pieces, the largest being about ½ inch (1½ cm); refrigerate until you are ready to bake the soufflé. Chop the shells (after reserving those for final decoration).

Film a large saucepan with oil, set over high heat, and when very hot add the chopped lobster shells. Stir and toss for 2 to 3 minutes, then add the diced carrot and onion, tossing and stirring for 2 minutes more. Pour in the Cognac, ignite with a lighted match, and let flame for several seconds, shaking the pan; extinguish with the stock, bouillon, and wine. Stir in the tomatoes, tomato paste, tarragon, garlic, ¼ teaspoon salt, pepper, and drops of hot pepper sauce. Cover and simmer 30 minutes, stirring up once or twice. Turn into a large sieve set over another saucepan; stir and shake sieve to loosen vegetables from shells. Then remove shells and press juices out of vegetables in sieve. (Reserve shells and vegetable residue.)

You should have about 1½ cups (3½ dL) of rosy-colored wine-flavored lobster juices, which will need a light thickening with *beurre manié* as follows: Blend the butter and flour into a paste, and whip into the hot lobster juices. Simmer, stirring with wire whip, for 2 minutes, and correct seasoning. (Sieved tomalley-butter will go in just before serving.) Refrigerate until you are ready to assemble the soufflé.

(Simmer reserved shells and vegetables in lightly salted water to cover for 25 to 30 minutes. Strain, and you will have a good lobster stock to put in your freezer.)

The Soufflé:

3½ Tb butter
6 croutons (rounds of crustless white bread sautéed in clarified butter, see page 368)
The lobster meat, sauce, tomalley, and shells
3 Tb flour
1 cup (¼ L) hot milk
½ tsp salt
⅛ tsp white pepper
⅔ cup egg whites (5 "large" whites or 1½ dL)
A pinch of salt
¼ tsp cream of tartar
3 egg yolks
¾ cup (1¾ dL) lightly pressed down, coarsely grated Swiss cheese

Equipment:

A large ovenproof platter, such as a shallow oval about 16 inches (40 cm) long; a very clean dry bowl and beater for the egg whites (notes on beating them are on page 373)

Half an hour or so before you wish to bake the soufflé (which will take 15 to 18 minutes), you may prepare the platter: smear it with 1 tablespoon butter, arrange the croutons upon it, and divide the lobster meat over the croutons. Dribble ½ tablespoon of the lobster sauce over each portion of lobster. (Refrigerate the platter if you are not proceeding.)

Cheese Soufflé Base:

Preheat oven to 425°F/220°C. Prepare the rest of the ingredients listed. If egg whites are cold, pour into their beating bowl and set bottom of bowl in hot water, stirring the whites until they are just tepid to your finger—cold egg whites do not mount properly.

Heat 2½ tablespoons butter in a 2½-quart (2½-L) heavy-bottomed saucepan, and when melted stir in the flour; cook, stirring slowly until they foam and froth together for 2 minutes without coloring more than a buttery yellow. Remove from heat, and when this *roux* has stopped bubbling, vigorously beat in the hot milk with a wire whip and add the salt and pepper. Bring to the boil, stirring, for 1 minute. Remove from heat, clean sauce off sides of pan with a rubber spatula, and at once start in on the egg whites. Beat them at moderate speed until they start to foam, beat in the pinch of salt and cream of tartar; gradually increase speed to fast and continue beating until egg whites form stiff shining peaks when a bit is lifted up.

Immediately beat the 3 egg yolks into the hot sauce, then stir ¼ of the egg whites into the sauce (to lighten it). Scoop the rest of the egg whites onto the sauce and fold them together, alternating with sprinklings of cheese (but save 2 tablespoons for top of soufflé); operate deftly and rapidly so as to deflate the egg whites as little as possible.

Assembling and baking

Mound the soufflé over the lobster-topped croutons, topping each with a pinch of cheese. Bake immediately in the upper middle level of the preheated oven. Set timer for 15 minutes. Soufflé is done when nicely puffed and browned—it does not puff up like a soufflé in a dish, but rises at least 3 times its original volume. Tuck the shell and claws at one end of the platter, the tail at the other, and rush to the table.

While soufflé is baking, reheat sauce to the simmer, and correct seasoning; just before serving, remove from heat, whisk in the tomalley butter, and pour into a warm serving bowl. Surround each serving of soufflé with a ladleful of sauce.

A Remark on the Sauce:

Another trick for the sauce, after you have sautéed the shells and simmered them with wine and vegetables, is to remove the little legs, chop them and purée them in a blender with a cup of the sauce. Then rub this through a sieve and back into the sauce, thus catching a little puréed lobster meat in there, to act as a light thickening. (I felt the recipe was long enough without adding this to it!)

To Boil or Steam Live Lobsters:

Whether to boil or steam lobsters is, I think, a question of personal preference, number of lobsters, and equipment. If you are to boil them you need a large enough pot to hold them, and a strong heat source that will bring the water rapidly back to the boil when the lobsters go in.

To boil them, plunge them headfirst and upside down into enough rapidly boiling water to submerge them; cover the pot and weight it down if necessary. As soon as the water comes back to the boil remove cover, and boil slowly but steadily until the time (below) is up.

To steam lobsters, place a rack in a kettle or roaster, add 1½ inches (4 cm) water, and bring to the boil. Place lobsters on rack, cover closely—weighting down cover if necessary to make a tight seal—and when water starts steaming, set your timer according to the following chart:

1 to 1¼ pounds 450 to 565 g	10–12 minutes
1½ to 2 pounds 675 to 900 g	15–18 minutes
2½ to 5 pounds 1¼ to 2¼ kg 20–25 minutes	

When is the lobster done:

It is done when the meat will just separate from the shells, and when the tomalley inside the lobster has coagulated. But how can you tell that without opening the lobster? I remove one of the little legs if I have any doubts; and if the leg meat is white and lobsterlike, I conclude the whole is cooked. Some experts can tell immediately by the look and feel of the underside of the tail section.

Removing the meat from a lobster

1) To separate the tail from chest, hold chest firmly with one hand and gently twist off tail with the other, drawing end of tail meat from chest.

2) Push tail meat out from the shell.

3) To remove intestinal vein or tube, cut a shallow slit down curve of tail meat, and pull it out—if you can see it.

4) Grab little legs, twist, and chest meat comes loose, along with legs, from chest shell.

5) Sand or stomach sac is inside chest cavity at the head; pull it out and discard it.

6) Delicious meat is in the chest interstices, but you have to dig it out bit by bit.

7) Bend the small claw down at right angles from the large claw and with it will come a large cartilage from the meat of the large claw. Then cut a window in the base of the large claw, and the meat can be removed in one piece. Dig the small sliver of meat out of the small claw.

1)

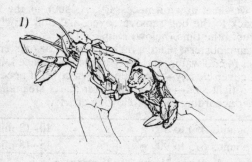

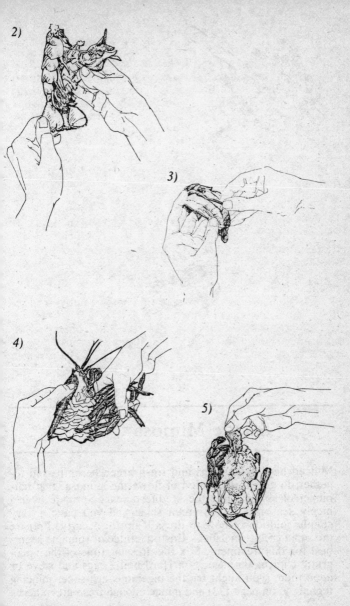

2)

3)

4)

5)

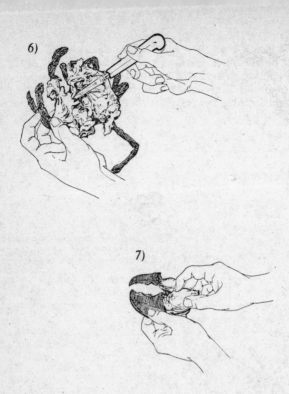

6)

7)

Salade Mimosa

Minced hard-boiled eggs and fresh green herbs tossed together do give a suggestion of flowering mimosa, that harbinger of spring along the Mediterranean. Sprinkle over a nicely seasoned tossed green salad and you have a very simple solution of how to dress it up for a party. Prepare the salad greens as usual—Boston lettuce or romaine seems best for this treatment. Mix the dressing (one of the vinaigrette choices on page 380). Hard boil 2 eggs and sieve or chop them (you might try the ingenious egg-slicer mincing technique on page 173) and mince enough fresh green herbs to make 2 to 3 tablespoons, using parsley, and chives, basil, or tarragon if you have them; toss herbs and eggs together in a small bowl with a sprinkling of salt and pepper. Just before serving, toss the salad with the dressing, taste, and correct seasoning; toss lightly with half the egg and herb mixture, and sprinkle the rest of it on top.

Pumpernickel Melba

Thin toasted cheese-topped pumpernickel, or rye

Southern California spawns many unusual and/or original edibles, from salads and avocado ice cream to this savory version of crisp, waferlike toast served in many a Beverly Hills restaurant—a dusky Melba of pumpernickel or rye bread, sprinkled with cheese and sometimes herbs as it crisps. The only actual problem, besides being capable of slicing it almost paper thin, is that of finding storebought unsliced bread if you've none homemade. That, as we found in the previous volume of J.C. & Co., seems to be the ever-present Melba drawback.

For an unspecified amount

Stale unsliced pumpernickel or rye bread
Finely grated Parmesan cheese, or a mixture of hard
   cheeses like Cheddar, Swiss, etc.
Dried herbs, finely ground, such as oregano, thyme,
   or an herb mixture (optional)

Slice the bread as thin as possible, less than ⅛ inch (½ cm)—if it's not thin it will not curl as it bakes, the way Melba toast should. Lay the slices in one layer on a baking sheet or sheets, and place in a preheated 425°F/220°C oven. In 3 or 4 minutes, when bread has begun to crisp, sprinkle each slice with ½ teaspoon or so cheese and a pinch of the optional herbs. Continue baking a few minutes more, until crisp and, you hope, somewhat curled.

❷ Any leftovers may be packaged and frozen; warm again in the oven to crisp before serving.

Pears Poached in White Wine

Compote de poires au vin blanc

A compote of fresh fruit seems a far more European than American dessert, yet it is so simple to do and delicious to eat that we should think of it more often. Also, it solves the problem of how to cope with those pears and peaches that are ripe and ready to eat, and won't keep another moment without spoiling: once compoted, they will keep well a goodly number of days in the refrigerator, ready to be served up as is, or dressed in all manner of plain or fancy ways.

The Poaching Syrup for Raw Fruits:

The proportions of sugar to liquid for poaching raw fruits are 6 tablespoons per cup of liquid, which makes 1½ cups sugar per quart (6 Tb per ¼ L; 3½ dL per L).

For 6 pears of the Anjou, Bartlett, Comice size

3 cups (¾ L) dry white wine or dry white French vermouth
1 cup (¼ L) water
The zest (yellow part of peel) of 1 lemon, and 4 Tb of its juice
1 stick or ½ tsp powdered cinnamon
1½ cups (3½ dL) sugar
6 firm ripe unblemished pears

If you are to poach the pears whole, as for this recipe (rather than halved or quartered as in many other recipes), you may not have enough liquid for 6 large pears to be submerged; in that case, either poach them in 2 batches or make more poaching syrup according to the proportions noted.

Choose a saucepan that will be large enough to hold the pears submerged in the syrup, place the syrup ingredients in the pan, and bring to the simmer; simmer 5 minutes (to bring out the various flavors into the liquid), then remove from heat.

One by one, with an apple corer or grapefruit knife, core the pears from the bottom—however, you may leave them uncored if you wish. Peel the pear neatly and drop at once into the syrup to prevent discoloration. When all pears are done, bring just to the simmer and maintain liquid at the not-quite-simmer for 8 to 10 minutes, until pears are tender through when pierced with the sharp point of a small knife. (Careful not to boil them, since that can break them apart.) When done, cover pan and leave the pears to absorb the flavors of the syrup for 20 minutes, or until you are ready to use them.

❷ May be done several days in advance; cover and refrigerate them.

Serving suggestions

Serve the pears in an attractive bowl, along with their poaching syrup; you may wish to accompany them with heavy cream, lightly whipped cream, fresh strawberry or raspberry sauce, chocolate sauce, custard sauce. Or you may drain them, set them on a round of sponge cake or a macaroon that has been sprinkled with some of the poaching syrup and a few drops of Cognac or rum, then spoon sauce over them. Or serve them on vanilla ice cream or sherbet, and top with a chocolate, custard, or fruit sauce. Or combine them with other fruits and serve in a savarin. Or serve them in chocolate cups, as described here.

A Pear and Chocolate Dessert

Les délices aux poires

Whenever you have pears poached in wine, maca-roons, chocolate cups, and caramel sauce all at hand at one moment, this lovely dessert is a fast assembly job. However, because the chocolate cups can soften and collapse in a warm room, and the caramel topping will lose its sheen as it gradually slides off the pears, you cannot assemble all of it ahead of time. You can set the pears in their choc-olate cups well ahead, however, if you have room in the refrigerator to store them on their dessert plates, but the sauce should either go on the last minute in the kitchen, or be spooned over each pear as you present it at the table.

Note: Directions for the chocolate cups, maca-roons, and sauce follow this recipe.

For 6 people

6 chocolate cups
6 macaroons (optional)
Droplets of pear poaching liquid
Droplets of rum, Cognac, or bourbon whiskey (optional)
6 pears poached in white wine (preceding recipe)
About 1 cup (¼ L) caramel sauce

An hour or so before serving, if you wish to ready things ahead, set the chocolate cups on individual dessert plates. Choose, or trim, macaroons, if you are using them, to fit the bottom of the cups, and place them in upside down. Dribble over each a few drops of pear liquid and the optional rum, Cognac, or bourbon. Trim bottoms of pears if necessary, so they will sit solidly, and set the pears on the macaroons.

❂ Must be refrigerated at this point if prepared in advance.

Just before serving, or at the table, spoon a tablespoon or 2 of the caramel sauce over each pear.

Chocolate Cups

To hold ice creams and sherbets, Bavarian creams, poached fruits

About 12 ounces or 2 cups (340 g or ½ L) chocolate bits or morsels for 6 chocolate cups

---

Choose fluted paper cupcake molds of any size you wish—the ones here have a 2¼-inch (5¾-cm) bottom, and were bought in a local supermarket. Because you want a wide cup to hold the fruit, press out the flutings between your thumb and forefinger. Provide yourself with several custard cups, shells, small bowls, or large muffin tins in which to set the chocolate-lined cups to congeal, later.

Then melt your chocolate—after numerous experiments we found chocolate bits more satisfactory than semisweet bars—bits, they say, have more viscosity, and that means spreading ability, which you need for this enterprise. To melt the chocolate, set it in a smallish saucepan; bring another and larger saucepan with about 2 inches (5 cm) water to the boil, remove from heat and let cool a moment, then cover the chocolate pan and set it in the hot water. In 4 to 5 minutes the chocolate bits will have melted; stir them up and they should form a shining liquid mass. (Be very careful not to use too much heat here, or the chocolate will harden into a lumpy or granular mess.)

Using the back of a teaspoon or a small palette knife, spread the chocolate up the sides of the cup, and in a layer on the bottom. Set each, as done, in a bowl or shell, and refrigerate until set—about 15 to 20 minutes. Carefully peel off the paper. Keep chilled until you are ready to fill and serve them.

Rosemary Manell's Almond Macaroons

Made in a food processor

My friend Rosie has conducted a good number of cooking classes featuring the food processor; this is the recipe for marvelous macaroons that she developed, and has kindly contributed. I've tried it in the blender without success; one could certainly adapt it to a large mortar and pestle in the time-honored hand-pounded way. But the processor is so quick and easy for macaroons that I've not gone into other methods seriously. By the way, Rosie prefers either Reese or "Red-E" almond paste, and brands of almond paste do vary in sweetness and consistency. Thus, if your first batch is too sweet, add less sugar the next time.

For 2 dozen macaroons 2 inches (5 cm) in diameter

8 ounces (225 g) almond paste
1 cup (¼ L) sugar
¼ tsp pure almond extract
A pinch of salt
¼ to ⅜ cup egg whites (2 to 3 whites; ½ to ¾ dL)

Equipment:

A food processor with steel blade; 2 baking sheets lined with brown paper (the shopping-bag kind); a pastry bag with ⅜-inch (1-cm) tube opening (optional)

Prepare cookie sheets, but do not grease them or grease the paper. Preheat oven to 325°F/165°C, and set racks in lower and upper middle levels.

Cut almond paste into ½-inch (1½-cm) pieces. Put into container of processor and cut up finely, turning motor on and off in 2-second spurts. When almond paste resembles coarse brown sugar, add the granulated sugar and process again in spurts, stopping several times to scrape down sides of container with a rubber spatula. Add the almond extract, salt, and ¼ cup (½ dL) egg whites, and process until no lumps of almond paste remain. The mixture should not be stiff, but should hold in a mass on a spatula. (If too stiff, add a little more egg white and process again.) This is the consistency for macaroons that are crunchy on the outside and chewy inside; if you like them softer and chewier, add more egg white by half teaspoons—after a batch or 2 you will arrive at the consistency you prefer.

Remove the mixture to a bowl and beat well with a wooden spoon, to be sure all is smooth and well blended. To form the macaroons, either drop mixture from a spoon, or use a pastry bag. If they are to fill chocolate cups, they should be small enough to fit inside easily; form ¾-inch (2-cm) blobs on the brown paper, spacing them 1½ inches (4 cm) apart because they spread a little as they bake. For larger macaroons, make the blobs 1½ inches (4 cm) across. Smooth tops of blobs with the back of a spoon dipped in cold water.

Bake in preheated oven for 25 to 30 minutes, switching sheets on the racks halfway through. The macaroons are done when lightly browned and crusty on top. Remove baking sheets from oven and let cool on cake racks. When cold, turn paper with macaroons attached upside down and dampen the back of the paper with a wet cloth or a brush; when macaroons loosen easily, peel away the paper. If they do not come off easily, dampen paper and wait a few minutes more. Set macaroons on cake racks for half an hour or so to dry.

❷ Store in an airtight tin, or wrap airtight and freeze.

Remarks:

We tried forming and baking the macaroons on floured and buttered nonstick pastry sheets. They came off all right, but the bottoms were concave, and they were very crisp. Silicone baking paper was also unsatisfactory.

Caramel Sauce

This is a rich and pure caramel sauce that you can serve either hot or cold—it thickens as it cools. You can also combine it with whipped cream or custard sauce, or use as a base for caramel ice cream.

For about 1 cup or ¼ L

1 cup (¼ L) granulated sugar
⅓ cup (¾ dL) water
An additional ⅓ to ½ cup (¾ to 1 dL) water
1 cup (¼ L) heavy cream

Boil the sugar and ⅓ cup (¾ dL) water in a small heavy saucepan, swirling pan by its handle until sugar has completely dissolved and liquid is perfectly clear. Put a lid on the pan and boil slowly until sugar bubbles thicken considerably. Then uncover, and boil undisturbed for a moment or so, until syrup begins to caramelize. Immediately swirl pan slowly by its handle until syrup has turned a nice walnut brown. Remove from heat, swirling (if pan is very heavy, set bottom in cold water to stop the cooking) until bubbling has ceased. Avert your face, pour in the additional water, and simmer, stirring frequently, until caramel has melted into the water; boil down until it is a light syrup. Add the cream, blend in thoroughly, and boil, stirring, for 2 to 3 minutes, to reduce the cream slightly. Serve cold, for the pears.

❍ May be made several days in advance; can be frozen, but may need boiling up and/or more cream before using.

❍ Timing

The pumpernickel Melba, the chocolate cups, and the macaroons can be made any time and frozen.

Buy your pears several days ahead, since they usually aren't sold ripe; if you do have ripe ones, you may poach them several days in advance. At this time, make the caramel sauce, and you can sauté and freeze the croutons for the soufflé.

The day before your party, you can prepare your lobsters and their sauce. The chocolate cups may be peeled and re-chilled.

In the morning, prepare your salad, and store the lettuce wrapped in damp towels in the refrigerator. Prepare the vinaigrette.

An hour or so before your guests come, prepare the soufflé platter with its croutons and mounds of lobster meat; cover and refrigerate it.

Half an hour before serving time, make the soufflé, which takes only 15 to 18 minutes to bake. Assemble the dessert, except for the sauce. Crisp the pumpernickel Melba in the oven if you have made it early and frozen it.

The salad is tossed just before you serve it. Same for saucing the dessert, so that the caramel keeps its sheen.

Menu Variations

The soufflé: as long as you have your fine lobster sauce, you can mix some fin fish with your lobster, like monkfish or halibut—this is an old Norwegian trick I learned when we were living there. The flavor of lobster is so strong and fine that it pervades other fish, too. You may use the same sauce system for live crabs and for fresh or frozen shrimp in the shell. You must be very careful with frozen shrimp, how-ever, to be sure they have not been adulterated with pre-serving chemicals—I've run into some loathsome examples that really exude a smell like that of floor-cleaning fluid. Read the label on the package! Rather than shellfish and sauce *à l'américaine*, you could use sole poached in white wine, to flake over the croutons, and turn the poaching liquid into a *sauce au vin blanc*—a hollandaise made with the re-duced white-wine fish stock. Another idea is to place a cold poached egg on each crouton, and a piece of ham or a dollop of cooked spinach on the crouton first, if you wish. When the soufflé is cooked, the egg has miraculously just warmed through; serve the soufflé with a hollandaise sauce, and you have a beautiful dish. (A recipe for the fish soufflé is in *The French Chef Cookbook*, as is a conventional, rather than platter, one for poached eggs and spinach.)

The salad: to follow a subtle soufflé, I'd always choose a salad on the delicate side—perhaps Rosie's spectacularly arranged lettuce salad in *J. C. & Co.*, or a salad of Belgian endive (if it's affordable) with watercress. Something like a *salade niçoise* would be too much, as would most vegetable combinations—tomatoes especially, since they'd repeat the sauce *à l'américaine*. You could certainly serve pita bread triangles, toasted and cheesed, instead of the *pumpernickel Melba*.

The dessert: apples, peaches, etc., could be poached in the same way as the pears and used instead. Rather than chocolate cups, you could use the vacherin meringue cases on page 43, or cookie cups. (A recipe for the latter is in *The French Chef Cookbook*.) Other fruit sauces are very easy to make: use frozen strawberries or raspberries and purée in a blender or processor, adding fresh lemon juice and more sugar as needed. For fresh berries, purée, beating in lemon juice and sugar to taste; raspberries need sieving, I think. See recipes for custard sauce (page 355), and for whipped cream Chantilly and chocolate sauce (page 370).

Leftovers

Little to say here! Any cook who would not promptly devour the last scrap of leftover lobster meat must be certifiably mad. Other uses for poached fruit and chocolate cases are in the recipes themselves. As for caramel sauce, who needs telling?

Postscript: Lunch or luncheon?

If you are requesting the pleasure of Mr. and Mrs. John Doe's company then you call it "luncheon." The added syllable gives extra employment to needy engravers, I guess, and anyway the word seems nicely old-fashioned to me. It does make one stop and think about menu planning for formal entertainment nowadays, when "tummy time," as Winston Churchill called his interior clock, has been reset by the press of our obligations.

Except on holidays, few of us can take our time at midday, whereas a dinner party can sprawl on into the wee hours. (Do we admit to sleeping off lunch?) If you and your guests are coring the heart out of a busy day, and devoting it to a meal that so many people are apt to skip or skimp, you are declaring an Occasion. A modern lunch*eon* menu should be light, and as compact and elegant as a sonnet. It is a good time to focus on one artful and unusual dish. And, since at midday people (a) come on time, and (b) don't want much to drink, you are secure in planning something that won't wait, like fish, or a grill, or a soufflé. No wonder so many enthusiastic cooks rise, like the sun, to their zenith at this hour.

Picnic

Menu

For 8 or more people

*Gazpacho Salad—Layers of colorful freshly cut vegetables
with bread crumbs and garlic dressing in a cylindrical glass
bowl*

*Fish Terrine, Straight Wharf Restaurant—A tri-color
mousse of sole and scallops with watercress and salmon*

*Pâté en Croûte—Spiced and wine-flavored ground meats
baked in a decorative pastry crust.*

*A selection of accompaniments—Carrot sticks, cauliflow-
erettes, and olives, as well as rare mustards and pickles*

*A variety of fine fresh breads—French, sourdough rye both
light and dark, and whole-grain loaves*

A platter of cheeses, and bunches of grapes

Plantation Spice Cookies

Suggested drinks:

*Chilled dry white wine (riesling, Muscadet, Chablis, or
chardonnay), and a picnic red—Beaujolais or zinfandel;
beer; iced tea; selected soft drinks; a large Thermos of hot
coffee*

The best picnic I've ever read of was given during World War II by an Englishman of legendary courage, the Duke of Suffolk. This black-bearded daredevil had recruited and trained a squad of volunteers for the most blood chilling of all wartime duties, the defusing of live bombs. Having been called down to one of the Channel ports after a Nazi air raid, the duke and his men, tense and exhausted, were returning to London after a grisly day on the docks. Suddenly, on a muddy road in what must have seemed the middle of nowhere, Suffolk signaled the truck convoy to stop. He then blew a whistle and lo, out from behind a hedge purred his Rolls Royce, laden with hampers, crystal, silver, damask, and a butler who unpacked and served a noble feast. Unbeknownst to the men, their road home passed close to Suffolk's country seat.

It wouldn't have been possible, in those lean and rationed years, to offer the meal we're having today—although, goodness knows, no picnickers ever deserved it more than the bomb squad. But at any rate the party possessed the three characteristics I most enjoy at a good picnic: surprise, luxury, and plenty. It's not worthwhile eating too much—which you can't help doing outdoors—unless the food is marvelous. In our family, we all love hard-boiled eggs and tuna fish sandwiches. But that's not picnicking, that's brown bagging, something we all do once in a while when we're too busy to fix ourselves a fine lunch.

Paper plates and plastic forks have their place—in a brown bag. At a real picnic I like real cutlery, but don't of course insist on damask and porcelain. Our bright plastic plates travel nicely, as does every dish on the menu...*pâté en croûte* snug in its mold, and the fish mousse in its thick-walled, chill-conserving terrine. For the gazpacho salad, we have used a straight-sided glass bowl, to show off the rainbow layers of vegetables. The whole works goes into insulated chests—how did we ever manage without?

Gazpacho in its primal state is a soup. But why not keep the gazpacho idea and serve it in a compact form? As a soup, gazpacho is an ancient dish, mentioned in both Old and New Testaments, and known in early Greece and Rome. Nowadays, however, most of us associate it with Spain, especially with the hot climate and searing summer sun of Andalusia, and in particular with the city of Seville. As with cassoulet and bouillabaisse, and even with our own Indian puddings and fish chowders, there are dozens of versions. Some thirty classic gazpachos exist, according to Barbara Norman in her *Spanish Cookbook* (New York: Atheneum, 1966; out of print). And there are variations on the thirty, she notes; a gazpacho can be thick or liquid, it can be served at any time during the meal, and rather than the traditional tomato red, it can even be white—when made with olive oil, garlic, and almonds. Alice B. Toklas, after the death of her friend Gertrude Stein, made a sort of gazpacho-quest of an Andalusian tour, and although she ate some marvelous examples, she could find no historical information on the subject in Spain itself. According to her lively account in *The Alice B. Toklas Cookbook* (New York: Harper, 1954; out of print), one clerk at a bookstore said to her, "Oh, gazpachos are only eaten in Spain by peasants and Americans." A final quote on the matter comes from M. F. K. Fisher, in *The Art of Eating* (New York: Vintage, 1976): "Above all it should be tantalizing, fresh, and faintly perverse as are all primitive dishes eaten by worldly people."

The word "gazpacho," it says in *The Cooking of Spain and Portugal* (New York: Time-Life Books, 1969), comes from the Arabic, and means soaked bread. And indeed bread appears in almost every version one runs into. Bread was much employed in the recipes of yore, not only as a thickener and nourisher, but simply so as not to waste a crumb. The recipe for the herb and bread crumb stuffing for chicken (page 138) is ancient too, as is the use of bread in onion soup, especially in its many-layered version on page 171.

Bread crumbs appear again in this meal, in the fish terrine—but I have no qualms about it because in the two dishes the taste and effect are so different that the crumbs become just another staple element, like salt. (Just be sure to get very good bread with body. Soft, squashy white bread will disintegrate.) A few years ago, the fish terrine would have been an unthinkable luxury at any but a princely picnic, because it took hours to purée the fish finely, pounding it in a mortar, sieving it, and finally adding cream, almost drop by drop. Even now, like the duke's crystal and silver in a brambly English lane, a fish mousse lends a note of slightly incongruous finesse, which I vastly enjoy, to an outdoor meal. It has a lovely texture; the flavor is unique, and suave to a degree, and the colors make one think of a subtle French painting—ivory-white, pearl-pink, and the green you sometimes see just after sunset. Celestial—and with a food processor, almost shockingly easy to do.

Equally luxurious, but in a quite opposite way—a portly burgher versus a court lady—is the hearty, handsome, porkily perfumed *pâté en croûte*. To call it a meat loaf baked in dough is true to the letter but not the spirit. Its rich meat laced with Port and brandy, spices, and herbs, its darkly gleaming aspic layer, and its greatcoat of heavy pastry, decorated fatly and fancifully—a traditional folk art—it is always the *pièce de résistance* on a table. Molds come in many shapes, but I find our corset-waisted one especially amusing. Set about with cheeses and big fresh country loaves, and grapes and bottles of wine, it looks almost pompously self-satisfied.

We wind up our feast with a delightful old-fashioned sort of cookie, a spice-ball variation containing peanuts, with the aroma of spices and dark molasses. Making these big savory cookies is easy, and children love to do it. The old meaning of the word "picnic" is a party to which everyone contributes, and I've purposely chosen every dish on our menu to be something one could easily carry to a friend's party as a welcome gift. If the children make the cookies, have them double the recipe, or they'll all disappear on the way.

Preparations and Marketing

Recommended Equipment:

A mincing meal indeed! Of course you can do it all by hand, but it's light work if you have a food processor for making bread crumbs and puréeing the fish for the terrine. A heavy-duty electric mixer with a flat beating blade is fine for both the crust and the filling of your *pâté en croûte*. Either a processor or a mixer will help with the cookie dough.

The gazpacho, however, demands good knife work: paring knives for trimming the vegetables and a very sharp French knife for mincing them and dicing them. You'll need 3 or 4 mixing bowls and 3 large sieves, and a 2-quart (2-L) cylindrical glass bowl is ideal for showing off your handiwork.

The mousse recipe was designed for a 5- to 6-cup (1¼- to 1½-L) terrine or loaf pan for baking and serving. (The mousse and its stripes could be adapted to a melon mold, however.)

A special spring-form mold, hinged and latched for easy removal, is ideal for baking *pâté en croûte*; the mold can be had at fancy cookware shops and comes in a variety of shapes. If you can't find one, don't be deterred; see recipe for other possibilities. You do need a pastry brush for glazing, and a bulb baster.

To chop peanuts for the cookies: blenders and processors won't work on the peanut shape. A nut chopper or grater is best, or a wooden bowl and an old-fashioned hand chopper. Have several baking sheets, since the recipe is for 24 cookies, and each sheet will take only 9.

Staples to Have on Hand:

Salt
White peppercorns
Sugar
Powdered cloves, cinnamon, nutmeg, allspice,
    and ginger
Ground imported bay leaves
Ground thyme
Fresh basil leaves, or dried oregano
Hot pepper sauce

Prepared Dijon-type mustard
Dark unsulphured molasses
Red wine vinegar
Prepared horseradish
Optional: capers, olives, anchovies
Baking soda
Gelatin (4 Tb or 4 packages)
Unsalted butter
Olive oil
Lard
French- or Italian-style bread (½ loaf)
Garlic
Lemons (2)
Scallions
Optional: shallots
Parsley; basil and chives if available

Specific Ingredients for This Menu:

Lox or smoked salmon (¼ pound or 115 g) ●
Fillets of white fish (1½ pounds or 675 g) ●
Scallops (½ pound or 225 g) ●
Ground veal (1½ pounds or 675 g) ●
Ground lean pork (1½ pounds or 675 g) ●
Ground fresh pork fat (1 pound or 450 g) ●
For optional pâté garnish: chicken livers, or
    boiled ham for dice or strips, or veal for strips,
    and/or truffles, or pistachio nuts, or your own
    choice (1 cup or ¼ L)
Optional: pig's caul (1 sheet) or strips of fresh
    pork fat ⅛ inch (1 ½ cm) thick (about 1 pound
    or 450 g) ●
Best-quality clarified brown stock (page 76), or
    canned consommé (4 cups or 1 L)
Cucumbers (2 or 3)
Green bell peppers (2 or 3)
Red bell peppers (2 or 3), or red pimiento
Mild red onion (1 large)
Avocados (2 or 3), ripe and firm
Onions (4 to 6 medium)
Fresh tomato pulp (3 cups or ¾ L; 12 tomatoes),
    and/or canned Italian tomatoes
Celery (2 or 3 stalks)
Watercress (1 large bunch)

Heavy cream (3½ cups, or 8 dL)
Sour cream (1 cup or ¼ L)
Unbleached all-purpose flour (7½ cups; 2 pounds,
    3 ounces, or 1 kg)
Eggs (1½ dozen "large")
Unsalted peanuts (1 cup or ¼ L)
Cognac or Armagnac; dry Port wine
Additional items as you wish: raw vegetable
    snacks, pickles, olives, mustards, grapes,
    cheeses, breads

---

❷ Remarks:

Fish fillets: you can choose among sole, flounder, conger eel, tilefish, petrale sole, monkfish, and halibut. For general remarks on buying and storing fish, see page 294. *Scallops*: even more perishable than fin fish, these should ideally be used the day you buy them. Sniff them in the market to be sure they're very fresh. *Fresh pork shoulder butt* has the correct proportion of fat to lean; buy a 2½-pound (1350-g) piece. *Pig's caul*: you don't have to have it, but if you want to use it, you may have to special-order this unless you live in a neighborhood that makes sausage cakes and caters to a European trade. It is the lining of the pig's visceral cavity, and every porker has one: a thin membrane streaked with cobwebby lines of fat that serves as an edible wrapping in sausage making, or for holding stuffing or flavoring around meat or poultry, or for lining pâté crusts. If more of us demanded pig's caul from our markets, we'd find it there. It freezes nicely, too. For pig's caul, substitute strips of *fresh pork fat*: this also may be hard to get. I generally trim mine from pork roasts, and freeze it. If the strips are too thick, cover them with wax paper and pound them with a rubber hammer, bottle, or whatever. If you can't get fresh pork fat, blanch bacon strips in a large pot of boiling water for 10 minutes.

Gazpacho Salad

Layers of diced peppers, onions, celery, cucumbers, avocados, and tomatoes interspersed with fresh bread crumbs and an herbal oil and garlic dressing

All the refreshing flavors of a gazpacho, but rather than being a soup it has become a mixed raw vegetable accompaniment to picnic food—a crudité combo in a pretty bowl. And it is equally delicious on any summer table with cold meats or fish, or with poached or scrambled eggs.

Manufacturing Note:

There is lots of dicing here—good practice—and it is far more attractive done evenly by hand than roughly by machine. Cut and flavor each item separately, and you want the tomatoes and cucumbers to drain well before they go into their final phase or they will exude so much water you will have soup rather than salad.

For 2 quarts (2 L), serving 8 or more

The Vegetables and Bread Crumbs:

3 cups (¾ L) tomato pulp—fresh in season or a combination of fresh and canned Italian plum tomatoes (see directions in recipe)

Salt and red wine vinegar as needed

2 or 3 cucumbers

¼ tsp sugar

2 or 3 each green bell peppers and red bell peppers (or, lacking red peppers, use a jar or so of canned red pimiento)

1 large mild red onion

2 or 3 celery stalks

About 2 cups (½ L) lightly pressed down, fresh crumbs from crustless nonsweet French- or Italian-style white bread (see directions in recipe)

The Herbal Oil and Garlic Dressing:

2 or 3 large cloves garlic
1 tsp salt, more if needed
Zest (yellow part of peel) of ½ lemon
Herbs: fresh basil leaves most desirable, otherwise
    fragrant dried oregano, or another of your
    choice
2 tsp prepared Dijon-type mustard
2 to 3 Tb lemon juice
½ cup (1 dL) or so good olive oil
Wine vinegar if needed
Freshly ground pepper and drops of hot pepper
    sauce

Other Ingredients:

2 or 3 ripe firm avocados
2 or 3 minced shallots or scallions
4 to 5 Tb fresh minced parsley
Capers, olives, anchovies for final decoration
    (optional)

Equipment:

3 sieves; 3 or 4 medium mixing bowls; a medium
    mortar and pestle, or heavy bowl and a masher
    of some sort (wooden spoon); a blender or food
    processor for making the bread crumbs; an
    attractive glass bowl of about 2 quarts (2 L) to
    hold the layered gazpacho

The tomatoes

Peel, seed, and juice the tomatoes and cut into neat dice
about ¼-inch (¾-cm) size. Out of season, include a judicious
amount of canned peeled Italian-style plum tomatoes—halve
them, scoop out seeds with your fingers, and dice the flesh;
they are usually rather soft, but they add color and flavor.
Fold together in a bowl with about ½ teaspoon salt and 1
teaspoon or so of wine vinegar, let stand 5 minutes, then
turn into a sieve set over a bowl to drain while you continue.

The cucumbers

Peel the cucumbers, cut in half lengthwise, and scoop out their seeds by drawing a teaspoon down their lengths. Cut into strips, then into dice about the same size as the tomatoes. Toss in a bowl with 1 tablespoon wine vinegar, ½ teaspoon salt, and ¼ teaspoon sugar. Let stand 5 minutes, then turn into a sieve set over a bowl to drain.

The peppers, onions, and celery

Halve the peppers, remove their seeds and stems, dice the flesh the same size as the tomatoes, and place in a bowl. Peel and dice the red onion (you should have about ⅔ cup or 1½ dL), drop for 15 seconds in a pan of boiling water to remove strong bite, drain, rinse in cold water, and drain again; add to the peppers. Dice the celery, add to the peppers, and then toss the three vegetables together with salt and drops of wine vinegar to taste. Set aside.

The bread crumbs

Cut off crusts, tear bread into smallish pieces, and crumb a handful at a time in a blender or food processor. (A good recipe for using the crusts is on page 368.)

The herbal oil and garlic dressing

Peel the garlic cloves, chop fine (or purée through a garlic press), and then pound in the mortar or bowl with 1 teaspoon salt until the consistency of a paste. Mince the lemon zest, add to the mortar, and pound until puréed, then add and pound the herb into the purée. Beat in the mustard with a small wire whip, then the lemon juice, and finally, by droplets, the oil—hoping for a homogenized sauce (but no matter if elements do not cream together: beat up before each use). Season well with more salt, drops of vinegar if needed, pepper, and hot pepper sauce to taste.

The avocados

Halve, seed, peel, and dice the avocados, as directed on page 173. Rinse in cold water to prevent discoloration, and set aside.

Arranging the gazpacho salad
4 to 6 hours before serving

Be sure the tomatoes are well drained; toss the cucumbers and the pepper-onion mixture in paper towels to dehumidify. The ingredients are to be spread in layers, to make an attractive design when you look through the glass; I shall specify 3 layers here.

Spread ¼ of the crumbs evenly in the bottom of the bowl, cover with ⅓ of the pepper-onion mixture, then ⅓ of the avocados, ⅓ the tomatoes, ⅓ of the cucumbers, then ¼ of the dressing. Continue with crumbs, pepper-onion mixture, avocados, tomatoes, cucumbers, dressing, and so on, ending with a layer of crumbs, then the remaining sauce. Toss the shallots and parsley together and spread over the top. Cover closely with plastic wrap and refrigerate. Just before serving, decorate with capers, olives, and anchovies, if you wish.

❶ Once the vegetables are prepared, arrange the salad in its bowl so that the ingredients may commune together to make an interesting whole. Leftovers are still good the next day, or may be ground up in a blender or food processor (or stirred together) with tomato juice to make a gazpacho soup...in which you might include the preliminary vegetable drainings, which are full of flavor.

Fish Terrine, Straight Wharf Restaurant—Terrine de Sole aux Trois Mousses

Mousse of sole and scallops layered with watercress and salmon

Here is a lovely terrine indeed, an ivory mousse of sole and scallops puréed together with cream and eggs interlaced with strips of green watercress and of pink salmon. Serve it hot as a first course or for a luncheon dish, or take it cold, in its terrine or baking dish, on a picnic.

Note: A fish terrine—or pâté—is almost invariably a purée of raw fish that is bound together with eggs, and made light and, in fact, mousselike, with cream. Sometimes the fish mousse stands alone, having enough bodily gelatin and strength to need no other base. This always sounds stylish, but I like a panade (thick cream sauce or bread crumbs) in my mousses and I particularly like the use of fresh bread crumbs here; they absorb the fish juices that would otherwise exude in a sometimes distressing quantity.

Before deciding on this particular mousse, our cooking team tried out quite a number of others. I had myself worked on numerous versions of a scallop mousse and found that it was either rubbery when it had no panade, or it was lacking in scallop flavor when it did. Chef Sara and I tried a mousse of scallops and sole with cream and gelatin that had a delicious flavor—but the unappealing texture of fish gelatin pudding. Finally chef Marian suggested we try her fish terrine, the one she does in Nantucket, where she is summer chef at the Straight Wharf Restaurant. We all liked hers immensely and this, with one or two jointly arrived-at modifications, is it.

Manufacturing Note—Molded Mousse:

The recipe here is for a fish mousse served directly from its terrine or baking dish, since that is great for a picnic or a covered-dish party. If you want to serve it unmolded, however, just line the inside of the terrine with buttered wax paper, and the mousse will come out easily after it has baked.

For a 5-cup (1¼-L) terrine or bread pan, serving 8 to 10 people

The Garnish—Watercress and Salmon:

1 large bunch fresh watercress
4 or 5 scallions
2½ to 3 Tb butter
¼ pound (115 g) excellent lox or lightly smoked salmon

For the Fish Mousse:

1½ pounds (675 g) of the finest, freshest-smelling fillets of sole or flounder (or other lean white fish such as conger eel, tilefish, petrale sole, monkfish, halibut)
½ pound (225 g) of the freshest-smelling scallops, washed rapidly and drained
2 "large" eggs
1 Tb (or a bit less) salt
2 cups (½ L) lightly pressed down crumbs from crustless nonsweet French- or Italian-style white bread (see gazpacho recipe for directions)
2 to 3 cups (½ to ¾ L) heavy cream
4 Tb fresh lemon juice
Freshly grated white pepper
A speck or so of nutmeg

Equipment:

A food processor; a 5- to 6-cup (1¼- to 1½-L) terrine or loaf pan; several rubber spatulas and soup spoons (useful); 2 or 3 medium mixing bowls; an instant (microwave) meat thermometer (useful)

Preliminaries

Preheat oven to 350°F/180°C and place a roasting pan half full of water in it, for baking the terrine. Cut a piece of wax paper a little larger all around than the terrine, and a piece of aluminum foil slightly larger than that. Butter one side of the wax paper.

Pull the tender leaves and top stems off the watercress (you may save the rest for watercress soup), and chop them into very fine mince with the white and tender green of the scallions; sauté slowly in 2 tablespoons butter for a minute or so, until limp. Set aside in a bowl. Look over the salmon to be sure there are no bones or other debris.

The fish mousse

(If you have a processor with a small container, divide the mousse ingredients in half and do in 2 parts, then beat together in a bowl to blend.)

Cut the fillets into 2-inch (5-cm) pieces and purée with the scallops, using the steel blade. Remove cover and add the eggs, salt, bread crumbs, 2 cups (½ L) cream, the lemon juice, 10 grinds of pepper, and nutmeg. Purée for 30 seconds or so. Remove cover; scrape and stir contents about, and purée longer if not smooth. When you spoon a little up, mousse should hold its shape softly—if you think it could take more cream, start the machine again, and add more in a thin stream, checking that you have not softened the purée too much. Remove cover, and taste carefully for seasoning— it should seem a little oversalted and overseasoned if you are to serve it cold, since the seasonings will become less strong once a mousse is cooked and cooled.

Assembling the terrine

(The mousse is arranged in layers in the terrine: plain mousse, green, plain mousse, salmon, ending with plain mousse. Some of the plain mousse is blended with the watercress and with the salmon; otherwise the layers would separate when the mousse is sliced.)

Spread a layer of plain mousse in the terrine, filling it by ¼. Smooth out with the back of a soup spoon dipped in cold water. Stir a dollop of mousse into the watercress (about twice the amount of mousse to cress) and spread into terrine, smoothing it also with a wet spoon. Spread on another layer of plain mousse, then remove all but a large dollop of mousse from the processor bowl. Place salmon in processor with the remaining mousse and purée for several seconds until smooth; spread the salmon in the terrine, and top with a final layer of plain mousse, filling the terrine to the top. Cover with wax paper, buttered side down, then foil—paper and foil should not come too far down sides of mold, or water from baking pan may seep into mousse.

❷ Assembled terrine should be baked promptly, since raw fish deteriorates rapidly even under refrigeration.

Baking
1¼ to 1½ hours

As soon as possible, set the terrine in the preheated oven in the pan of hot water. When mousse starts to rise above rim of terrine, after an hour or more, it is almost done—and not until then. At that point, also, you will begin to smell the delicious aromas of cooking fish. It is done at an interior temperature reading of 160°F/71°C—top will feel springy not squashy, and mousse can be gently pulled away from side of terrine.

To serve hot

Leave in pan of water in turned-off oven, door ajar, until serving time. Cut slices directly from the terrine and serve with the sour cream sauce described farther on, or with melted butter, white butter sauce (page 369), or hollandaise (page 301).

To serve cold

Remove mousse from oven and let cool. When tepid, drain off accumulated juices—there will be several tablespoons that you may use in your sauce. When cool, cover with plastic wrap and refrigerate.

To serve, cut slices directly from terrine, and accompany with the following sauce. (Spoon a dollop of it onto the plate, place the slice over the sauce, and decorate with a sprig of parsley or watercress.)

❶ Baked terrine will keep for several days under refrigeration.

Sour Cream Sauce for Fish:

When you are serving a sauce with something as delicate as a fish mousse baked in a terrine, you want a sauce that will go nicely with it but not mask any of its subtle flavors. Go easy on the seasoning here, then, hoping to make it just right for that mousse.

For about 2 cups (½ L)

**The mousse cooking juices
1 cup (¼ L) sour cream
2 egg yolks (optional, for color)
½ cup (1 dL) heavy cream
1 tsp, more or less, prepared horseradish
½ tsp, more or less, prepared Dijon-type
    mustard
Drops of lemon juice
Salt and white pepper**

If you have more than about 4 tablespoons of cooking juices, boil them down until they have reduced to that amount. Then pour into a mixing bowl, beat in 2 or 3 tablespoons of sour cream, then the egg yolks if you are using them. Stir in the rest of the sour cream and the heavy cream, and season to your taste with the horseradish, mustard, lemon juice, salt, and pepper.

❷ Store in a covered bowl in the refrigerator; will keep for several days.

Variation—Sour Cream Sauce with Herbs:

In some cases, minced green herbs would go well in the sauce, especially if you are serving it with plain boiled fish. Stir in minced chives, chervil, tarragon, parsley, basil—according to your particular fish and your own desires.

Pâté en Croûte

Spiced and wine-flavored ground meats baked in a pastry crust

For a 4- to 5-pound (1¾- to 2¼-kg) pâté, serving 10 to 12 people or more

Although you can form the crust on an upside-down bowl, and you can make it of any size or shape you wish—a pâté baked in its own special spring-form is particularly appealing because it looks as if it came straight out of a French *charcuterie*.

Manufacturing Notes:
Measuring capacity of mold

To determine the capacity of your mold, set it on a large piece of newspaper or plastic wrap on a tray, and measure into it beans or rice by the cupful.

Dough talk

You need a dough that will stand up to 2 hours of baking, that will be strong enough to hold up after baking, and yet that will be reasonably good to eat—pâté doughs are not epicurean delights anyway, but should be palatable. Be sure you roll it thick enough, or it will crack either during or after baking, and will be very difficult to line with aspic. (There will be an aspic layer between top of meat and crust: aspic is poured in through holes made in top crust, after pâté has baked and cooled.)

Fat content

A meat pâté is just not successful if you cut down on the amount of pork fat needed to make it tender and to give it the quality it should have. A great deal of the fat renders out during cooking, but if you are restricted as to fats, pâtés are not the kind of food you should even consider in your diet. Fat proportions in classic French recipes can be as high as one to one, or at least 1 part fat to 3 parts meat; I am suggesting that ¼ of the total amount be fat, which is as little as I think one can use successfully.

Pig's caul—caul fat

In most recipes, a thin sheet of pork fat lines the inside of the dough, before the meat mixture goes in. This not only bastes the outside of the meat, but reinforces the crust. If your crust is solid enough, you do not need that extra fat, but I have included a pig's caul lining—mostly because I like to use it, and also to show you that it exists. (See notes, page 234.)

Dough for Pâté:

For an 8- to 10-cup (2- to 2½-L) spring-form

5¼ cups (¾ kg) all-purpose flour, unbleached preferred (measure by dipping dry-measure cups into flour and sweeping off excess)

1 Tb salt

2 sticks (8 ounces or 225 g) chilled unsalted butter

8 Tb (4 ounces or 115 g) chilled lard

1½ cups (3½ dL) cold liquid: 6 egg yolks plus necessary ice water, plus droplets more water if needed

Equipment:

A heavy-duty electric mixer with a flat beater is useful here

If you do not have a mixer of the right type, rub flour, salt, and fats together with balls of your fingers, rapidly, without softening fat, until fat is broken into the size of small oatmeal flakes; rapidly blend in the liquids, to make a moderately firm dough. Knead into a rough cake. Wrap in plastic and refrigerate.

If you have a mixer, blend flour, salt, and fats at slow speed until mixture looks like coarse meal; blend in liquid, still at slow speed, until dough masses on blade. Turn out onto work surface, adding droplets more water to any un-massed bits in bottom of mixing bowl. Dough should be moderately firm. Knead into a rough cake. Wrap in plastic and refrigerate.

Dough should be chilled for at least 2 hours, to give flour particles time to absorb the liquid, and to relax the dough after its mixing.

❶ May be made in advance, but dough containing unbleached flour will turn gray after a day or so under refrigeration—it keeps perfectly in the freezer, however.

Veal and Pork Filling for Pâtés and Terrines:

For about 9 cups (2¼ L)

3 cups (1½ pounds or 675 g) ground veal
3 cups (1½ pounds or 675 g) lean pork ground
**   with 2 cups (1 pound or 450 g) fresh pork fat***
4 "large" eggs
2½ to 3 Tb salt
4 large cloves garlic, puréed
1½ Tb thyme
½ tsp ground imported bay leaves
1½ tsp ground allspice
1 tsp freshly ground pepper
1½ cups (3½ dL) cooked minced onions
**   (sautéed slowly in butter)**
½ cup (1 dL) Cognac or Armagnac
⅓ cup (5 Tb) dry Port wine

Garnish for Interior of Pâté:

1 cup (¼ L) chicken livers sautéed briefly in
**   butter, or diced boiled ham, or strips of ham**
**   alternating with strips of veal, and/or truffles,**
**   pistachio nuts, etc., etc., etc.**

Equipment:

A heavy-duty mixer with flat beater is also useful
**   here for filling (not garnish)**

---

*Note: Fresh pork shoulder is ideal because it contains just
about the right proportion of lean and fat.

Beat all filling ingredients together until very well mixed.
To check seasoning, sauté a spoonful, turning on each side,
for several minutes to cook through; taste very carefully—
salt and seasonings should seem almost twice as strong as
normal, since they become very much milder after the pâté
has baked and cooled. We found the listed proportions right
for us, after a too mild pâté or two—but spices vary in their

savor; measurements, as always, are only indications and suggestions from one cook to another.

Fitting the Dough into the Spring-form Mold:

The chilled and rested dough
Flour for rolling out, etc.
A little lard, for greasing mold

Equipment:

The spring-form mold; a heavy rolling pin; a cup of water and a pastry brush; an edged baking sheet or jelly-roll pan

Make a paper pattern to guide you in forming dough cover, later; grease inside of mold.

The dough is to be formed into a pouch that will fit into the mold so there will not be extra folds of dough. Here is a clever system invented by some ancient and nameless *croûtiste*:

Place the chilled dough on a lightly floured work surface and roll rapidly out into a rectangle about 1 inch (2½ cm) thick, and several finger widths larger and longer than the top and side of the mold. (1) Paint short sides of dough with a strip of water, and spread a thin layer of flour on bottom half; (2) fold the dough in half and press dampened sides together to seal (flour prevents interior flaps of dough from sticking together).

1)

To start forming the pouch, bend the two sides down toward you, as shown, then roll the dough away from you, gradually lengthening it into a pouch shape. Careful here not to thin out the dough too much—combined thickness of the 2 layers should be no less than ¾ inch (2 cm).

Lightly flour the baking sheet, and place the greased mold upon it when you have lengthened the pouch to the right size. (3) Lift the dough into the mold, and fit it gently onto the baking sheet and side of mold, being careful not to stretch or thin out the dough—which could cause leakage or cracks during baking. Fold edges of dough down outside of mold, and trim off with scissors, leaving a 1-inch (2½-cm) over-hang. If by any chance you feel dough is too thin in places, patch with strips of raw dough—painting surface lightly with cold water, and pressing new dough in place.

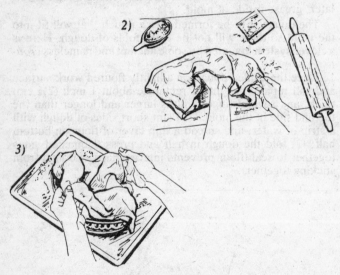

❷ Mold may be lined an hour or more in advance; cover closely with plastic wrap and refrigerate.

Roll out the leftover dough to a thickness of about 3/16 inch (approximately ¾ cm). Cut 2 pieces the size of the paper pattern (for covers), and whatever decorative cut-outs you have decided to use. Place on a plate, cover with plastic wrap, and chill.

Filling the Dough-lined Mold, and Finishing the Pâté:

A sheet of pig's caul, or strips of fresh pork fat
  ⅛ inch (½ cm) thick, to line sides and
  bottom of mold (optional)
About 9 cups (2¼ L) meat filling—veal and
  pork, or other
A garniture, like sautéed chicken livers, or other
  (optional)
The dough-lined mold and decorative dough pieces
Egg glaze (1 egg beaten with a pinch of salt and 1
  tsp water)

Equipment:

1 or 2 pastry brushes; aluminum foil or pastry-bag
  tubes (for funnels)

4)If you are using caul fat, drape it into the mold; or line bottom and sides with pork fat, if using.

4)

5)Pack half the meat filling into the mold, press the optional garniture over it, and cover with the rest of the filling, reaching to the rim of the mold.

6)Press one of the cover pieces of dough over the filling, and fold the overhanging edges of the dough lining up over it. Paint with water, and press the second dough cover in place.

Paint top with water, and press decorations in place; press designs on top of the larger pieces with the back of a knife.

With a sharp-pointed knife, make 2 steam holes in top of dough cover, going right down into the meat. Wind 2 bits of

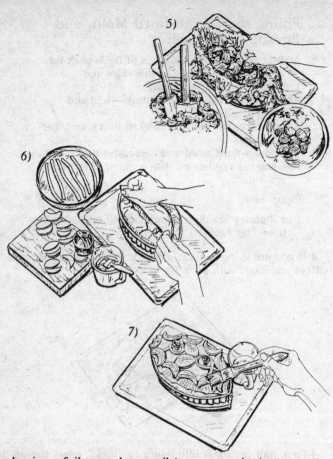

aluminum foil around a pencil (or use metal tubes) to make funnels; butter them, and insert in the holes. (Needed to prevent crust from cracking as pâté steams and bubbles during baking.)

❷ Pâté may be formed and decorated in advance, or may even be wrapped and frozen at this stage...thaw for a day in the refrigerator before baking.

7) Just before baking, paint with egg glaze, and make light crosshatchings in the glaze, over the dough, with the point of a knife.

Baking
Oven at 425°F/220°C and 350°F/180°C

Set in lower middle level of preheated oven and bake for about 20 minutes, or until pastry has started to brown lightly. Then turn the oven down and continue baking to an internal temperature of 155–160°F/67–71°C—which will usually take about 2 hours and 15 minutes for a 2-quart (2-L) mold of this general shape. Keep checking every 10 minutes after 1¾ hours, and if crust begins to brown too much, cover loosely with aluminum foil. Juices, bubbling up from pâté, should almost entirely lose their rosy color—being a faint pink at most, or a clear yellow. (Several times during baking, remove accumulated fat with a bulb baster or spoon from pan holding pâté mold.)

When done, remove from oven and let cool—2 hours or so are needed for the meat filling to consolidate itself, and for the crust to firm. After that time you may carefully remove the spring-form mold—or you may leave it on until pâté is cold. Then remove it.

Chill the pâté for 6 hours or longer, covered with plastic or foil. When thoroughly cold it is ready for its aspic lining—which fills the space between crust (where meat has shrunk during cooking) and meat.

❷ A pâté (without aspic) will keep for 10 days under refrigeration. I do not think a cooked pâté freezes well, and do not recommend it—it has a damp quality when defrosted that cannot be disguised. However, I have not yet tried freezing, thawing, and reheating—it might help!

Filling the Spaces with Aspic:

4 cups (1 L) beautifully flavored aspic (see note next page)
The chilled pâté en croûte

Equipment:

A small-ended funnel or the metal tube from a pastry bag; a bulb baster

Note on Aspic: If you have no homemade beautiful clarified beef or brown poultry stock (page 109), use best-quality canned consommé: flavor it with dollops of Port or Madeira and Cognac to taste. Then dissolve 4 packages (4 Tb) plain unflavored gelatin in part of the cold liquid; when soft, heat it with the rest of the liquid, stirring, until gelatin is completely dissolved and there is not a trace of unmelted gelatin to be seen or felt. Very carefully correct seasonings, accentuating their strengths—remembering that flavors die down when foods are served cold. This is a stiff aspic, befitting an outdoor picnic pâté. Chill half of it, over ice, until cold but not set.

Aspic is now to be poured into the pâté, through the funnel holes; make sure they are not clogged, by poking down through them with a skewer to reveal the meat below. Place funnel or metal tube into one of the holes, and drop down through it dribbles of aspic, stopping now and then to tilt pâté in all directions. Continue until you see that aspic has come up to level of both holes. (Sometimes top of dough has not risen from top of meat, and you will not succeed in making the aspic enter—you may be sure crust has separated from meat in some places, however; you can only try your best to make it penetrate. If you do not succeed, pour the aspic into a pan, let it congeal in the refrigerator, then chop it up—crisscrossing with a knife in the pan—scoop the chopped aspic into a bowl, and serve along with the pâté, as a most pleasant accompaniment.)

To serve a pâté en croûte

How to cut up a *pâté en croûte*? You have to be daring when faced with fancy shapes like the fluted ogival—the one we have made here. My system is to cut it in half crosswise with a serrated knife, then to cut the half lengthwise, and to cut each half of that into bias slices. Don't expect the slices to be neat and the crust to remain whole, especially with an edible crust such as this one. The crust may break, and the aspic may separate from the top, but you can arrange the slice neatly enough as you put it on the plate.

❷ A pâté baked in a crust with aspic filling will keep safely under refrigeration only for 3 or 4 days. If you wish to keep it longer, remove crust and aspic, and wrap meat filling securely in foil, where it will keep several days longer, and will always be welcome as a delicious plain ordinary marvelous pâté... or fancy French-type meat loaf.

Another Way to Make the Crust—Upside-down Molds:

If you don't have a spring-form hinged pâté mold, or want to make individual pâtés, a fine system is to form your dough on any kind of handy container that you turn upside down. Prick the dough all over, then set it in a preheated 400°F/205°C oven for 15 to 20 minutes to bake until set and barely browned. Unmold the crust, turn it right side up, fill it with pâté mixture, top it with a raw dough cover and decorations, and bake it as usual. The bottom crust is formed on an upside-down ovenproof jar. When filled, baked, and chilled, you may wish to pour in cold aspic, to fill empty spaces between meat and crust. Make pâtés this way in any shape and size you wish.

Plantation Spice Cookies

Sugar and molasses spice-ball cookies rolled in chopped peanuts

Variation on an old theme, this type of cookie is sometimes called a spice ball because it starts out round—though it ends up flat. They come in all sizes, but not many have these particular flavors. Easy to make and to bake, they are perfect for picnics or to serve with afternoon tea to sylphlike friends.

For 24 cookies 3½ inches (9 cm) in diameter

1 cup (4 ounces or 115 g) unsalted peanuts
1¼ cups (8½ ounces of 240 g) sugar
1½ sticks (6 ounces or 180 g) unsalted butter
1 "large" egg
⅓ cup (5 Tb) dark unsulphured molasses
2 cups (10 ounces or 285 g) all-purpose flour
  (measure by dipping dry-measure cup into flour
  container and sweeping off excess)
2 tsp baking soda
1 tsp powdered cinnamon
¾ tsp powdered cloves
½ tsp each powdered ginger and powdered
  nutmeg
¼ tsp salt

Equipment:

A nut chopper or grater (blenders and food
  processors do not work with peanuts); an
  electric mixer is useful; a flour sifter or a sieve;
  2 or 3 large baking sheets, buttered

Grinding the nuts

Because of the peanut's shape and smoothness, it does not chop up evenly in a blender or food processor—you could chop the peanuts first in a bowl and finish in a processor, but that seems like double work. Buy them already chopped, or chop with one of the patent gadgets, or in an old-fashioned wooden bowl with a curve-bladed chopper. They should be in pieces of about ¹⁄₁₆ inch (¼ cm). Reserve half in a bowl with ¼ cup (50 g) of the sugar, for later.

Mixing the cookie dough

Place second half of peanuts in the mixer bowl with the rest of the sugar and the butter cut into pieces; cream together until light and fluffy. Beat in the egg, then the molasses. Put flour, soda, spices, and salt into sifter or sieve, and stir to blend; sift, then beat or stir into the cookie dough.

Forming the cookies
Oven preheated to 350°/F/180°C

(The cookies are formed by rolling the dough into balls, rolling the balls in sugar and ground peanuts, then placing on baking sheets. If dough is too soft to form easily, chill for 20 minutes or until it has firmed up.)

Spread the reserved ground peanuts and sugar on a sheet of wax paper. With a tablespoon, take up a lump of dough and roll it into a Ping-Pong-sized ball. Roll ball in the sugar and chopped nuts, and place on a buttered baking sheet. (A 12-by-15-inch or 30-by-38-cm sheet will take 9 cookies—they spread as they bake.)

Baking

When one sheet is filled, place in middle (or lower or upper middle) level of preheated oven, fill the next sheet, and place in the oven, then the third. Cookies this large take about 15 minutes, and are done when set around the edges but still soft in the center   they swell as they bake, and the tops will crack. Take the cookies from the oven as done, and in 2 to 3 minutes they will crisp enough to be removed to a cake rack. Let cool.

❷ To store the cookies, place in a cookie tin or airtight plastic bag, where they will keep nicely for several days. Or, for longer storage, freeze them.

❷ Timing

There are no last-minute or even last-hour jobs on this picnic, except to pack it, and that's easy if you have enough ice, or an insulated chest.

Your last job, which can be done 6 hours in advance, is to assemble the gazpacho salad. Allow at least half an hour for the trimmed vegetables to drain and to release some of their moisture. As you trim them, you can also trim and refrigerate the crudités.

The *pâté en croûte* can be baked as much as 3 days beforehand; the terrine, too. The cookies can be baked even a day or 2 earlier than that—or bake way ahead and freeze them.

The dough for the pâté crust can be mixed at any time, and so can the breads, if you are making them yourself. Both freeze well.

Menu Variations

Instead of having *gazpacho* in salad form, take gazpacho soup; among other good cold soups are cucumber, beet, mushroom, asparagus, peapod, spinach, green herb, celery, zucchini, turnip, tomato, watercress, and vichyssoise. If you're omitting the fish terrine, try cold scallop soup; cold white bean soup is delicious, too. Or, to return to salads, consider the skewered vegetable salad, potato salad, or cold braised topinambours (all in *J. C. & Co.*), or the cold artichoke hearts filled with shellfish or a vegetable mixture (page 266), or cold eggplant cases stuffed with mushrooms, or a cold ratatouille.

You can vary the fish terrine by coating it with aspic and serving it unmolded—though perhaps not on a very hot day! You can stuff it into edible sausage casings and serve "fish dogs," page 374. You can take along a whole poached fish, like salmon or striped bass, or poached fish steaks (page 299), or lobsters (page 213). Or if it's a boat picnic, take hook, line, and sinker, and good luck to you.

Pâté en croûte can be infinitely varied, or served crustless, as a terrine; most books, including my own, are full of recipes. And of course you can stuff a boned bird with a pâté mixture (such as the Chicken Melon in *J. C. & Co.*). You can bake it with or without a crust, and/or coat it with aspic. The crust can be varied too, as in *Mastering II*, which has a pâté baked in brioche dough in a round pan (you cut it like a pie). Going a little further afield, you could serve a quiche, or a noble puff pastry Pithiviers stuffed with ham, or Cornish pasties, *chaussons*, and other meat turnovers.

As for the *cookies*, I do think it's nice to finish off with a crunch! The hazelnut wafers on page 280 are probably too fragile, but you could use the chocolate fudge cake recipe, page 151, in brownie form; the meringue-nut dough in *J. C. & Co.*'s Los Gatos cake makes a delicious crisp cookie; or, instead of forming meringue into *vacherins* (page 43), bake and serve it in cookie shapes. *Mastering I* and *II* both have *sablé*, or sugar, cookies (not sand cookies, as I've heard them called in English; they're named for Madame de Sablé, who invented them in the seventeenth century). *Mastering II* has cat's tongues, almond *tuiles* (fragile again), and two delightful puff pastry cookies; *J. C.'s Kitchen* has *tuiles* made with walnuts, cat's tongues, gingerbread, and two kinds of madeleines (really little sponge cakes—these would be delicious, though not crunchy).

Leftovers

The *gazpacho salad* will keep 3 to 4 days, but does lose a little of its charm. I think it might be nicer served as a soup, either hot or cold, with tomato juice added plus any other flavorful juices you saved when draining the trimmed vegetables.

The *fish terrine* keeps for several days; let's say 3 to play safe. If you have quite a bit, you might unmold it and serve it coated with aspic, as a beautiful first course for a fancy dinner, or turn the remains into a fish soup.

Once aspic'd, the *pâté en croûte* will not keep longer than a few days (see recipe).

On keeping *cheeses*: they vary, but remember to wrap then separately and they'll last much longer in the refrigerator. Cheese molds seem to turn each other on.

The *cookies* will keep for several days in a closed tin, or can be frozen.

Postscript: Picnic packing

Everybody has his own bag of tricks for this cheerful job; here are a few hints.

In case of damp or hard ground to sit on, take a rainproof poncho and a blanket. Our own green treasured blanket has accompanied us on picnics the world over, and is almost a talisman. Take extra water for drinking and hand washing, especially if the dog's coming along, and don't forget his favorite nibbles. We pack a roll of paper towels, extra—and extra-large—paper napkins, and we use insulated chests. If you like wicker hampers, line them with ant foilers (plastic dry-cleaner bags), so that if the basket is set on the ground, ants can't wriggle in through the crevices. I know families with children who pack light, compact amusements with every picnic, usually in a special box for just that purpose; a bat and ball, a kite, a Frisbee, horseshoes to pitch, cards, and a few books. Tied to one family's playbox, there is a whistle, for calling the children in. And speaking of tying, we've attached a bottle opener and a corkscrew permanently to our insulated chest, on long strings so they need never be detached—and lost. We always take rope or strong string when we plan to feast near an icy stream, so bottles can be suspended in the water—just as they can be lowered over the stern on a boat picnic.

Good gadgets to know about: one is a liquid, sold in metal containers; put them in the freezer, and they get ultracold and stay that way for an amazingly long time. We put a frozen one in the ice-cube chest, to delay melting. On chilling generally: since cold air moves downward, have flat-topped containers on which you can heap ice cubes.

Finally, as always: don't forget the salt!

Rack of Lamb for a Very Special Occasion

Menu

For 6 people

Artichoke Scoops Garnished with Shellfish—A cold appetizer

Roast Rack of Lamb
Buttered New Carrots
Tomatoes Moussakaise—Baked tomatoes stuffed with lamb and eggplant
Gratin of Potatoes à la Savoyarde—Scalloped potatoes with onions and cheese

Fresh Strawberries and Hazelnut Cornucopias—Delicate rolled nut wafers filled with lightly whipped cream

Suggested wines:

Although some people avoid the combination of wine and artichokes on the theory that artichokes make wines taste sweet, I have fortunately never found that to be the case and would certainly serve a light dry white, like a riesling. Bring out your very best red Bordeaux—a Graves—or a well-aged cabernet, for the lamb. A sparkling wine on the sweet side, or a gewürztztraminer, Vouvray, or Sauternes, could go with the dessert.

Before we go on to splurge on rack of lamb, that acme of expensive chic, please note that the back porch of this chapter, the Postscript, is comfortably occupied by two cozy, homey recipes for budget cuts of lamb. But tonight we're celebrating with all the stops out. Our guests are great travelers and restaurant connoisseurs, and in fact our first thought was to take them out for the kind of dinner they most appreciate. There are fine new restaurants around here, often run by young women chefs (our chefs Marian and Sara, for example), which have raised local standards to a much higher level of sophistication than we used to see. We *could* go out—but afterward, where would we install ourselves, as the French say, for the second half of the affectionate reunion that we all expect to go on until midnight?

And think of the price! Rack of lamb is not cheap at home, but it's half what it would be in a restaurant. And the nice thing is, it involves very little effort or last-minute preparation. (We've noticed about meat that the fancier the cut, the less trouble for the cook.)

So, home it is, and our easy menu gives us plenty of time to gussy up the place for that soigné look one enjoys in a top restaurant. Pat Pratt of the J.C. & Co. team, whose happy taste and light hand create the graceful, unfussed flower arrangements you see on our shows, folded our napkins into the fleur-de-lys shape she learned from her Danish grandmother (see page 377 for her way of doing it). Tonight, we've tucked the crisp white flower-forms into big goblets—clear ones, not tinted, so we can enjoy the color of the wine. When we choose things for the table, our first thought is whether they make the food look appetizing (as some magnificent china does not), and our second, whether they involve much fuss. The time we'd have to spend polishing silver we'd rather spend cooking.

At this dinner the food itself is so ornamental that it needs only the simplest setting. We left an inch of deliciously edible stem on the hollowed artichoke halves so that, heaped with the gold and pink of shrimp in an eggy vinaigrette, they'd have the air of bounteous little scoops. Interlaced like two Spanish combs, the racks of lamb are sculpturally elegant, yet the serving is not hindered at all. The crisp emerald green watercress sets off the perfect trim of the slim ribs, and the little golden carrots, gleaming with butter, provide a soft contrast in color and form. For the dessert, we found a bowl with a deeply scalloped rim to support the fragile cookie cornucopias around the rosy heap of strawberries; if one were lucky enough to own a Monteith, one of those punch bowls with crenelated sides that holds glasses, a truly splendorous effect could be achieved here.

The nicest food of all—I've said it before and will doubtless say again—gratifies all the senses at once, not just taste and scent, but sight, and even touch. All three of these courses tempt one to use fingers: the artichoke leaves, the last nibbly bits on the lamb ribs, the plump strawberries you take by the stem and dip into the cream-filled cornets. Whether the crisp dry crunch of these delicate cookies is more pleasant to feel or to hear, one can hardly say....

"Our cat has a long tail tonight," once remarked Abraham Lincoln to dressy Mrs. Lincoln. Maybe it was Inauguration Night, for which that stout party wore enough purple velvet to drape a hearse, as you can see in the Smithsonian. Well, we're not that ambitious; but here we are with the house looking nice, an impeccable dinner well in train, a joyous reunion to come, and half an hour in hand. What about in a leisurely lemon verbena bath to honor *la vie en rose*?

Preparations and Marketing

Recommended Equipment:

To trim the lamb, you'll need a slicing knife, a paring knife, and possibly a small meat saw. To cook it, foil to protect the bare bones, and a roasting pan; to serve it with the racks interlaced and garnished, a wide platter.

A food processor is useful but not essential for grinding lamb to stuff tomatoes, for slicing onions and potatoes. For grinding nuts for the Plantation Cookies, you could use a knife or a nut chopper. You need a baking dish for the tomatoes, a baking-and-serving dish for the gratin, and a good-sized saucepan for the carrots.

To bake the cookies, you need a wide flexible spatula or a pancake turner. To form them, use metal cookie horns, or make your own out of brown paper. Since baking is brief and precisely timed, a kitchen timer is a must.

I almost forgot cookie sheets. My oven repairman tells me that he often has calls from cookie cookers who complain that their oven thermostats are not working properly. It turns out that the cooks were apt to shove such large cookie sheets into their ovens that the heat could not circulate properly, and naturally the thermostats and the ovens themselves could not function as they should. He advises using a cookie sheet (or a baking sheet for any purpose) that will leave at least 1 inch (2½ cm) of air circulating all around its edges.

Staples to Have on Hand:

Salt
White peppercorns
Optional: hot pepper sauce
Granulated sugar
Confectioners sugar
Cream of tartar
Imported bay leaves
Dried thyme
Dried tarragon leaves
Optional: mixed herbs
Dijon-type prepared mustard
Pure vanilla extract
Wine vinegar

Light olive oil or best-quality salad oil
Optional: fresh peanut oil
All-purpose flour
Butter
Eggs (4 "large")
Heavy cream (1 pint or ½ L)
Fresh white nonsweet bread for crumbs
Garlic
Shallots or scallions
Parsley
Lemons (1)
Celery (1 stalk)
Dry white wine or dry white French vermouth
Dark Jamaica rum

Specific Ingredients for This Menu:

Cooked shellfish (see recipe); or use raw
    mushrooms (1½ cups; 12 ounces or 340 g) ❷
Racks of lamb (2, plus meat trimmings from them;
    see buying notes, page 268)
Artichokes (3 large fine)
Carrots (36 to 48 if 2 inches; 12 to 13 if large)
Eggplant (1 firm shiny, about 9 by 5 inches)
Tomatoes (3 large firm ripe)
"Boiling" potatoes (12 to 16 medium)
Onions (8 or 9 large)
Optional: watercress
Strawberries (about 2 quarts or 2 L)
Hazelnuts (¾ cup; 3 ounces or 85 g), shelled (also
    called filberts)
Grated Swiss cheese, or a mixture (1½ cups or
    3½ dL)
Chicken stock (6 to 7 cups or 1½ to 1¾ L)

Some Mournful Remarks on Shellfish:

What filling to choose for the artichokes is a question of
what is best and freshest-tasting in the market. I am sorry
to report my growing disillusion with frozen shrimp, which,
if I buy them peeled, have a pervasively chemical taste that
seems slightly less pronounced in the frozen shrimp in shell
that I find. Canned shrimp can be mushy, and fresh shrimp

are rare indeed. The canned lobster I have sampled has been unthinkably bad in texture and taste, but I have tried some acceptable frozen lobster meat. Canned pasteurized refrigerated crabmeat, though terribly expensive, has been reliable in sauced dishes, but I have suffered some very poor examples of ordinary canned crab in the lower price ranges. Some frozen crabmeat has been excellent—when properly frozen and stored, and eaten soon—but frozen crab (and lobster too) must be thawed slowly in the refrigerator for a day or 2 to prevent it from becoming watery; I am told this has something to do with ice crystals that pierce the flesh if the thawing is too abrupt. If you cannot find good shrimp, crab, or lobster, switch to scallops, lightly poached in wine, or fresh raw mushrooms diced and tossed in the sauce.

Artichoke Scoops with Shellfish

Halved boiled artichokes and shellfish in egg yolk vinaigrette

For 6 people as a first course

Egg Yolk Vinaigrette:

½ Tb very finely minced shallots or scallions
½ tsp or more salt
¼ tsp dried tarragon leaves
1 raw egg yolk
1 tsp Dijon-type prepared mustard
1 Tb each lemon juice and wine vinegar
6 Tb light olive oil or best-quality salad oil
Freshly ground pepper
Drops of hot pepper sauce (optional)

Other Ingredients:

About 1½ cups (12 ounces or 340 g) cooked
    shellfish meat, or raw mushrooms
Salt, pepper, oil, lemon juice—as needed
3 large fine boiled or steamed artichokes

The vinaigrette

Mash the shallots or scallions in a small bowl with the salt, then with the tarragon. Beat in the yolk and mustard, then the lemon juice and vinegar. In a small stream, beat in the oil. Season to taste with pepper, hot pepper sauce, and more salt if needed. Sauce should be a pale yellow cream with a light thickening so that it will film the shellfish but not mask it.

❶ Best made shortly before using. If it separates, shake in a screw-topped jar.

Assembling

Turn the shellfish (or mushrooms) into a bowl, and pick over to remove any possible debris. Fold in the dressing and let sit 10 minutes, folding several times. Taste, and add lemon, oil, and/or seasonings if you feel them necessary. Slice the artichokes in half lengthwise, and scoop out the central core of leaves and the chokes with a teaspoon. Shortly before serving, pile sauced filling into each cavity.

❷ It is best not to sauce the filling too far ahead for fear the sauce might separate. Instead, toss the shellfish with salt, pepper, and drops of lemon juice and oil; cover and refrigerate. Fold in the sauce and assemble 10 minutes before serving.

To Boil or Steam Artichokes the Simplest Way:

First hold each artichoke head under a stream of cold water, spreading the leaves gently apart to give a thorough washing. Slice off ½ inch (1½ cm) from the bottom of the stems, and pull off any small or withered leaves at the base. To boil, drop them into a large kettle of enough boiling salted water to submerge them completely, and boil slowly for 30 to 40 minutes, or until bases of artichokes are tender, and the bottom of a leaf is tender when you pull it through your teeth. To steam them, place in a vegetable rack in a covered kettle with 2 inches (5 cm) of water, and steam 30 to 40 minutes or until tender. Drain the artichokes bottom up, and serve them hot, warm, or tepid—or cold for the preceding recipe.

Buying and Trimming a Rack of Lamb

The rack of lamb is the whole rib chop section from one side of the lamb, going from the tip of the shoulder blade to the beginning of the loin, and comprising ribs number 6 through 12. (The official name for the rack is "lamb rib roast.") Although not as expensive as the saddle, which is the whole loin chop section from both sides of the lamb, the rack is a luxurious cut of exquisitely flavored tender meat. But there is not very much of it: 1 rack will serve only 2 to 3 people.

If you look closely at the photograph of our lamb here, which is indeed a fine specimen, you can see the purple grading stamp on the fat, U.S.D.A. Prime, which is the official federal classification for the very best grade of meat, more often reserved for restaurants than for the retail markets where most of us shop. Choice, the next grade, is very good too, but just not quite as perfect in every category and therefore not quite as expensive.

How to recognize quality in a rack of lamb

Look for the purple grade stamp, which should be left on the meat. The color of the meat should be fresh and deep bright red, with almost a silky sheen to it; the fat should be hard and creamy white; the eye of the meat—the large, most edible part of it—should be reasonably big and rounded. When you turn the rack over and look on the underside, the bones should be tinged with pink, and slightly rounded— they whiten and flatten with age. The best way to pick fine meat, for most of us, is to find a good meat market and make friends with the head butcher. Butchers are human, and most of them blossom into real friendliness when they find an interested customer who, too, is serious about meat.

To trim a rack of lamb

A rack of lamb is easy to trim, and it is not a bad idea to do it yourself—then you know it will be done right. Besides, you will get all the meat scraps to use, and the bone for making your sauce.

1)Removing backbone. The backbone should be very carefully detached from the tops of the ribs (on the underside or rib side of the rack), in such a way that the eye of the meat, lying right under the backbone, is not disturbed. If you don't have a saw, you can ask the butcher to do this for you, but ask him please to be very careful. When the tops of the ribs are loose, very neatly detach the meat from the under part of the backbone, then detach the backbone from the strip of fat covering the top side of the meat.

2)Trimming rack to expose lower ribs. Cut right down to the rib bones, about halfway from their tip ends to the eye of meat, as shown, cutting straight across, then slicing against ribs and down to rib ends.

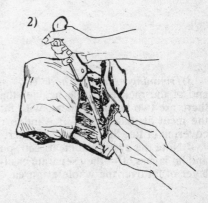

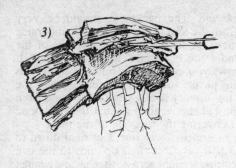

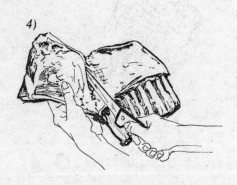

3)Trimming excess fat and "cap" meat off the rack. One end of the rack is a little heavier than the other, because there are two layers of meat, with fat, covering the eye of the meat at that end. You want to remove all but a thin covering of fat. Start at the shoulder, or heavier, end.

*4)*Note the eye of the meat. Lift, pull, and cut extra meat and fat layers off—they separate easily—leaving only a thin layer of fat over the whole eye area.

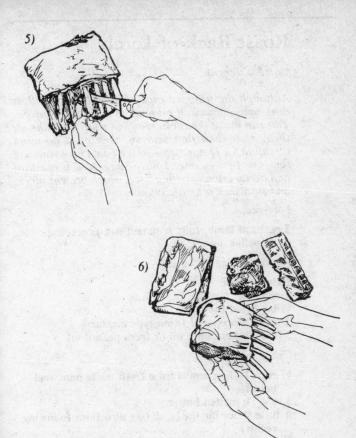

5) *Frenching the bone ends*. Cut the meat out from between the rib bones, then scrape the bones clean—this is picky work, but worth it if you want the rack to look its luxury price.

6) *The trimmed rack*. The fully trimmed rack illustrated here weighs less than 1½ pounds (¾ kg) with the fat, the cap meat, and the backbone removed. An untrimmed rack weighs 3½ pounds (1½ kg). However, you do have the backbone to use, and you can also recuperate a handful of usable meat between the fat layers you removed from the top and from between the ribs.

Roast Rack of Lamb

Carré d'agneau

Although the trimmed rack of lamb looks small, it does take about half an hour to roast in the oven. You can make the racks ready to roast well ahead; then, after their first searing, they need no more attention for 15 minutes—which could give you time for your first course. I have suggested a mustard and bread crumb coating here, which browns nicely and furnishes a gentle crunch.

For 6 people

2 racks of lamb, fully trimmed (see preceding directions)

For the Mustard Coating:

1 clove garlic
½ tsp salt
½ tsp dried thyme
2 to 3 Tb prepared Dijon-type mustard
3 to 4 Tb light olive oil or fresh peanut oil

Other Ingredients:

½ cup (1 dL) crumbs from fresh white nonsweet bread
3 to 4 Tb melted butter
A little sauce for the lamb (see directions following recipe)
Watercress leaves or parsley, for garnish

Equipment:

Aluminum foil to cover rib ends; a kitchen timer and an instant (microwave) meat thermometer are useful

---

Preparing the lamb for the oven

Score the tops of the racks lightly—making shallow criss-cross knife slashes in the covering fat. Mash the garlic and salt together in a small bowl, mash in the thyme, then beat in the mustard and the oil. Paint mixture over tops and meaty ends of racks.

Set racks meat side up on an oiled roasting pan, and fold a strip of foil over the rib ends to keep them from scorching.

❷ May be prepared several hours in advance; cover and refrigerate.

Roasting the racks of lamb
25 to 30 minutes

Preheat oven to 500°F/260°C and set oven rack in upper middle level. The first part of the roasting is to sear the lamb; when oven is ready, put the racks in and set timer for 10 minutes. When time is up, slide out oven rack and rapidly spread a coating of bread crumbs over the top of each rack, and baste with dribbles of melted butter. Turn thermostat down to 400°F/205°C, and roast for 15 minutes more, then begin checking. Lamb is done to a nice rosy rare at 125°F/52°C on an instant meat thermometer—or when the meat, if pressed with your finger, begins to show a slight resistance rather than being squashy like raw meat. (When you have a special, expensive roast like this, it is better to err on the side of rareness, since it is a shame to serve it overdone unless, of course, your guests prefer their lamb that way.)

❷ Although you are safer serving the lamb soon after it is done—giving it a few minutes before carving for the juices to retreat back into the meat—you can let it wait. Be sure, however, that you set it at a temperature not over 120°F/49°C so it cannot overcook—use a reliable warming oven, or let your roasting oven cool off with the door open and check with an oven thermometer before you put the racks back again. You can also do the preliminary searing, then set the lamb at room temperature and continue the final roasting in half an hour or so. The crucial consideration is that it not overcook. (I made the terrible mistake, once, of setting my beautiful, madly expensive, perfectly roasted ribs of beef in the upper part of a double gas oven combination to wait for half an hour. The lower oven was on, and although the upper oven was off, that lower oven overheated my upper oven and the waiting roast came out well done. Tears of rage, but a lesson learned.)

Serving

An interlaced rib arrangement is attractive for 2 racks of lamb, and carving is easy. You cut down between the ribs on each side, and each guest gets 2 perfectly trimmed chops. Spoon a little sauce around the chops, garnish with watercress or parsley, and the buttered carrots.

A Little Sauce for the Lamb:
About 2 hours' simmering time

There will be little or no juice in the roasting pan because the lamb is cooked rare and no juices escape. But it is nice to have a little sauce to moisten the meat, and you can easily make one—but you will have to plan ahead for it—using the backbones you removed from the racks.

Whack the bones into convenient chunks and brown them in a medium-sized saucepan with 2 tablespoons oil, and a chopped onion and carrot. Sprinkle on 2 tablespoons flour and let brown for several minutes, stirring. Remove from heat and blend in ½ cup (1 dL) or so of dry white wine or vermouth, and 2 cups (½ L) chicken stock. Bring to the simmer, skim off scum for several minutes, then add a small celery stalk, a mashed garlic clove, ½ teaspoon dried thyme, and an imported bay leaf. Cover partially and simmer about 1½ hours, skimming occasionally and adding water if liquid evaporates below ingredients. Strain into another saucepan, degrease, and carefully correct seasoning. You should end up with a cup or so of delicious slightly thickened light brown sauce that tastes like lamb, and that will complement but not in any way overpower the delicate flavor of your roast.

Buttered Carrots

As a garnish

Your carrots must be delicious to eat, as well as providing color on the platter. Frozen or canned carrots simply will not do because they are, in my experience, mushy, and they certainly lack the flavor of fresh carrots. Baby fresh carrots, however, unless one has them fresh from a neighboring garden, can often be flavorless and textureless, too. Far better in many instances to trim mature fresh carrots, and have them taste as they should.

For 6 to 8 carrot pieces per person

Either 36 to 48 baby carrots about 2 inches (5 cm) long, or 12 or more mature carrots
Cold water
2 Tb butter for cooking, plus 2 to 3 Tb for final flavoring
1 Tb very finely minced shallots or scallions
½ tsp salt, more as needed
Freshly ground white pepper
1 tsp sugar

Trim and peel the carrots. If you are using mature carrots, halve or quarter them and pare to nice baby carrot shapes (save trimmings for salads or soup). Arrange in a roomy saucepan with enough water to come halfway up the carrots. Add the initial 2 tablespoons butter, the shallots or scallions, salt, pepper, and sugar. Cover the pan and boil for 5 minutes (or longer for mature carrots) until liquid has evaporated and carrots are just tender—careful at the end that carrots don't scorch. Correct seasoning.
❷ May be cooked ahead. Set aside uncovered.
  Shortly before serving, toss the carrots with the additional butter, so they are warmed through and glistening.

Tomatoes Moussakaise

Baked tomatoes stuffed with lamb and eggplant

I call these "moussakaise" because the stuffing is lamb and eggplant, and that's what makes a mous-saka, a good accompaniment since there is not much meat on a rack of lamb. These stuffed tomatoes beef up the meal, so to speak.

For 6 tomato halves

1 firm shiny eggplant about 9 by 5 inches (23 by 13 cm)
Salt
A handful of parsley sprigs
1 or 2 cloves garlic, peeled
1 large onion, peeled and quartered
Olive oil or other cooking oil
The meat trimmings from the racks of lamb, or about 1½ cups (3½ dL; 12 ounces or 340 g) lean raw lamb stew meat
½ cup (1 dL) dry white wine or dry white French vermouth
1 cup (¼ L) chicken stock
½ tsp thyme (or rosemary, or mixed herbs, or tarragon)
3 large firm ripe tomatoes
Freshly ground pepper
½ cup (1 dL) crumbs from crustless fresh white nonsweet bread

Equipment:

A food processor with steel blade makes quick work of the chopping.

Salting and draining the eggplant

Peel the eggplant and cut into dice ⅜ inch (1 cm) to a side; toss in a large sieve with 1 teaspoon salt and let drain.

Chopping onion and lamb

Meanwhile, if you have a food processor, start it running, and drop in the parsley, letting machine run for a few seconds until parsley is chopped; scrape parsley into a small bowl and reserve. (Do not bother to clean out processor too thoroughly.) Start running it again, and drop in the garlic; when minced, drop in the onion, turning machine on and off in several bursts until onion is chopped fairly fine. Film a medium-sized frying pan (nonstick preferred) with oil, turn the onion and garlic into it, and sauté slowly. Divide the lamb into 2 batches and grind 1 batch at a time with on-off spurts in the processor, adding each as done to the onion. (Otherwise, chop ingredients by hand, using a meat grinder, if you wish, for the lamb.)

Simmering the lamb

Sauté the lamb with the onion for a few minutes over moderately high heat, tossing and turning, until lamb has browned lightly and turned from red to gray; pour in the wine and stock, and stir in the herbs. Cover and simmer slowly for about half an hour, or until lamb is tender and liquid has evaporated. Turn lamb into a sieve set over a bowl, to drain out accumulated cooking fat.

The tomato shells

With a grapefruit knife, potato baller, or teaspoon, hollow out the tomatoes, leaving just the outer flesh. Salt lightly, and reverse on a rack to drain.

Finishing the stuffing

Dry the eggplant in paper towels; film the frying pan again with oil, and sauté the eggplant, tossing and turning, for several minutes until tender. Return the lamb to the pan with the eggplant and sauté a few minutes more, tossing and turning and letting the mixture brown very lightly. Toss with the minced parsley, and carefully correct seasoning.
❷ Stuffing may be prepared a day in advance; refrigerate in a covered container.

Filling the tomatoes

Arrange the tomatoes hollow side up in an oiled baking dish. Fill them with the stuffing, spread on a spoonful of bread crumbs, and drizzle a little oil over the tops.
❷ May be prepared several hours in advance. Cover and refrigerate.

Baking—or broiling
10 minutes or less

The tomatoes need just a thorough heating through, since the stuffing is all cooked and you don't want the shells to burst. Set them in the oven with the lamb, during its last bit of cooking. (Or bake 10 minutes or so in a 400°F/205°C oven, or set under a low broiler.)

❷ Tomatoes should be cooked only at the last minute or they lose their shape.

Gratin of Potatoes à la Savoyarde—or à la Lyonnaise

Scalloped potatoes baked in broth with onions and cheese

Some kind of potato dish is very good with lamb, and I like this one cooked in broth, rather than in milk like the famous potatoes dauphinoise, since it is less rich—although the cheese does add a certain heft. However, the lamb morsels are so small!

For 6 people

Several Tb soft butter
2 to 3 cups (½ to ¾ L) thinly sliced onions
12 to 16 medium "boiling" potatoes, peeled and thinly sliced
Salt and freshly ground pepper
1½ cups (3½ dL) coarsely grated Swiss cheese
2 to 3 cups (½ to ¾ L) chicken stock

Equipment:

A food processor is useful for slicing onions and potatoes, or a hand slicer; a flameproof 2-quart (2-L) baking-and-serving dish, such as an oval one 9 by 12 by 2 inches (23 by 30 by 5 cm)

Assembling

Preheat oven to 425°F/220°C. Melt 2 tablespoons butter in a frying pan and sauté the onions slowly, stirring occasionally, while you peel and slice the potatoes. Smear the baking dish with butter and spread in a layer of potatoes, season lightly with salt and pepper, and spread in ⅓ of the onions (which need not be fully cooked), then ⅓ of the cheese. Continue with 2 more layers of potatoes, onions, and cheese, ending with the last of the cheese. Dot top with 2 tablespoons butter, and pour in enough chicken stock to come only halfway up the potatoes.

Set dish over moderately high heat on top of the stove, bring to the simmer, and place in lower middle level of preheated oven. Bake for 30 to 40 minutes. Ideally the liquid will have been almost entirely absorbed when the potatoes are tender; if not, remove baking dish from oven, tilt it, and draw out excess liquid with a bulb baster. Boil it down rapidly in a saucepan until thickened, pour it back into the dish, tilting in all directions, and return to oven for a few minutes to finish baking.

● If potatoes are to stay warm for half an hour or so, remove from oven when they are tender but there is still a little unabsorbed liquid in the dish; keep warm, loosely (never tightly) covered, over a pan of simmering water, on an electric hot tray, or in a warming oven.

Hazelnut Cornucopias

Rolled cookies—cookie horns—tuiles aux avelines

This is the type of cookie that is soft and pliable when it has just come from the oven, giving you several seconds to roll or form it into a shape before it crisps. The formula makes a nicely delicate wafer, and the flavor of toasted hazelnuts is particularly delicious. If you cannot find fine fresh hazelnuts, however, substitute walnuts—which can be ground without toasting. (Note: All shelled or ground nuts keep freshest in the freezer.)

For about 16 cookies 4½ inches (11½ cm) in diameter

¾ cup (3 ounces or 85 g) shelled hazelnuts
½ cup (3½ ounces or 100 g) sugar
½ stick (2 ounces or 60 g) unsalted butter
⅛ tsp salt
2 Tb heavy cream
¼ cup (4 Tb or ½ dL) egg whites (about 2 whites)
4 level Tb (1¼ ounces or 35 g) all-purpose flour in a sifter

1 Tb dark Jamaica rum
A little soft butter

Equipment:

A blender or food processor (or nut chopper); 2
lightly buttered nonstick cookie sheets; a kitchen
timer; a wide flexible spatula or a pancake
turner; 3 or 4 metal ~~~~~~ horns, or cornucopia
shapes m~~~~~~~~~~~~per. I used metal
cooki~~~~~~~~~~~~ and 2 inches in
di~~~~~~~~~~~~~~ by 5 cm); other
~~~~~~~~~~~~~~~~ssed at the end of the

Toasting and grinding the hazelnuts

(The hazelnuts are toasted to give additional flavor and also
to loosen the outside skins; taste several to be sure they are
not rancid.) Place them in a roasting pan and toast for 10 to
15 minutes in a preheated 350°F/180°C oven, stirring 2 or 3
times, until lightly browned. Rub by small handfuls in a towel
to remove as much of their brown skins as you easily can.
When cool, grind ⅓ of them roughly in a blender or food
processor and set aside in a small bowl. Grind the rest of
them with the sugar, and reserve for the following cookie
mixture.

The cookie mixture

Preheat oven to 425°F/220°C, and set rack in middle level.
Cream the butter in a mixing bowl (if chilled, cut into pieces
and beat with a wooden spoon in a metal bowl over warm
water; if it softens too much, then beat over cold water until
a creamy mass). Blend in the sugar and hazelnut mixture,
the salt, and the cream. Add the egg whites, stirring only
enough to blend. Sift and fold in the flour by thirds, then
fold in the rum. Mixture should look like a heavy batter.
❷ Batter should be used promptly.

Forming, baking, and rolling the cookies

Before forming the cookies, be sure the oven is preheated,
have your spatula and your metal or paper molds ready, and
have your kitchen timer handy. Drop a 2-tablespoon blob of

cookie mixture on a buttered cookie sheet, and spread it out, as illustrated, into a 4½-inch (11½-cm) circle with the back of a tablespoon, making sure that the edges are the same thickness as the rest of the shape, or about ¹⁄₁₆ inch (¼ cm). Form 1 or 2 more cookie shapes, leaving a good inch (2½ cm) between them. Sprinkle a pinch of chopped hazelnuts over each. Place in oven and set timer for 4 minutes, meanwhile forming another sheet of cookies.

Cookies are done when about ¼ inch (¾ cm) around edges is lightly browned (if they seem to be cooking too fast, lower oven thermostat slightly). Set cookie sheet on open oven door and let cool a few seconds. One at a time gently slither spatula or pancake turner under a cookie all around to loosen it, lift it off, turn it upside down on your work surface, and roll it around the metal or paper horn. Rapidly repeat with the other cookies—leaving them on the oven door keeps them pliable until you are ready to roll them.

Close oven door and wait for oven to come up to temperature again, then bake the other sheet, and form another batch. Meanwhile, in less than a minute, the rolled cookies will have crisped and you can gently dislodge the molds. Let cookies cool on a rack.

❷ These cookies are fragile, and soften rapidly in damp weather. Bake them shortly before serving, or store in a warming oven at around 100°F/38°C, or freeze them.

Variations:

You can roll the cookies into other shapes, such as cylinders, using the end of a wooden spoon or a cylindrical cookie form. You can press the limp cookie over the outside of a small bowl or inside a teacup to make cookie cups. You can make the classic tile or *tuile* shape, when you drape the limp cookie over a rolling pin to crisp. Or, of course, you can serve them perfectly plain and flat—which makes them easier to store, and nice with tea or sherbets.

Fresh Strawberries and Cream-filled Hazelnut Cornucopias

The reason for rolling the preceding hazelnut wafers into cornucopias is so that you can fill them with a light whipped cream and serve them with strawberries. You dip the berries by their stems into powdered sugar, and then into the cream—lovely finger food for all ages. However, plain whipped cream all by itself is, I think, so rich that I like it lightened with some beaten egg whites, which also serves to stabilize the cream.

For 6 people

About 2 quarts (2 L) beautiful fresh ripe
    strawberries
2 egg whites, a pinch of salt, and a pinch of cream
    of tartar
½ pint (¼ L) heavy cream, chilled
About 2 cups (½ L) confectioners sugar, sifted
Pure vanilla extract, or dark Jamaica rum, or
    kirsch
6 hazelnut cornucopias (preceding recipe), plus
    more, if you wish, to pass with the berries
2 Tb chopped toasted hazelnuts (preceding recipe)

Equipment:

A clean dry bowl for whipping egg whites, and a
    large wire whip or portable beater; a second
    bowl, of metal, for whipping cream, set into a
    larger bowl with a tray of ice cubes and water to
    cover them

The strawberries

If strawberries are sandy, drop them into a bowl of cold water, swish them gently, then lift out immediately and drain on a rack. Pick them over to be sure each is perfect, but do not stem them.

Whipped cream lightened with egg whites

Shortly before serving, beat the egg whites until they start foaming, then beat in the salt and cream of tartar, and continue beating until egg whites form stiff peaks. Set egg whites aside and immediately start whipping cream, using the same beater—circulate it all around the bowl, incorporating as much air as possible, and whip until cream holds its shape nicely but is not too stiff. Fold in enough of the egg whites by dollops to lighten the cream, but it should hold its shape sufficiently to be spooned into the cornucopias. Fold in confectioners sugar to taste—2 to 3 tablespoons, and 1 teaspoon or so of vanilla, rum, or kirsch. (Complete information on egg whites, page 373; on cream, page 370.)

❶ Strawberries may be prepared and left on their rack an hour or so in advance—refrigerate them on a hot day. If the cream is made somewhat ahead, turn it into a sieve lined with washed cheesecloth and set over a bowl; cover with plastic wrap and refrigerate—it will exude a little milky liquid.

Serving

The moment before serving, arrange the berries in a bowl or on plates. Fill the cornucopias with the cream, using a teaspoon or a pastry bag, and sprinkle a pinch of chopped nuts over the top of the cream; arrange the cornucopias in a bowl. Serve at once, passing separately bowls of powdered sugar and the remaining cream plus, if you wish, additional cornucopias or, better, the same cookie but in one of the other shapes described on page 282.

❷ Timing

You will need a few—a very few—extra minutes between each course of this dinner. Before dessert, you'd fill and arrange the cookies; take your time, they're fragile. Before the main course, first you'd take the lamb out of the oven. It will sit and re-absorb its juices while you change plates, toss the carrots in hot butter, garnish your warm platter, and bring forth the gratin. Surely you'll want to parade the stylish lamb platter around the table and then carve it right there, which takes seconds. Courses like these shouldn't follow like railroad cars anyway, jolt, jolt, jolt; they should be set apart by a tender moment of memory and anticipation.

If you have only one oven, do the potatoes ahead, and keep them warm while roasting the lamb. Or cook them partially and let them finish with the lamb. Ideally, the lamb should undergo its second stage of roasting, accompanied with the tomatoes, while you're enjoying the first course.

Just before dinner, then, set the crumbled and basted lamb back in the oven with the tomatoes. Just before that, sauce the shellfish and spoon into the artichoke halves, and arrange the strawberries in their bowl (strawberries can bruise each other so they're better fixed not too far ahead).

An hour before dinner (on the one-oven plan), the lamb gets seared; then the oven temperature is lowered and the potatoes are sliced and the gratin mixed and baked, while the lamb sits at room temperature. At this time you'd whip the cream and refrigerate it in a cheesecloth-lined sieve over a bowl, and make the sauce for your shellfish.

That morning, you would prepare the lamb for the oven and refrigerate it, cook the onions for the gratin, cook the carrots, and hollow, stuff, and refrigerate the tomatoes.

The day before, you trim the lamb, make sauce with the bones, and prepare the tomato stuffing. That day, or even the day before that, you can cook and refrigerate the artichokes.

The cookies can be made any time and frozen; just bear in mind that the batter should be baked right after mixing.

Menu Variations

See Mournful Remarks preceding the *artichoke scoops* recipe for artichoke-filling possibilities (and problems). Mayonnaise alone might be too rich, but you could simply spoon a little vinaigrette into the artichoke cavities. Or mound the scoops with highly seasoned egg or fish salad. An alternative would be asparagus, either hot or cold, or tucked into puff pastry rectangles as we did on the first series of the *Company* shows.

I can't think of any main dish so elegant as *rack of lamb*— and that's the point of this whole dinner.

As for *vegetables*, we chose the potato gratin for ideal flavor, and the others chiefly for their looks. You could stuff onions with the delectable lamb and eggplant mixture, and serve cherry tomatoes in butter with herbs (page 16). If they're small enough to be served one apiece, stuff your eggplant cases. I think you do want something tangy, so tomatoes in some form are good, and something hearty and rich; what about potatoes Anna or doing those "straw mat" potatoes (page 14), but in a square form, in an electric frying pan? Their tangly look would set off the sculptural symmetry of the lamb racks. The old-fashioned thing was to carve the racks and make a palisade, like a crown roast, around a heap of mashed potatoes, then put a paper frill on each rib end. Too thumby-looking for me.

The *cookie* recipe works perfectly with walnuts, if you can't get really fresh hazelnuts; and the cookies can be formed into several shapes, as suggested at the end of the recipe. If you make cookie cups, you might fill them with raspberries or blueberries, and pass whipped cream separately. Or you could make the *vacherins* on page 43, but very small ones, fill them with the cream, and surround each with strawberries. Various other cookies are suggested on page 257.

Leftovers

Cooked *artichokes* keep for 2 or 3 days. If you have spare ones, try slicing the bases and serving them in a thickened vinaigrette with scallops "cooked" in lime juice, as in *J.C. & Co.* Or mix artichoke bits into a salad. Extra shellfish can be minced and mixed with mayonnaise for a cocktail dip or spread.

Extra cooked *lamb ribs* are the cook's precious property. Bare your teeth and snarl, until lunch tomorrow.

Cooked *carrots* can be reheated, briefly. Or wash them off and dice them for a cold vegetable *macédoine*, or for a soup garnish. The *potato gratin* can be reheated, and so can the *tomatoes*—chop them and serve on toast.

As for the *dessert*, cookies freeze, and you can purée the strawberries, mix with extra cream, and freeze for a strawberry mousse.

Postscript: Two budget cuts of lamb

Flanks and Breast of Lamb:

Although a rack of lamb is costly indeed, the lamb flank, which is the continuation of the rack down the belly of the beast, sometimes comes free with the rack. If not, it costs ⅕ as much, which is very reasonable. The breast of lamb corresponds to the brisket of beef; it is the flank and its continuation toward the front.

Broiled or Barbecued Lamb Flanks

Epigrammes d'agneau

For 4 to 6 people—2 lamb flanks

Peel and cut fell (outside membrane) and fat from top of flanks; slit open and remove excess fat from inside. Cut the flanks into serving pieces, leaving riblets in the meat. Brown lightly in a frying pan in a little oil, with a chopped carrot and onion. Pour out browning fat, add half-and-half white wine or vermouth and chicken stock barely to cover the meat. Add a clove of garlic, an imported bay leaf, and a little dried thyme. Cover and simmer slowly for about an hour, or until lamb is tender. Remove to a platter, arrange in 1 layer, and set a pan and weight on top, to flatten the meat, which will have curled out of shape during its cooking. Leave for 20 to 30 minutes.

When ready to broil, cover 1 side of each piece with the mustard coating described for the racks of lamb, page 272, and spread on a layer of fresh bread crumbs and a drizzle of melted butter. When ready to cook, set for several minutes under a hot broiler until heated through and nicely browned.

You could boil down the braising liquid, after degreasing it, and serve it as a sauce; or keep it in the freezer for the next time you need a sauce for lamb.

Stuffed Braised Breast of Lamb

For 4 to 6 people

The breast of lamb contains the boat-shaped breastbone with a number of auxiliary bones attached, and some riblets. Leave the riblets in, but detach the breastbone from them; remove breastbone after cooking. Slice off the fell and fat from outside the meat. Cut a pocket the length of the meat going under the rib bones, removing any fat layers you can reach inside.

Use a rice and lamb or sausage stuffing, or bread crumb stuffing, or the lamb and eggplant stuffing suggested for the tomatoes on page 276. Sew or skewer the stuffing into the pocket you have made in the meat. Brown and braise the breast for about an hour, as described for the flanks in the preceding recipe—you may wish to add a peeled and chopped tomato or 2 along with the rest of the ingredients. Serve with a dish of fresh beets (page 95) or a salad, for a hearty informal meal.

Summer Dinner

Menu

For 6 people

A Platter of Chicken Livers Molded in Aspic

Individual Fresh Salmon Steaks, Poached, and Served with Hollandaise Sauce
New Potatoes
Cucumber Triangles Sautéed in Butter and Dill

Savarin au Rhum et aux Fruits Exotiques—The giant ring-shaped cousin of rum baba, filled with a selection of tropical fruits

Suggested wines:

A light dry white with the first course, like a riesling or muscadet. A fine full white with the salmon, like a Meursault, Corton Charlemagne, or well-aged chardonnay. A sparkling wine with the dessert—semisweet Champagne, Vouvray mousseux, Asti spumante

If we were serving this meal in cool weather, when it would certainly taste just as good, we might begin with hot consommé. But in warm weather, what could seem more piquant and inviting than these small oval aspics, clear as fine amber, set around a jackstraw pile of finely slivered crisp string beans? These fanciful trifles have a festive air, though their decoration is a simple matter, and the poached chicken livers, mysteriously brooding within, are delicately flavorful. Delicacy is, indeed, crucial, because salmon has so much character that it must dominate any menu on which it appears.

Since salmon has become increasingly expensive, we rarely buy a whole fish anymore; rather, we offer salmon steaks. In America, green peas from the garden are the classic accompaniment, especially on the Fourth of July, when salmon is traditionally eaten. Some prefer it with fresh asparagus; some like it cold, with mayonnaise and a cucumber salad. I like the cucumber idea, and agree with Scandinavian cooks that dill is the herb of choice with salmon. So we'll have our cukes cooked very lightly in dill and butter, dished up fragrant and crisp, with a golden hollandaise for pink fish and green vegetable. Cold salmon is delightful, but, now that this great fish is a rare luxury, we want it at its most glorious— in other words, hot. The platter looks particularly appetizing—appearance matters so much in summer meals! And you can't have boiled salmon without boiled potatoes, especially new ones cooked in their tender skins.

Our fish is a Pacific salmon, *Oncorhynchus*, 3 of whose species, the silver, sockeye, and pink, are most commonly found in fishmarkets. To acquire its Atlantic cousin, *Salmo salar*, you generally have to pack up your waders and head for Nova Scotia or Iceland. All salmon are rare these days, because for a century we failed to take into account their very special habits, and to preserve the complex environment they require. They're anadromous, meaning that they live and grow in the ocean but spawn in fresh water: always in the very water where they themselves were spawned. This may mean a tremendous journey upstream, leaping up falls or fish ladders built into dams. If the stream is obstructed or polluted, the salmon can't make it. Just lately, though, salmon have been found in rivers that had not known them for a century: children of spawn planted there by the U.S. Fish and Wildlife Service. Hope springs eternal!

Strawberries follow salmon on so many menus; though they'd be delicious with a savarin cake, we've opted this time for the doubly summery taste of tropical fruits, adding enormous black grapes to set off the green of kiwi fruit and the orange of mango and papaya. A few black grapes are saved, to be lightly frosted with sugar and set becomingly around the glazed, gleaming, rum-soaked cake. The traditional decoration is crystallized fruits, but I haven't found good ones here lately, and I wasn't foresighted enough to order replenishments from France. If you want the real thing, fruits big and brilliant as crown jewels and tasting intensely *like* fruit—not like rubber baby-buggy bumpers—you can write to Maiffret, Fabrique de Fruits Confits et Chocolats, 53, rue d'Antibes, 06400, Cannes, France, a house of master craftsmen that does a worldwide mail-order business.

As for the cake itself, it's made of the same simple batter as the more familiar small *babas au rhum*, a confection that is supposed to have been invented in the seventeenth century by the amiable king of Poland, Stanislas Lesczczynski, the French queen's father. Some say he named it for Ali Baba; but "baba" in Polish means "little granny," and I like the cozy thought. In the nineteenth century, a Parisian pastry cook baked the batter in a large ring mold and named it "savarin" in honor of the gastronome Brillat-Savarin. This too is a cozy thought: Savarin was a delightful man who named his favorite horse Joyous, who traveled in the American colonies and loved both us and our food. While here, in the woods near Hartford, he even shot a wild turkey, which he cooked and served to his American hosts. His book, *The Physiology of Taste*, translated by M.F.K. Fisher (New York: Alfred A. Knopf, 1971), is well worth any food lover's time some fragrant summer evening, made serene by a dinner like this one.

Preparations and Marketing

Recommended Equipment:

To jell small, manageable amounts of aspic, use a small saucepan you can quickly chill in a bowl of ice and water. To form the aspics, we used 6 oval molds, metal for easier unmolding, of ½-cup (1-dL-plus) capacity; you could use round molds, or large muffin tins. You'll need a tray to put the molds on.

To cook the salmon, use a pan big enough to hold all 6 steaks in 4 inches (10 cm) water, plus a kitchen timer, a skimmer, and a clean kitchen towel.

To make hollandaise, have 2 small stainless-steel saucepans and a wire whip.

For the cucumbers, a large frying pan, not of cast iron, and for the potatoes, a deep saucepan with lid.

The savarin recipe is for a 4-cup (1-L) mold. You don't need a special one; even a bumpy ring mold will do, or a cake pan or soufflé dish. The dough can be made by hand, but an electric mixer with a dough hook is helpful (dough is too soft and sticky for a food processor). To drench the cake with syrup, have a bulb baster; to glaze it, a pastry brush.

Staples to Have on Hand:

Salt
White peppercorns
Sugar
Dried tarragon
Optional: pure vanilla extract
Wine vinegar
Strong consommé or beef bouillon (1 cup or ¼ L, or more)
Butter (3 sticks; 12 ounces or 340 g)
Eggs (5 "large")
Dry-active yeast (1 package or 1 Tb)
All-purpose flour (1⅓ to 1½ cups or 190 to 215 g)
Carrot (1 large)
Fresh dill or parsley
Lemons (1)
Port or Madeira wine (½ cup or 1 dL)
Dark Jamaica rum, kirsch, or bourbon whiskey

Specific Ingredients for This Menu:

Perfect whole chicken livers (6)

Salmon steaks (6, weighing 8 ounces or 225 g
each, and ¾ inch or 2 cm thick) ❷

Wine-flavored aspic (recipe on page 00; 4 to 6
cups or 1 to 1½ L)

Fresh green peas (1 cup or ¼ L podded)

Cucumbers (3 large)

New potatoes (18 to 24, 1½ inches or 4 cm in
diameter)

Apricot jam (1½ cups or 3½ dL)

Fruits to fill savarin ❷

Optional: green beans (½ pound or 225 g)

---

❷ Remarks:

Salmon: except for the color of skin and flesh, what follows
applies to the buying and storing of any fresh fish. The scales
should be shiny and fresh, and the skin color bright—bright
silver for the lovely salmon. The eyes are bright and bulg-
ing—never buy fish when the eyes are flat or sunken—and
the gills red . . . that is, if the head is on. The meat is red-
orange—a deeper color if you can get the sublime King or
Chinook Pacific salmon—and has a glossy sheen, and it feels
firm and fresh to the touch, with a little give when pressed.
A fish that is past its prime of freshness will begin to soften,
its skin will lose its bright silvery color, the scales will be
dry and dull, and the flesh will pale—an enzyme action is
taking its toll on texture and flavor. Smell it; perfectly fresh
fish has either no odor, or else a very mild, delicious one.

A good fishmarket doesn't stop at refrigerating its wares;
the fish are bedded on ice. Do likewise. Rush it home (or
have a plastic ice container with you), and place it in a plastic
bag surrounded with ice, in a bowl, and refrigerate it. Drain
out accumulated ice water, renew ice 2 or 3 times a day, and
really fresh fish will keep well for 2 or 3 days; but, of course,
the sooner you cook it the better.

Fruits to fill savarin: if you decide to use the tropical
fruits shown here, be sure to buy them several days in advance. Kiwi fruit, mangoes, and papayas are all sold unripe;
put them in a closed paper bag or a ripening container at

room temperature, with a ripe apple or tomato for company if you want to hasten the process. You can judge the ripeness of mangoes, papayas, or kiwis by giving a gentle squeeze. They should feel like a ripe peach.

Chicken Livers in Aspic

Jellied anything, from consommé to eggs in aspic, is an inviting summer prospect, and these attractive chicken liver molds could serve as the main dish for a luncheon in any season, as well as being the first course for our summer dinner.

Timing: if you have never done this kind of thing before, it may seem too difficult for any but a professional to tackle. However, it is purely an assembly job, the sole requirements being plenty of time, ice, room in the refrigerator, and quite a bit more aspic than you think you will need. You can take as little as an hour or as much as a day or 2 to complete the very simple steps here—5 in all—which consist of making layers of aspic and objects layered in aspic: each layer has to chill in the refrigerator until it sets—a matter of 10 to 15 minutes. Then the molds need an hour or more of overall setting time to be sure they are thoroughly jelled and can safely be unmolded. Aspic, by the way, is a liquid—consommé in this case—that has gone through a clarification process to render it clear and sparkling, and gelatin has been added to it so that it sets or jells as it chills.

Ingredients Note: The better your aspic, the more delicious your final result. You can make it all yourself, or use canned chicken broth or canned consommé plus Port or Madeira wine, or a simmering of either with white wine and aromatic vegetables. What you use depends on your resources.

For 6 people

6 perfect whole chicken livers
1 cup (¼ L) strong fine consommé or beef bouillon
½ cup (1 dL) Port or Madeira wine (or consommé)
½ tsp dried tarragon
4 to 6 cups (1 to 1½ L) wine-flavored aspic (page 109)
Decorative suggestions (see others in Menu Variations): 1 large cooked carrot and 1 cup (¼ L) cooked green peas

**Garnishing suggestions: ½ pound (225 g) green
    beans, blanched and finely julienned (optional)**

Equipment:

**6 oval or round molds or cups of about ½-cup
    (1-dL-plus) capacity, preferably of metal for
    easy unmolding—or you could use muffin tins; a
    small metal saucepan set in a bowl of ice and
    water**

Poaching the chicken livers
To be done in advance

Pick over the chicken livers, removing any discolored spots
and bits of fat. Place in a small saucepan with the consommé
or bouillon, the wine, and the tarragon. Bring to the simmer,
and cook at just below the simmer (water is shivering but
not really bubbling) for 8 minutes. Cover loosely and let cool
in the liquid—to pick up added flavor—for at least half an
hour, or overnight. Drain, and chill. (This delicious liquid
could be added to the rest, for clarification, as on page 109.)

The aspic

Prepare the aspic, and be sure to test it out—pour a little
into a saucer, chill for 20 minutes, then fork it out onto a
plate and leave 10 minutes or so at room temperature to be
sure it will hold its own. On a warm day you may find you'll
need a little more gelatin: 1 tablespoon for 1½ cups (3½ dL)
liquid.

The decorations

I have chosen some very simple decorations here: the carrot
slices go into the bottom of the mold over its aspic lining,
and the peas go in at the end, so that when the aspic is
unmolded all is reversed. Cut several gashes down the length
of the carrot, so that when you then cut the carrot into thin
rounds you'll get a decorative edging: if you wish, also make
half moons out of other rounds. Place on a saucer. Slip the
skins off the peas, and pick them in half—they separate
easily; place in a small bowl. Chill both carrots and peas.

Assembling

Have your main supply of aspic liquefied in a pan or bowl;
the reason for the small saucepan over ice is so that you can

chill just what you need, until it is almost syrupy and about to set. When you have used that up, you pour a little more into the pan, chill, and continue. Otherwise you will be warming and then chilling such a large amount that your assembling would take hours to do.

Set your molds on a tray, and pour a ¼-inch (¾-cm) layer of aspic into them. Make room in the refrigerator, and set tray on a perfectly level place; chill until set—10 to 15 minutes.

Pour a little aspic into the small saucepan, chill over ice until cold to your finger but not jelled. Spear a carrot round with the point of a small knife, dip into the cold aspic, and center into a mold, adding other carrot pieces if you wish. When all decorations are in place, set in the refrigerator for a few minutes until anchored.

Arrange the chilled livers in the molds, pour in ½ inch or so (1½ cm) cold aspic, and chill. (If you poured in tepid aspic, that could melt the bottom layer and the decorations would float up.)

When set, spoon in more cold aspic to cover the livers.

When that has set, in 10 to 15 minutes, spoon on a layer of peas, and fill the molds with cold aspic.

Chill for at least an hour, until thoroughly set.

❷ May be assembled 2 or 3 days in advance of serving; cover with plastic wrap and keep chilled.

Serving

If you have allowed for enough aspic, you can use the remainder to decorate your plates or platter. Pour it into a pan to make a layer about ⅜ inch (1 cm) thick, and chill. Just before arranging the serving, cut the chilled aspic, still in its pan, into dice or diamonds or other shapes, or simply turn the whole sheet of aspic out onto your work surface and chop it with a knife. The molds can be dipped, one by one, into hot water for 8 to 10 seconds, or just long enough to loosen the aspic, and unmold them onto a serving platter, with chopped aspic all around and a central spray of cooked shredded green beans.

Fresh Salmon Steaks, Poached

Plain poaching, or boiling as it is sometimes erroneously called, is certainly one of the easiest and most delicious ways to cook perfectly fresh fine salmon. Nothing disturbs its lovely natural flavors, and there are no pitfalls I can think of in its cooking.

For 6 people

6 salmon steaks 8 ounces (225 g) each and about
   ¾ inch (2 cm) thick (I prefer boneless steaks
   cut from the fillet, skin on)
2 tsp salt and 2 Tb wine vinegar per quart or liter
   cooking water
Sprigs of fresh dill or parsley
Ready accompaniments: the hollandaise sauce,
   boiled new potatoes, and sautéed cucumbers
   (following recipes)

Equipment:

Pliers or tweezers; a wide saucepan, chicken fryer,
   or roaster with about 4 inches (10 cm) boiling
   water; a kitchen timer; a large skimmer for
   removing the fish; a clean kitchen towel; a soup
   spoon and fork; a heated platter and something
   to cover it with

Preparing the salmon

Run your finger searchingly over tops and sides of fish, and if you feel any big or little bones, pull them out with pliers or tweezers. Otherwise there is nothing to do, since the fish will be skinned after poaching. Keep on ice until the moment of cooking.

Poaching the fish
8 to 10 minutes

About 15 minutes before you plan to serve, have the water at the boil, and pour in the salt and vinegar. Bring back to

Julia Child & More Company / Summer Dinner

the boil, and lay in the salmon, piece by piece and skin side down. Set timer for 8 minutes. Regulate heat so water never comes near the boil again but stays at the shiver—no real bubbles, but a slight movement in the water to show it's cooking. When time is up, turn off the heat and let salmon rest for 2 minutes (or a few minutes longer if you are not ready to serve).

Peeling the salmon and placing it on the platter

With a folded towel in one hand, lift a piece of salmon out of the water with your skimmer; turn fish flesh side down on the towel. Place on your work surface, and lift off the skin with spoon and fork. Using the towel, reverse the steak right side up on the skimmer, and set on the hot serving dish. Cover and proceed rapidly with the rest of the salmon steaks. If your platter is large enough, you may wish to spoon a garland of cooked cucumbers around the fish, lay a ribbon of hollandaise down the center, and decorate that with wisps of fresh dill or parsley. Then pass the rest of the sauce, and the potatoes, separately.

❶ The cooked fish can safely wait in its cooking water for 15 minutes or so, but once peeled and plattered serve it immediately.

Hollandaise Sauce

*Although blenders and food processors do a quick
and easy hollandaise, a good cook should be ab-
solutely confident about whipping up a hollandaise
by hand. It not only takes less than 5 minutes, but
you are saved the time-consuming and messy task
of scraping as much sauce as you can off prickly
machine blades while getting it all over your fingers.
With a handmade sauce all you need do is bang the
whip on the side of the pan, scrape the sauce up in
2 or 3 scoops with a rubber spatula, and it's out in
a neat matter of seconds. Counting everything from
start to clean-up, I conclude it's faster by hand.*

For about 1½ cups (3½ dL), serving 6

**1½ to 2 sticks (6 to 8 ounces or 180 to 225 g)
    butter**
3 egg yolks
The grated rind of 1 lemon (optional)
1 Tb fresh lemon juice; more if needed
1 Tb water or fish-poaching liquid
¼ tsp salt, or more as needed
Big pinch white pepper; more as needed
2 Tb additional butter
**1 Tb or so fish-poaching liquid and/or cream
    (optional)**

Preliminaries

Have all your ingredients and equipment at hand. Melt the
1½ to 2 sticks butter in a small saucepan, and you are ready
to begin.

Thickening the egg yolks before heating

To prepare the egg yolks for their ordeal, place them in a
stainless-steel pan and beat vigorously with a wire whip for
a good minute, until they have thickened into a cream.

Adding the flavorings

Beat in the optional lemon rind, the lemon juice, and the
water or fish-poaching liquid, along with the ¼ teaspoon salt

and pinch of pepper. Add the 2 tablespoons additional butter as is; by melting slowly as you proceed in the next step, the butter will discourage the eggs from suffering heat shock, which might curdle them.

Thickening the yolks over heat
1 to 2 minutes

(Your object here will be to warm the yolks slowly enough so that they will thicken into a smooth creamy custard—too sudden or too prolonged heat will scramble them, and they cannot then absorb the melted butter to come. Remember you have complete control of your pan: you can lift it up from the heat, or set it aside, or even set the bottom of the pan in cold water to stop the cooking process at any time.)

Set pan over moderate heat and stir with your wire whip, reaching all over bottom of pan and taking about ½ second to complete each circuit. As the yolks slowly heat they will begin to foam—keep testing them with your finger, and when they feel hot, they are almost ready. Watch for a wisp of steam rising from the surface, which will also indicate their almost readiness. As soon as egg yolks have warmed, thickened, and creamed—which will happen suddenly—remove from heat and beat for a minute to cool them and stop the cooking.

Adding the butter
1 to 2 minutes

By droplets, beat the melted butter into the warm egg yolks, just as though you were making a mayonnaise—it is important to go slowly here, particularly at first, or the yolks cannot absorb the butter. Use as much butter as you wish, up to the maximum, to make a thick creamy sauce. Taste carefully for seasoning, adding more lemon juice, salt, and pepper as needed. To lighten the sauce, if you wish to, beat in droplets of warm fish-cooking liquid and/or cream.

❶ *Ahead-of-Time Notes*: If you are doing the sauce in advance, beat in only 1 stick butter; then, just before serving, heat the remainder and beat it into the sauce. Less butter makes the sauce safer to hold, and the hot butter at the end will warm it nicely. To hold the sauce, leave at room temperature if the wait is but a few minutes, since hollandaise is served barely warm, never hot. Otherwise set it near a gas pilot light, or near a simmering pot, or in a pan of tepid (not hot) water. Remember that too much heat will gradually coagulate the egg yolks, they will release the butter from suspension, and the sauce will curdle. Remember also that it is dangerous to let a hollandaise sit around in the kitchen for more than an hour or so because egg yolks are fine breeding grounds for nasty bacteria.

Trouble Shooting:

If sauce refuses to thicken or if finished sauce thins out or curdles, sometimes the beating in of a tablespoon of cold water or an ice cube will bring it back. If not, beat a teaspoon of lemon juice and a tablespoon of the sauce in a small bowl until they cream and thicken, then drop by drop at first, beat in the rest of the sauce until you again have a creamy mass. However, if you have overheated the sauce and curdled the yolks, the best thing to do is to heat it more until they release most of their butter; strain it out, then start over using fresh egg yolks but the same butter.

Boiled New Potatoes

I like boiling rather than steaming for new potatoes because it seems to me that steaming can discolor them. In any case, they are easy indeed to cook and any leftovers can make a happy reappearance in a salad.

For 6 people

18 to 24 small new potatoes about 1½ inches (4 cm) in diameter
Salt
2 to 3 Tb butter

Equipment:

A saucepan large enough to hold potatoes comfortably, and with a lid; a larger saucepan to hold the first if potatoes must wait a bit

Wash the potatoes and pick them over, removing any blemishes with a knife. Arrange in saucepan and cover with cold water, adding 1½ teaspoons salt per quart or liter of water. About 35 minutes before you plan to serve them, cover and bring to a boil and maintain at a slow boil for about 25 minutes, or until potatoes are just tender when pierced with a sharp knife—eat one as a test if you are not sure. Drain out water, roll about gently over heat to dry them off, then roll with a little butter to glaze them.

❂ These potatoes are at their best when served soon after cooking. If they must wait a bit, bring a little water to the simmer in the other pan, and set the potato pan in it, covering it loosely—potatoes must have air circulation or they will develop an off taste.

Cucumber Triangles Sautéed in Butter and Dill

The light fresh crunch of cucumbers and the flavor of dill seem always wedded to salmon. Here the cucumbers are cut, then tossed in butter and seasonings, with a sprinkling of dill. They still retain a bit of a crunch, and gain yet a different degree of cucumber flavor from being cooked.

For 6 people

**3 large fine cucumbers
2 Tb or more butter
Salt and white pepper
2 to 3 Tb minced fresh dill, or a little dried dill
     weed and minced fresh parsley**

Equipment:

A large frying pan, not of cast iron

Peel the cucumbers, slice in half lengthwise, and scoop out the seeds. Cut each half in half lengthwise, and then into triangles, as shown.

❂ May be prepared several hours in advance; refrigerate in a covered bowl.

Not more than 10 minutes before serving, melt the butter in the pan, add the cucumbers, and toss over moderately high heat, seasoning lightly with salt, until cucumbers are almost cooked through but still retain some crunch. Season to taste with more salt, pepper, and, if you wish, toss with a tablespoon or 2 more butter. Then toss with sprinklings of dill.

❂ Cucumbers should be served promptly or they lose both their crunch and their freshly cooked look.

Savarin aux Fruits Exotiques

A large ring-shaped yeast cake drenched in rum syrup and filled with a mixture of tropical fruits

Timing and Manufacturing Notes:

The savarin is made of a simple yeast dough that when cooked makes a plain, dry cake that is strangely tasteless and coarse—purposely so, since its role is to be a sponge that will absorb an enormous amount of flavored syrup without collapsing. Given time to drink its fill, the savarin's every bite is deliciously moist, quite unlike anything else but the rum babas following this recipe.

Timing: you will need a minimum of 4½ hours: 1½ to 2 hours for the dough to rise in a bowl, 1 hour for it to rise in its mold, ½ hour for it to bake and cool, and a final hour for it to absorb its syrup and to drain before you can glaze and serve it. However, you can bake it ahead and freeze it; you can syrup and drain it in advance; you can glaze it ahead, as well.

Avoiding dough troubles: be sure to dissolve your yeast in tepid water—hot water can kill it—and see that it is fully liquefied or it cannot do its work. Do not kill the yeast, either, by pouring hot butter on it. Give the dough time to rise; it may take longer than the amounts specified—it's the volume of the rise that you're looking for, not the time it takes to rise. Measure your flour correctly.

For 6 to 8 people

Dough for a 4-cup (1-L) Mold:

1 package (1 Tb) dry-active yeast
3 Tbs tepid water (not over 110°F/43°C)
2 "large" eggs
2 Tb sugar
⅛ tsp salt
4 Tb tepid melted butter
1⅓ to 1½ cups (190 to 215 g) all-purpose
**   flour—scoop dry-measure cups into flour and**
**   sweep off excess**

The Rum Syrup:

2 cups (½ L) water
1 cup (¼ L; 7 ounces or 190 to 200 g) sugar
½ cup (1 dL) dark Jamaica rum, kirsch, or
    bourbon whiskey, or 2 to 3 Tb pure vanilla
    extract

Glazing and Filling:

1½ cups (3½ dL) apricot jam
4 Tb sugar
Mixed fruits such as 1 or 2 ripe mangoes, papayas,
    and kiwis, plus a small bunch of black grapes
Additional sugar as needed
Rum, kirsch, bourbon, or lemon juice to flavor the
    fruits (optional)
1 or 2 egg whites

Equipment:

A 2-quart (2-L) mixing bowl, or an electric mixer
    with dough hook; a 4-cup (1-L) savarin mold
    (illustrated), or other ring mold (or a cake pan
    or soufflé dish); a skewer; a bulb baster; a
    pastry brush

The Dough:

About 3 hours

Preliminaries

Stir the yeast into the tepid water and let dissolve completely
while preparing the rest of the ingredients as follows. If eggs
are chilled, warm them for 2 minutes in hot water, then break
into mixing bowl. Blend in the sugar, salt, and butter. Measure the flour into the bowl, and stir in the completely liquefied yeast mixture.

Method for kneading by hand

Blend ingredients together with a rubber spatula or wooden
spoon, and when too heavy to stir, begin kneading by hand:
lift the dough with one hand, your fingers held together and
curved like a spoon. Slap the dough against the side of the
bowl, and vigorously repeat the process for a dozen sticky

passes or more, until the dough begins to take on some body, and finally enough for it to be removed from the bowl. (This is supposed to be a soft and sticky dough, but if it is still too soft after vigorous kneading, work in a little more flour; if too stiff, knead in droplets of milk.) Remove dough to your work surface, and let rest 2 to 3 minutes while you wash and dry the bowl. Knead the dough again by slapping it against your work surface, pushing it out with the heel of your hand, and continuing vigorously for a minute or 2 until it begins to peel itself cleanly from your fingers—it should stick to them if you hold a pinch of it, however. It will have enough elasticity so that you can grab it in both hands, pull it out, and give it a full twist without its breaking.

Method for kneading by electric mixer

Knead at moderate speed for several minutes until dough has enough body to ball on the dough hook or beater. (If too soft or too stiff see preceding paragraph.) Remove from mixer, wash out bowl, and finish by hand, as described.

The initial rise
About 2 hours

Roll the dough into a ball and return it to the mixing bowl. Cover with plastic wrap and let rise at around 75°F/24°C until the dough has doubled in bulk and feels light, spongy—1½ to 2 hours, or longer if cooler.

❷ If you are not ready to form the dough now, deflate it by pulling the sides toward the center, cover with buttered plastic, a plate, and a weight of some sort, and refrigerate. Push down again if it starts to rise before it has chilled and its butter content has congealed. Will keep 12 hours or more.

Final rise in the mold
About 1 hour

Butter inside of mold. Form the dough into a rope 10 to 12 inches (25 to 30 cm) long, rolling it under the palms of your hands, and gradually separating them to extend the dough. Cut crosswise into half, cut each half into thirds, and then halve each third. Drop the pieces into the mold, and press together lightly with your fingers—no need to be too careful since dough pieces will come together as they rise. (Mold should be about half filled with dough.) Cover with plastic and let rise until dough has filled the mold—about 1 hour at 75°F/24°C. (Chilled dough will probably take an hour more.) Meanwhile, preheat oven to 375°F/190°C in time for baking.

❶ You can delay the rising by refrigerating the mold; you can freeze it. Before baking, let chilled dough come to room temperature; thaw frozen dough and let warm to room temperature.

Baking
About 20 minutes at 375°F/190°C

Set mold in lower middle level of preheated oven. It is done when nicely puffed and browned, and when it comes easily out of the mold. If sides and bottom are not golden brown, return to mold and bake 4 to 5 minutes more. Unmold and let cool upside down on a rack.

❶ When cool, you may wrap the savarin airtight in a plastic bag and refrigerate for a day or so; it will keep for weeks in the freezer.

The Savarin Imbibes the Syrup:
About 1 hour

Both the syrup and the savarin must be tepid for this step, since a cold savarin will not imbibe easily, and a hot one might disintegrate. If savarin is cold, then, set it in a warming oven or a 200°F/95°C oven for a few minutes. To make the syrup, pour half the water into a saucepan, stir in the sugar, and heat gently until sugar has completely dissolved, then pour in the rest of the water (to cool it); add the rum or liqueur or vanilla. Prick the savarin all over at 1-inch (2½-cm) intervals with a skewer, and set the savarin in a dish. Pour the syrup over it, and dribble the syrup over the top a number of times with a spoon or bulb baster. In several minutes, repeat the process. After about half an hour of frequent basting the savarin will have absorbed all of the syrup; it will look swollen and feel spongy. Transfer onto a rack set over a dish to drain for half an hour, and it is ready to glaze.

❶ May be done several hours in advance; leave savarin in its dish, and cover with a bowl or with plastic, and refrigerate. Then drain on a rack; if it seems dry, make a little more syrup and baste it several times before glazing.

Apricot Glaze, and Glazing the Savarin:

Heat the apricot jam in a small saucepan with the sugar, stirring until sugar dissolves completely, then boil rapidly, stirring, until jam is quite thick and the last drops falling from your spoon are thick and sticky (the "thread stage," or 228°F/109°C). Push through a sieve to remove skin debris, and return the glaze to the pan.

❶ If not to be used immediately, set pan in another pan of simmering water; it must be warm or it will not spread. Leftovers may be bottled, reheated, and used again.

Paint the glaze all over the surface of the savarin. Then set the savarin on its serving dish.

❶ If the glaze has been properly cooked to the thread stage, it should set or jell on the savarin and act as a waterproofing seal; then the savarin can sit for several hours.

Finishing the Savarin:

Cut up the fruits (reserving some of the grapes), toss in a bowl with sugar and, if you wish, rum, liqueur, or lemon juice to taste. To frost grapes, beat the egg whites lightly with a fork to liquefy them, dip in the grapes one by one, roll them in granulated sugar, and let dry on a rack.

Just before serving, pile the fruits into the savarin, and decorate outside with the frosted grapes. To serve, cut wedges out of the savarin, and spoon a serving of fruit on the side. (You may wish to pass additional fruit with the savarin, and a bowl of lightly whipped and sweetened cream, on page 284.)

Variation: Babas au Rhum

Exactly the same dough makes babas, those individual rum-soaked yeast cakes. Use 12 well-buttered baba tins or muffin cups about 2 inches (5 cm) high and 2 inches across, and after the dough has risen in its bowl, form it into a rope, and cut it into 12 even pieces. Drop 1 piece into each cup, let dough rise just above the rims of the cups, and set on baking sheet. Bake about 15 minutes in the middle level of a pre-heated 375°F/190°C oven. They are done when they unmold easily, and are nicely browned. When tepid, imbibe with the same rum syrup, drain, glaze, and decorate if you wish. Serve as is, with whipped cream, or fruits flavored with the same liqueur.

❷ Timing

This is an easy and relaxed dinner. Fill the center of the savarin with previously trimmed fruit just before you serve it. Before the main course, peel the salmon steaks (a matter of seconds if you chose the fillet, rather than cross-section, type), finish the cucumbers, give the potatoes a toss over heat in their butter, and arrange your platter.

Before sitting down, poach the salmon and leave it in its cooking water. Set the cucumbers in butter over heat, then set aside. Everything can wait off heat while you enjoy the first course. At this time, you can either make the hollandaise sauce (a 5-minute job once you've got the knack), or have it half made and beat in warm melted butter just before serving.

Half an hour before sitting down, start the potatoes boiling.

Several hours beforehand, prepare the fruit for the savarin, and dose the cake with syrup, then glaze it.

Two or 3 days before your party, make the aspics.

The savarin can be baked and frozen long beforehand, or baked the day before and kept in the refrigerator.

Menu Variations

Aspic does for any cold food what pearls do for any complexion. Instead of chicken livers, you could use poached eggs—a classic dish—or lobster claw meat poached in wine, or crab, or shrimp, or pieces of *foie gras* and truffle, or liver pâté. Or dress up a cold mousse in an aspic jacket. You might prefer one large mold to individual small ones—though perhaps not a ring mold if you're having the savarin. Decorations, of course, can be very varied; just bear in mind the color of the aspic. Instead of carrots and peas you could use crossed fresh tarragon leaves that have first been dipped in boiling water; or strips of boiled ham, pimiento, black or green or stuffed olives, blanched green pepper, the whites of hard-boiled eggs, and/or the yolks sieved with a little butter and pushed through a paper cone to form designs. Or don't decorate the molds at all; they're handsome as is.

Fish for poaching: if salmon seems too expensive or is unavailable, use some other firm solid fish that has good natural flavor. (Monkfish has the right texture but is altogether too bland.) Halibut and striped bass are delicious poached, as is swordfish. Large cod steaks can take to it but might be more successful in a court-bouillon (a mixture of water, wine, and seasonings simmered for half an hour with 1 or 2 finely sliced carrots, onions, celery, and herbs). Instead of *hollandaise sauce*, you could use melted butter with herbs, or lemon butter or white butter sauces (recipes are on page 369). Dieters could use a decoration of dill sprigs and thinly sliced lemon, more fresh lemon on the side, and perhaps a bowl of sour cream or yogurt brightened with a little mustard, horseradish, fresh pepper, and minced herbs.

Cucumbers are the first thing I think of for salmon, but asparagus, peas, zucchini, or green beans would do very well.

New potatoes are ideal with poached fish, but can't always be had. You might substitute buttered and parslied potato balls, but I don't think any of the richer potato dishes (fried, scalloped, mashed, etc.) would suit. In season, just-picked sweet corn might be nice.

Tradition being what it is, you cannot call anything a *savarin* unless you bake it in the traditional ring mold. But the same dough in another mold will taste the same, and you can call it a rum cake, or a strawberry shortcake if you split it, drench it with strawberry juice, decorate it with sliced berries, and serve it with whipped cream. It is also delicious with rhubarb, sliced peaches, wild berries, and raspberries— for which you might drench it with framboise, the delicious raspberry liqueur. Or have babas!

Leftovers

The *chicken liver aspic* will keep for 2 to 3 days. Or you might buy more chicken livers than you need, make a little extra aspic, and use it to coat a delicious pâté, for which a recipe is included in this section.

For leftover cooked *salmon*, I also include a recipe here,

following the one for pâté. Cold poached salmon is delicious with cucumbers and sour cream or mayonnaise, but its beauty is fleeting. Eat it the next day; 2 days later, it'll be better in the nice old-fashioned gratin I've suggested. To stretch it, you can turn it into a sort of kedgeree by adding rice to the mixture.

Leftover *cucumbers* go into soup. But the *new potatoes* can be rinsed of their butter in boiling water, peeled, and used in salad. A slice of cold boiled new potato makes a better carrier than toast for some hors d'oeuvre—for instance, salmon roe with sour cream.

Hollandaise sauce must be discarded if it has sat at room temperature for an hour or more, since it is so vulnerable to bacterial action you can't detect. If it hasn't sat long, you can refrigerate it and reheat it cautiously.

A *savarin* loses its bloom rather quickly, but will still be good the next day. Or you can layer slices of it with custard, to make something resembling an English trifle.

Chicken Liver Pâté

For a 3-cup (¾-L) pâté

1 medium onion
1 Tb butter
2 cups (½ L) chicken livers
4 Tb Port or Madeira wine
½ cup (4 ounces or 115 g) plain or herbed cream
   cheese
6 Tb additional butter
½ cup (1 dL) aspic (page 110; or consommé and
   ½ Tb dissolved gelatin)
Salt and pepper
Herbs and spices: pinch of allspice or special spice
   mixture (page 381), and/or thyme or tarragon
Cognac or Armagnac in dribbles, if needed

Equipment:

A food processor makes quick work of this; or use
   a blender, or a sieve and wooden spoon.

Mince the onion and cook slowly in the butter until wilted.
Meanwhile, pick over the livers, removing any discolored
spots and fat. Stir them into onion and sauté several minutes
just until stiffened. Pour in the wine and boil for a moment.
Purée the livers with the cheese, additional butter, and aspic.
Taste very carefully for seasoning to make a marvelous-
tasting mixture, overseasoning a little since it will lose some
of its flavor when it is cold. Pack into a mold or bowl, cover,
and chill several hours.

*Will keep for about a week under refrigeration. May be
frozen, but will lose something in texture when thawed.

Gratin of Poached Salmon

For 4 people

2 poached salmon steaks (or about 2 cups or ½
    L salmon, cooked or canned)
4 hard-boiled eggs
1 large onion
4 Tb butter, more as needed
½ Tb curry powder
5 Tb flour
2 cups (½ L) milk, heated in a small pan
4 to 6 Tb dry white wine or dry white French
    vermouth
Salt and white pepper
1 tsp or so fresh minced dill weed, or big pinches
    of dried dill
About ⅔ cup (1½ dL) grated Swiss or mixed
    cheese (page 370)

Equipment:

A buttered 6-cup (1½-L) baking dish 2 inches (5
    cm) deep

Flake the salmon, and slice or quarter the eggs. Mince the
onion and cook slowly in the butter in a 2-quart (2-L) saucepan; when limp, stir in the curry powder and the flour, adding
a little more butter if flour is not absorbed. Cook, stirring,
for 2 to 3 minutes. Remove from heat, and let cool a moment,
then blend in the hot milk with a wire whip. Return to heat
and simmer, stirring, for 2 minutes. Add the wine and simmer
several minutes more, stirring frequently. Season carefully
to taste.

Fold the salmon into the sauce, fold in the dill, and taste
very carefully again; it should be delicious. Spread half the
salmon mixture in the bottom of the buttered baking dish,
and spread half the cheese over it. Arrange the eggs over
the cheese, and spread the rest of the salmon over them,
covering with the remaining cheese.

❷ Baking dish may be arranged several hours in advance.
Cover and refrigerate.

About half an hour before serving, preheat oven to 400°F/205°C. Place dish in upper third level, and bake until contents are bubbling and cheese topping has browned lightly. Do not overcook, or salmon will dry out and eggs will toughen.

Postscript: Hot-weather food

When you think of the foods native to hot climates, like our own gumbos and barbecues and chili, or the curries of India, or the rijstafel of Malaysia, or the tomatoey, garlicky soups and sauces of the Mediterranean, what they seem to have in common is their high, poquant seasoning. It strikes me that hot-weather food should be light but rarely bland; if the appetite is excited, its satisfaction is more intense, and one can do with less. To think that cold food equals light food, however, seems to me an illusion. One double-dip ice cream cone is just as hearty as one steak.

What's called for, I think, is contrast and stimulus: hot and cold, sharp and bland, crunchy and creamy. Before a chicken salad, try a winy consommé, but piping hot, not jellied. And aim for variety. So often, all the dishes on a fancy cold buffet taste mostly of mayonnaise, vinaigrette, cream, and sour cream. One wearies of the ubiquitous lemon: sometime, instead of filling an avocado hollow with oil and lemon, try fresh orange juice spiked with hot pepper sauce. Try horseradish instead of mustard. Try a change of oil: fresh walnut oil, for example, is exquisite.

Our salmon dinner, though it would be nice in any season, seems to me to have a summery air, but temperately so. Of the menus in this book, "Fast Fish Dinner," with its cold beet and cucumber soup and the lively sauce over hot monkfish, would be ideal for a really sultry evening, though one might prefer a lighter dessert—fresh pear sherbet? In *Mastering I*, we devoted a chapter to the classical French cold buffet, and among good cookbooks, all with "summer" in their titles, are Judith Olney's (Atheneum), Molly Finn's (Simon & Schuster), and Elizabeth David's (Penguin).

In extreme hot weather, one can save jobs like baking and simmering for the cool of the evening, or use a hibachi set outside the kitchen door to avoid lighting the broiler. And one's eating as well as one's cooking patterns can be adapted: more for breakfast, and have it earlier, less for lunch, dinner after sundown.

In general, the best rule of thumb is that for dieters' food: in summer, meals should be exciting as well as delicious. Never forget, there was a record heat wave in Fall River, Massachusetts, on that fell morning when Lizzie Borden fetched her axe, and never forget what she had had for breakfast: overripe bananas, too-long-leftover cold mutton, and cookies. No wonder she couldn't keep her cool.

Buffet Dinner

An Expandable Menu

For 20 to 30 people or more

Sweet-and-Sour Sausage Nuggets
Tarama Brandade—*Carp roe with hints of garlic, olive oil, and Provençal mysteries*
Pissaladière Gargantua—*Giant onion and anchovy pizza*
Toasted Pita Triangles; Raw Vegetable Nibbles; Nuts and Crackers

Braised Pot Roast of Beef—*Bottom round of beef in red wine*
Potato Gnocchi—*Cheese and potato dumplings browned in the oven*
Old-fashioned Country Ham
A Cauldron of Home-cooked White Beans with Herbs
Fresh Vegetables à la Grecque—*Cold in aromatic liquid*
Tossed Green Salad
Hot French Bread

Orange Bavarian Torte—*Dressed in whipped cream and glazed orange peel*
Sliced Strawberries with Orange Liqueur

Suggested wines:

White wine—*French colombard or Chablis;* red wine—*a Beaujolais, zinfandel, or cabernet. Champagne or sparkling wine for the dessert*

A big bounteous party is fun for the cook the way a herbaceous border is fun for the gardener: you start with a gorgeous vision, make precise plans, execute them leisurely (smugly checking off item by item)—and lo! there it all is, right on time and a sight to behold. You really brought it off. Even for 30 people, this grand spread is entirely feasible for 1 cook—but if you want to vary it, there's a list of big-party dishes on page 361, all rated for their practicality. On this menu, the braised beef and the torte each serve 15, and the other recipes are for 10; so, for say 30 guests, braise 2 rounds, make 2 cakes, and otherwise multiply by 3.

Here's how I set party priorities:

1) *The End Result. Flavor*—will the meal be delicious, with each dish at its best? (This eliminates many pastas and hot fish things, which should be eaten soon after their preparation. At a very large buffet, plan on dishes that can sit around a bit.) *Appearance*—will everything look handsome and stay that way? By this token, do your own carving and slicing at table, or else appoint a friend to take it on; otherwise you'll have Devastated Areas. *Space*—if you haven't much, serve compact dishes, pots not platters. If you have lots, use several locations: one for appetizers, one for the main course, one for dessert. This keeps people moving and mingling, for one thing. *Temperature*—have you enough warming devices, and enough electric outlets to serve them? You can't use 2 on the same line, unless one is a low-voltage slow cooker. However, thick-walled casseroles stay warm a long time, and there are always chafing dishes and candle-heated stands. Have plenty of ice around for cooling wines and filling insulated chests, etc.

2) *Space*—not just for serving, but for storing dishes prepared in advance, and, before that, their components. Most refrigerators need a periodic clear out, and now's a good time. Anyway, we could all use our refrigerators more efficiently. Cake layers can be stacked with racks or strong cardboard in between. Square containers are more efficient than round ones. Flexible containers, such as plastic bags, fit anywhere. (A tip: having dried your salad makings, tear the greens and assemble the whole salad in 1 bag.) In winter, the back porch makes a good refrigerator annex; in summer, an insulated chest; perhaps your friends have space you can borrow.

3) *Equipment*—friends and space both count here. To my mind, it's pointless to have more than one rarely used, expensive, or space-consuming item per neighborhood. So why not a community duck press, lobster pot, fish steamer, *pâté en croûte* mold, spring-form pan? A portable tabletop oven is another very useful community item, as are slow cookers and electric hot trays. For the ham on this menu, as for, say, *gravlaks*, you need a fine slicing knife—expensive and not used every day—so share it! If you have only 1 oven, plan on dishes that can co-occupy it (cakes and soufflés can't), and that require the same temperature setting.

On ordinary staple equipment, my advice is not to stint yourself. Have plenty of bowls, strainers, spatulas, paring knives, and kitchen towels, so you don't have to waste time on petty calculations, or stop to wash single items.

4) *Rhythm and Timing*. It's very helpful to start a cooking bout by "doing your prep," as restaurant cooks say: squeezing lemon juice (keep refrigerated), chopping parsley, washing and drying salad greens, putting a kettle on to boil, starting a new batch of ice cubes. White wine can be chilled all day; red wine can be brought to room temperature early. Time savers: large flour, sugar, and salt containers, each with its own rarely washed set of measuring cups or spoons—otherwise, every time you open a package, you have to mop up spilled grains; a big pan of soapy water where used implements can soak; a portable pastry slab you can chill. Always read a recipe through beforehand, and assemble all the items and equipment before starting. Measure the capacity of molds and baking pans, and mark them.

Make and freeze "standard parts" like doughs, crêpes, and stock beforehand, and plan jobs for the time when something can simmer or bake unattended. (I know lots of cooks who budget their time but not their energy.) A job that takes 10 minutes when you're fresh can take 20 when you're not; you'll wind up livelier if you alternate sitting jobs with standing ones, chopping with paring, etc. Clutter is fatiguing; for me, frequent cleanups are more restful than one final bout.

5) *Cost Effectiveness*—really, Effort Effectiveness. Now, with a big party, is not the time to put in 100 percent more work for 5 percent more effect. Take this simple but sound braised beef. Old-fashioned recipes call for larding, marination, and a sauce slowly reduced to almost nothing, then

reconstituted with wine. This is all very well if you've nothing else to do; but basically what gives a braise flavor and tenderness is cooking and keeping meat and liquid together. Reheating this dish is not merely a convenience but an improvement.

On the other hand, put your effort where it does count. Whipped cream, for instance, is much better made by hand, over ice, than with a mixer; a custard sauce can't be beaten mechanically—so much foam builds up that you can't see what you're doing. You could use machines, in this menu, for making pastry, cutting onions, mixing the *brandade* and the gnocchi, and whipping egg whites, but it's not really a menu planned for machines. For buffet dishes that are, see the Postscript.

6) *Resources*, and Your Own Resourcefulness. There's usually more than one way to skin a rabbit; the Timing section of this chapter gives you only one. However you go at it, you can do this meal alone, and so well in advance that at the time of your party, your kitchen can be sparkling, uncluttered, and all ready for a glorious evening.

Preparations and Marketing

Recommended Equipment:

Serving: let's suppose you're planning for 20 or 30 people, and for the full menu. You have first to decide whether to carve the beef and the ham at table, and if you do, that means 1 or 2 large carving boards, and, for the ham, a first-rate, razor-sharp slicing knife. The ham is served cold or cool; the beef is best hot but is still good at room temperature. The sausage nuggets and the beans will stay warm in slow cookers, or you can use warming devices; 1 big electric tray would hold them, plus the gnocchi. Freshly baked *pissaladière* will probably be eaten before it cools off! Allow space for your big salad bowl, your platter of cold vegetables, and your smaller bowls of *brandade*, raw vegetables, nuts, crackers, and pita triangles—plus more space for dessert, sauce, dessert plates, your bar setup, and your coffee tray. Remember that carvers need elbow room, and consider the number and location of electric outlets for warmers. At one efficient buffet served in a roomy kitchen, I remember hot dishes were served from the counter tops, and cold ones were bedded on ice in the sink; used dishes and silver were slid—gently and unobtrusively—into trash barrels filled with soapy water, to soak. A cooled-off oven also makes a discreet repository for such items, as does your dishwashing or laundry machine.

Cooking: if you did each job in succession, using a minimum of pans, you'd need 1 skillet (preferably nonstick) for sausages and the pizza onions, and 1 large, heavy, stainless-steel saucepan to sauce sausages, simmer black olives, poach gnocchi, cook vegetables, and make custard sauce (the reason why it has to be stainless). For baking gnocchi and *pissaladière*, you need 2 jelly-roll pans (1 of which browned the beef), or 1, plus a baking sheet. A large, deep roaster, preferably with cover, will cook first the ham, then the beef. A food processor or mixer will help with several jobs. You need a casserole for the beans and a deep pan for the torte (10- by 3-inch, or 25- by 8-cm, spring-form preferred).

Be sure to check your supply of aluminum foil, plastic wrap, plastic bags, white kitchen string, and cheesecloth.

Small implements needed: meat thermometer, pastry bag with large star tube, skimmer or slotted spoon, giant spatula and flexible-blade spatula.

Obviously, the more saucepans, bowls, sieves, colanders, and paring knives you have, the faster you can go.

Staples to Have on Hand:

Salt
White peppercorns
Granulated sugar
Eggs (17 "large")
Butter (1½ pounds or 675 g)
Confectioners sugar (½ cup or 70 g)
Dried herbs: oregano, thyme, allspice berries, imported bay leaves, whole cloves, mustard seeds, coriander, saffron threads, and fennel seeds; mixed herbs (optional)
Grated nutmeg
Pure vanilla extract
Olive oil
Cooking oil, or rendered beef or pork fat
Wine vinegar
Soy sauce
Hot pepper sauce
Dijon-type prepared mustard
Cream of tartar
Arrowroot, or rice flour, or potato flour, or cornstarch
All-purpose flour
Milk (2¼ cups or 5½ dL)
Butter, clarified (about ½ cup or 1 dL)
Grated Gruyère, Parmesan, or Swiss cheese (1¼ cups; 5 ounces or 140 g)
Beef stock or bouillon (5 cups or 1¼ L)
White nonsweet bread for crumbs (½ loaf)
Lemons (3)
Carrots (1 bunch)
Celery (1 bunch)
Garlic (1 head)
Parsley (1 large bunch)
Red wine (1 bottle; see beef recipe)
Orange liqueur (3 Tb; plus 7 to 8 Tb, optional)
Optional: concentrated frozen orange juice

Specific Ingredients for This Menu:

Excellent sausage meat (1 pound or 450 g) ❷
Bottom round of beef (1 whole trimmed, 10 to 12
    pounds or 4½ to 5½ kg)
Country ham (1 whole; see recipe)
Chilled pastry dough (1½ pounds or 675 g) ❷
Gelatin (6 Tb or 6 envelopes)
Flat anchovy fillets, packed in olive oil (two 2-
    ounce or 60-g cans) ❷
Black Mediterranean-type or Niçoise olives
    (about 24) ❷
Dry white beans (1 pound or 450 g)
Optional: fresh basil (1 bunch)
Apricot jam or chutney (4 Tb)
Tarama (salt carp roe) (½ cup or 115 g) ❷
Heavy cream (5 half-pints, or 1¼ L plus)
Orange juice (1⅓ cups or 3¼ dL)
Oranges (3)
Optional: candied orange peel (see page 17)
Cakes: *génoise*, yellow, or sponge (can be
    storebought; 2 round, about 10 by 1 inches or
    25 by 2.5 cm, see page 352)
Vegetables for cold platter (see recipe)
Vegetables for raw nibbles
Greens for salad
Potatoes (about 6½ pounds or 3 kg; or can be
    instant—see recipe)
Yellow onions (about 3 pounds or 1350 g)
Ingredients for dessert sauce (see recipe)
Nuts, crackers, pita bread, etc. (ad-lib)
Plenty of ice cubes for cooling wine, etc.

---

❷ Remarks:

Sausage meat: a quick easy recipe for making your own is
in *J.C. & Co. Pie crust dough*: double the proportions for
the pie and quiche dough on page 371. *Olives*: the salt-and-
oil-cured Mediterranean type need blanching before you use
them, to remove excess salt—simmer in 1 quart (1 L) water
5 to 10 minutes (depending on how salty they are), drain,
and rinse. If you don't like to serve olives with pits, you'll

either have to pit them or switch to the relatively tasteless pitted black olives you can buy in any market. *Anchovy fillets*: don't use if decorating *pissaladière* in advance; use more olives. Always open anchovy cans at the last minute. *Tarama*: this is a salty orange-pink paste, often imported from Greece, that is sold in Middle Eastern markets and delicatessens.

Sweet-and-Sour Sausage Nuggets

You will note the perhaps odd addition of aspic to the sausage mixture here, a suggestion from chef Joe E. Hyde, whose straw potato pancake is described on page 14. His disciple, our own chef Marian, says he says the aspic makes the meatballs lighter, and indeed it does, since these have a delightfully unheavy texture.

For about 24 nuggets

The Sausage Mixture:

1 pound (450 g) best-quality well-seasoned prepared
    sausage meat
1 "large" egg
5 Tb crumbs from fresh white nonsweet bread with
    body
4 Tb strong liquefied aspic (a scant teaspoon plain
    unflavored gelatin, softened and then heated to
    dissolve in 4 Tb consommé)

The Sweet-and-Sour Sauce:

¾ cup (1¾ dL) well-flavored beef stock or
    broth
1 Tb wine vinegar
4 Tb strained apricot jam or chutney
1 Tb arrowroot, rice flour, potato flour, or
    cornstarch dissolved in 5 Tb orange juice
1 Tb soy sauce
1 Tb butter
1 Tb Dijon-type prepared mustard
6 drops hot pepper sauce
Salt and freshly ground pepper

Beat the sausage meat, egg, crumbs, and aspic together in a bowl. If too soft to form, chill for half an hour or so, or beat over ice. Using 1½ tablespoons of meat at a time, form into balls. Chill for 30 minutes. Brown slowly in a large, preferably nonstick skillet, and drain on paper towels.

Meanwhile, blend the sauce ingredients together in a large, heavy stainless-steel saucepan; simmer 3 to 4 minutes, and correct seasoning, adding salt and pepper to taste, and drops more of the listed ingredients if you think them necessary. Fold the sausage into the sauce.

❷ May be done a day or so in advance.

To serve

Reheat to the simmer for a minute or 2, then place in a decorative bowl or pan and set on an electric warmer, or in a pan of water over a chafing dish flame. Have a container of toothpicks at hand, for spearing.

Tarama Brandade

A spread or dip—salted carp roe puréed with potato, garlic, olive oil, cream, and seasonings

The most famous brandade *(it literally means "stirred vigorously") is a purée of salt cod, garlic, and olive oil, a marvelous concoction that originated in Provence, and there is every reason to put that brilliant concept to good use with other ingredients. The pink and salty carp roe, the kind you find in jars in Middle Eastern groceries, is a fine example. It is usually whipped up with soaked bread crumbs, but mashed potato makes an even smoother and more delicious mixture.*

For about 1 quart (1 L)

2½ cups (6 dL) warm cooked potatoes (baked, preferably, or boiled, or stiff instant mashed)
½ cup (115 g) tarama (salt carp roe)
1 or more cloves garlic, puréed
½ cup (1 dL) fruity olive oil
½ cup (1 dL) heavy cream
Fresh lemon juice to taste
Freshly ground white pepper
Drops of hot pepper sauce

Equipment:

A food processor makes quick work here; or use an electric mixer; or a potato ricer or vegetable mill, mixing bowl, and wooden spoon.

If you are using a processor, purée the potatoes, using the steel blade, then add the *tarama* and puréed garlic and continue processing while you add olive oil alternating with cream to make a heavy creamy paste that holds its shape lightly when lifted in a spoon. Season to taste with lemon juice, pepper, and hot pepper sauce plus a little more oil, cream and/or garlic if you think them needed. (Otherwise, purée the potatoes and whip in the *tarama* and garlic, then the oil alternating with the cream, and finally the seasonings.) Pack into a serving bowl, or chill and mound on a serving dish.

❷ May be made several days in advance; cover and refrigerate.

Variations:
Brandade de morue—purée with salt cod

Substitute 1 pound (450 g) cooked salt cod for the *tarama*, warming it first in a saucepan over moderate heat with 4 tablespoons olive oil, and beating with a large fork to shred it. Then purée with 1½ cups (3½ dL) cooked potato and 2 or more cloves garlic, puréed, adding alternate dollops of olive oil and cream, and seasoning with salt, pepper, and lemon juice. A marvelous mixture.

Avocado brandade

Use equal amounts of warm cooked potato and ripe avocado, puréeing them together with a small clove of garlic, puréed, and adding spoonfuls of heavy cream and olive oil. Season with salt, white pepper, and lemon juice. Makes a beautiful pale green creamy dip that keeps nicely in a covered jar in the refrigerator for a day or 2. I have added anchovies, chives, and capers to it, but I think the simpler version is more successful.

Pissaladière Gargantua

A party-sized onion and anchovy pizza

I always like to have a pastry something for large gatherings, and the pizza idea in rectangular form is a good one because it is not too rich—no eggs, just pie crust dough, cooked onions, anchovies, black olives, and a sprinkling of cheese for the top. Another plus is that you can assemble and freeze it, all except for the anchovy topping. Furthermore, 1 large sheet of it will give you 20 generous portions, or 40 small ones.

For 20 appetizer-sized servings

4 cups (1 L) sliced yellow onions
4 to 6 Tb olive oil
Chilled pie crust dough (proportions for 3½ cups, 1 pound, or 454 g flour; double the recipe on page 371)
Salt and pepper
1 tsp or so dried oregano or thyme, or mixed dried herbs
Two 2-ounce (60-g) cans flat anchovy fillets, packed in olive oil
About 24 black olives (the dried Mediterranean type or other salty imported smallish black olives)
About ½ cup (1 dL) grated Parmesan cheese, or mixed cheeses from your frozen collection (page 370)

Equipment:

A jelly-roll pan, nonstick preferred, about 11 by 17 inches (28 by 43 cm)

Cook the onions slowly in 4 tablespoons of olive oil in a roomy covered frying pan or saucepan, stirring frequently, until they are soft and thoroughly tender, but not browned—20 minutes or more.

❶ May be cooked ahead; cool, cover, and refrigerate for several days, or freeze.

Meanwhile, butter the bottom (not the sides) of the jelly-roll pan. Rapidly roll out the chilled dough into a rectangle ⅛ inch (½ cm) thick, and larger and wider than the pan. Fit it into the pan, and neatly trim off the overhanging edges. Fold edges of dough down against bottom all around; press a decorative border into them with the tines of a table fork. Prick inside surface of dough all over with 2 forks, as shown—to keep it from rising up during baking.

❶ Cover and refrigerate (or freeze) until you are ready to continue.

When onions are tender, season carefully with salt and pepper, and either let them cool or stir over cold water until cool. Spread them over the inside surface of the dough.

❶ Cover and refrigerate (or freeze) until you are ready to continue.

Baking
25 to 30 minutes at 425°F/220°C

While the oven is preheating, arrange a design of anchovies, such as the diagonal pattern illustrated, over the onions, with black olives at strategic intervals. Sprinkle the cheese over the onions and the design, and dribble on a tablespoon of olive oil (oil from the anchovy can, if you wish). Bake in lower third level of oven (where pastry will crisp better) until pastry has browned and is beginning to shrink from the sides of the pan.

Serving

Slide onto a serving board or work surface, and either let guests cut their own, or cut into serving pieces and arrange on a plate. Five strips across the *pissaladière* and 4 the length of it give you 20 pieces.

❶ I prefer not to arrange the anchovies more than 30 minutes or so before baking because I think they develop an off taste if they sit around out of their hermetically sealed can. And although it can be baked ahead, the *pissaladière* is at its most delicious served fresh and warm, rather than cold.

Variations:

Pizza

Use a regular pizza topping of tomato sauce, herbs, and cheese, plus, if you wish, diced cooked mushrooms, sausages, ham, and so forth. An interesting pizza additive is diced sautéed eggplant (use the recipe, on page 189, the garnish for our spaghetti squash).

Quiche

If you want a cheese and cream combination, which can be very good too, you will either have to make a prebaked crust with edging to hold the liquid quiche mixture or do as follows. Spread the surface of the dough with shaved or coarsely grated Swiss cheese, using about 2 cups (½ L). Beat 1 egg and 2 yolks in a bowl with ⅔ cup (1½ dL) heavy cream, season well with pepper, drops of Worcestershire, and a little sage or thyme. Just before baking, spread the egg and cream mixture over the cheese—it is to be a thick coating only; if you need more liquid, spread on a little more cream. Bake as described for the *pissaladière*. This makes attractively brown and cheesy mouthfuls.

Cocktail Miscellany

You will want the usual crackers and nuts, and something like potato chips or toasted pita triangles (there is a recipe for homemade ones in *J.C. & Co.*), plus some raw vegetable nibbles for those who are well-disciplined dieters. Since every household has its favorites, I shall not go into details.

Notes on the Braising of Beef

Beef cuts for braising

I like the bottom round for braising—the long outside muscle of the leg; it is a solid piece with no separations, and it cuts into neat pieces. Other braising parts, like chuck, top round, and tip (or face), break into separate muscles, and that makes for messy carving. The brisket is a possibility, but not my favorite for this dish, and I have never cared for the stringy quality of the usually overpriced eye of the round.

If you are braising more than one

You will need either 2 covered roasting pans unless you have a mammoth one that will hold 2 beef bottoms. Or you can braise the roasts 1 at a time, and cool 1 while you are cooking the other—or others. You can braise the meat on top of the stove if you are careful with the heat, and turn the meat every 45 minutes or so, but an oven is more even—2 ovens are ideal.

The red wine sauce for the beef

Any meat that needs long simmering, as in a braise or a stew, wants some kind of a sauce. The meat is no longer moist after cooking because its juices have gone into the braising liquid: both meat and liquid take from and give to each other, which is one of the principal reasons that braised meat has such fine flavor. In this recipe the braising liquid is lightly thickened; when the beef is done the sauce is made.

Braised Pot Roast of Beef

Daube de boeuf—Boeuf à la mode
Whole bottom round of beef braised in red wine

A fine large pot roast of beef is ideal for a group because you can cook it 1 or 2 days before serving. In fact, it is better that you do so because the meat not only will pick up additional flavor from sitting in its braising juices but will also slice more neatly, since the meat fibers will have compacted themselves as they cool, and will hold together nicely when reheated. Furthermore, braised beef is easy to cook, and it stands up well during the leisurely pace of most buffets.

For a 10- to 12-pound (4½- to 5½-kg) roast, serving 15 to 20 people

A whole trimmed bottom round of beef (10 to 12
   pounds or 4½ to 5½ kg)
Rendered beef or pork fat, or cooking oil
6 Tb all-purpose flour
About 4 cups (1 L) beef stock (page 167), or best-
   quality canned beef bouillon
Salt
2 carrots, roughly chopped
2 large onions, roughly chopped
1 large celery stalk, roughly chopped
4 cloves garlic, not peeled
1 large herb bouquet (10 parsley sprigs, 3 or 4
   imported bay leaves, 1 tsp thyme, 6 allspice
   berries, all tied in washed cheesecloth)
1 bottle healthy young red wine, like zinfandel,
   Chianti, or other of like quality

Equipment:

White string for tying the beef; a jelly-roll pan for
   browning it; a medium-sized heavy-bottomed
   saucepan, for starting the sauce base; a covered
   roaster, or a large roasting pan with sides 3 to 4
   inches (8 to 10 cm) high and heavy aluminum
   foil

Browning the beef

Wind white string around the beef down its length, to hold the meat in place firmly during its cooking. Paint on all sides with fat or oil, set in the jelly-roll pan, and brown slowly on all sides under the broiler, being careful not to let the meat burn. This is a process that needs close watching, but it is the easiest way to brown such a large piece.

❷ May be browned well in advance, if need be, and especially if you are doing more than 1 roast.

Preliminaries for the sauce base

Meanwhile, but keeping your eye on the beef as well, blend 5 tablespoons fat or oil in the heavy saucepan with the flour (if you are doing more than 1 bottom, double or triple this amount), and stir almost continuously, but rather slowly, with a wooden spoon over moderate heat as the flour gradually turns a quite dark nutty brown. Making a brown *roux* takes time and care—you don't want the flour to burn, just to darken slowly so it will not have a bitter taste. Time: about 10 minutes. Remove from heat and let cool several minutes, then blend in the beef stock and set aside.

Braising the beef
2½ to 3 hours

Preheat oven to 350°F/180°C. Salt the meat on all sides, using about 2 teaspoons, and set it in the roaster fat side up. Arrange the vegetables and garlic around the meat, add the herb bouquet, and pour in the wine and the beef stock—*roux*, plus a little more stock if necessary, to come almost halfway up the meat. Bring to the simmer on top of the stove; cover and set in lower third of oven. When contents are bubbling quietly, in about half an hour, baste the meat with the sauce and turn thermostat down to 325°F/165°C. Liquid should simmer quietly throughout the cooking; regulate oven accordingly. Baste and check on the cooking every half hour until 2 hours are up, then begin testing. The meat is done when a sharp-pronged fork can penetrate through the middle section with comparative ease. If you have any doubts, cut a piece off the large end and eat it: the meat should be somewhat firm, but not tough. Time of cooking will depend on quality of meat—a Prime well-aged piece will take a shorter cooking time, while a fresh Choice cut may take up to an hour longer.

• Meat may be carved and served after a rest of half an hour or so, but is really better cooked several hours or a day in advance.

Finishing Meat and Sauce:

Let the beef cool for half an hour, basting it every 10 minutes or so with the sauce, and turning it several times. Then remove it and drain contents of roaster through a colander or sieve into a large saucepan, pressing juices out of braising vegetables into pan. Bring liquid to the simmer, skimming fat off surface as you do so; continue to skim for several minutes as fat rises to the surface while sauce very slowly bubbles. You can serve it now, but the sauce will really taste best if you have time to keep simmering and skimming it for half an hour as it slowly reduces. Taste carefully for seasoning and strength, and boil down slowly until the sauce coats a spoon just enough so you know it will coat the meat. (If by any chance sauce is strong and fine but not thick enough, soften 2 or more tablespoons of arrowroot, rice flour, potato flour, or cornstarch—or even all-purpose flour—in several spoons of wine or stock; remove sauce from heat, beat in starch mixture, then simmer for 2 to 3 minutes. On the other hand, if sauce is too thick, thin out with more stock.)

Pour the sauce around the meat, cover with foil or wax paper, and refrigerate.

Reheating and Serving:

You may reheat the beef whole, as is, or sliced and sauced. Here are the two alternatives.

To reheat the beef whole

Cover the beef closely and reheat either in the oven at around 300°F/150°C, or by simmering very slowly over low heat on top of the stove, turning the beef every 15 minutes. It will take 30 to 40 minutes to reheat, and the internal temperature need be no more than 120°F/49°C. It is important that you do not let the meat overheat and overcook, as it will fall apart when sliced. However, you may keep it warm once it is reheated. Just before serving, cut and discard the trussing strings.

Carving at the table. If you have reheated the beef whole and there is a willing carver available, it is always appealing to have meat sliced at the table. Set the beef on a handsome board, and have the carver start his work at the large end, making bias slices, since a straight cut across the meat would make too large a piece for 1 serving. When he gets near the tail end and notices any overt tendency to shredding, he cuts the meat into chunks. He should have a bowl of sauce on a hotplate at his side, and will ladle a spoonful or so over each serving.

Carved meat presented on a platter

Carve the meat in the kitchen and return it neatly to the roaster or a large baking pan; baste with the sauce. Let it warm through slowly, and keep it warm, then arrange it on a hot platter with sauce over each piece, renewing with meat and sauce as necessary.

Potato Gnocchi

Cheese and potato dumplings

Although the gnocchi is of Italian origin, when it came to France it turned into a dumpling, at least in this version, where it consists of mashed potatoes, cheese, and a pâte à choux (a heavy eggy white sauce that swells when baked). You give them a preliminary poaching in salted water, after which the gnocchi may be refrigerated or frozen; to serve, you brown them in the oven. For a starchy something to go with a party meal such as this, I think the gnocchi are a fine solution just because of their amenability. Besides, they make good eating with the braised beef and its red wine sauce.

For about 30 golfball-sized gnocchi

For the Pâte à Choux:

> About 2 cups (½ L)

1 cup (¼ L) water
6 Tb (3 ounces or 85 g) butter
1 tsp salt
¾ cup (3½ ounces or 100 g) all-purpose flour
   (measure by dipping dry-measure cups into flour
   and sweeping off excess)
3 "large" eggs, plus ½ to 1 more egg if needed

Other Ingredients:

4 cups (1 L) firm warm mashed potatoes (see notes
   in recipe)
¾ cup (3 ounces or 85 g) finely grated Gruyère,
   Parmesan, or mixed cheese
A pinch of nutmeg
Salt and pepper
A little flour, for forming gnocchi
½ cup (1 dL) clarified butter (page 368), more if
   needed

Equipment:

A heavy 2-quart (2-L) saucepan; a wooden spatula or spoon; a hand-held electric mixer or a food processor is useful; 1 or 2 wide casseroles or saucepans, for poaching the gnocchi; a large bowl of cold water; a skimmer or slotted spoon; nonstick baking pans

---

The Pâte à Choux:

Measure out the ingredients listed. Bring the water to the boil in the 2-quart (2-L) saucepan, meanwhile cutting the butter in pieces and dropping it in, along with the salt. When water is boiling and butter has melted, remove pan from heat and immediately pour in all the flour at once, beating vigorously with wooden spatula to blend. Set over moderate heat, beating, until pastry cleans itself off sides and bottom of pan and begins to film the bottom of the pan. Beat for 2 minutes or so over moderately low heat to evaporate excess moisture. Remove from heat.

If you are continuing by hand or with a mixer, make a well in the center of the hot pastry with your spatula or mixer, break an egg into the well, and vigorously beat it in until absorbed. Continue with the next 2 eggs, one by one. Mixture should be quite stiff, but if too firm for easy beating, break remaining egg into a bowl, beat to blend, and beat driblets into the pastry to loosen it.

If you are using a processor, scrape the hot pastry into the container fitted with the steel blade. Turn on the machine and break the 3 eggs into it, one after the other. Stop the machine, test pastry for consistency, and add the fourth egg by driblets if pastry seems too stiff.

❶ Pastry should be warm when you use it; set over warm but not hot water, and cover loosely. (If pastry is kept too warm the eggs will cook, and lose their puffing abilities.)

The potatoes

Either use plain mashed potatoes here, boiling, peeling, and putting them through a ricer. Or use instant mashed, which work perfectly well in this instance; when making them, use the amount of milk specified on the package, a little less water, and no butter. Potatoes should be quite stiff.

Combining, forming, and poaching the gnocchi

Bring 3 inches (8 cm) salted water to the simmer in the poaching pans. Beat the warm pastry and warm mashed potatoes together to blend; beat in the cheese, nutmeg, and salt and pepper to taste. Flour your hands, and with a light touch, rapidly roll gobs of the gnocchi mixture into balls 1¾ to 2 inches (4½ to 5 cm) in diameter, and drop into the water. (A sticky business!) Maintain water almost but not quite at the simmer (not bubbling) throughout the cooking—an actual simmer or boil can disintegrate the gnocchi. Gnocchi are done in about 15 minutes, when they have risen to the surface and roll over very easily. Transfer them with the skimmer to the bowl of cold water, and in a minute or so they will sink to the bottom—the cold water firms them and sets the cooking. Remove and drain on a towel.

❷ The gnocchi may be prepared in advance to this point. Let them dry for half an hour, then chill for an hour. When thoroughly cold, arrange in a roasting pan between layers of plastic wrap; they will keep in the refrigerator 2 to 3 days, or may be frozen.

To serve gnocchi
20 to 30 minutes at 350°F/180°C

(The gnocchi need a final baking in the oven, and the conventional system is to arrange them in a buttered baking-and-serving dish with a covering of grated cheese and butter, or cheese sauce. Here, however, since they are to take the place of potatoes, they are rolled in butter and baked on a nonstick aluminum jelly-roll pan or pastry sheet so that they can be lifted off and placed on the meat platter for easy serving.)

Preheat oven, and heat the clarified butter to liquefy it; pour the butter into a dish or pie plate. Roll the gnocchi, a few at a time, in the butter, draining off excess with a slotted spoon. Arrange them ½ inch (1½ cm) apart on the pans and brown lightly in upper and middle third levels of the preheated oven, switching pans from one level to another for even cooking. The gnocchi are done when they have swelled gently, and they usually crack open a little bit; if they do not brown lightly on top, set for a few minutes under a moderate broiler, watching carefully that they do not brown too much.

❷ May be kept warm for 20 minutes or more, but do not cover them...warm potatoes need air circulation.

Old-fashioned Country Ham

Old Virginia Hams and Smithfield Hams:
These are very special hams, slow cured in the old-fashioned way and with a much drier, saltier, and more intense flavor than ordinary storebought hams. They are usually served cold, sliced paper thin, and make a delicious accompaniment to other dishes on a buffet table. I am particularly partial to a fine old ham served along with the remains of the Thanksgiving turkey, but here, on our buffet, the ham can take the place of a second helping of beef, to eat with the beans, or with bread and cheese.

Country Hams versus Virginia and Smithfield Hams:

What is the difference? Smithfield is easy: by law it can only be called a Smithfield ham if it has been processed in Smithfield, Virginia, by the Smithfield method—a dry salt cure followed by a coating of pepper, a long slow hickory smoking, and a final aging of up to a year or more. And the Smithfield hams have a different look than other hams because Smithfield hogs are of a special breed that produces longer and thinner hams. In addition, if the hogs are fed in the approved manner, they have a unique flavor because of the acorns and hickory nuts, among other delicacies, that make up their diet. A number of Virginia processors outside Smithfield produce the same kind of hams using the same type of hogs, feed, and methods; however, they must content themselves with the name "old Virginia" or "Smithfield type."

"The name Country Ham covers a multitude of sins," writes Colonel Bill Newsom of Kentucky, and he goes on to say that the Kentuckian's definition of a real country ham is one that is dry cured using salt and sugar, then smoked with hickory wood, and aged for 6 months or more. Todd's of Richmond, however, do not age their country hams, since in their opinion an aged ham does not lend itself to slicing thick and frying. In other words, you have to know your country hams because they differ widely in their manner of cure and in their aging. In general, though, I think it is true to say that the Virginias and Smithfields are older, drier, and saltier, as well as thinner and longer, than the country hams, and are really in a category by themselves.

Cooking Procedures:

An aged ham is not difficult to cook—a bit long and cumbersome perhaps, but not a tricky business. First you scrub it with a stiff brush under warm running water to remove any of the harmless mold that has collected on it due to its aging, and with it any pepper and other curing elements embedded in the surface. Then you soak it for a number of hours, depending on its type, to remove some of its salt. It is now ready to cook, either by simmering, or baking, or by a combination of both. When cooked, you slice off the rind and excess fat and, if you wish, you can bone it. Finally, to dress it up, you glaze it in a very hot oven either just as it is, or coated with bread crumbs, or brown sugar, or cloves, etc. A cooked dry-cured aged ham will keep nicely in the refrigerator for several weeks at least.

The exact details of its cooking are, of course, a matter of pride, family tradition, and very definite opinions among southern cooks, and I have no intention of pontificating on the subject. I have, none the less, cooked a good 2 dozen of these hams through the years and have some observations to offer. In the first place, anyone tackling this type of ham will do well to follow the directions of the packer, at least the first time, but keep notes on your results because next time you may want to change things a little, as I have.

Soaking

Soaking softens an aged ham to some extent, and does indeed remove a certain amount of saltiness. Packers' directions vary from 4 to 6 hours for many country hams on up to 48 hours for Smithfield types. I frankly do not like too salty a ham; I soak Smithfields for 3 to 4 days, and aged country hams for 2.

Simmering versus baking

Simmering (or "boiling") a ham takes a large container and a lot of water, but it does remove excess saltiness to quite an extent, and does make a slightly softer ham of a well-aged one. The usual rule is to simmer the ham about 20 minutes per pound (450 g), or until the bones from the hock (small end) can be pulled out of the ham.

The on-again-off-again baking system. Not too long ago an alternate method to simmering was developed. You put your scrubbed and soaked ham, fat side up, in a covered roasting pan with 5 cups (1¼ L) water, or part water and part wine or cider vinegar. You seal the roaster as airtight as you can with a sheet of aluminum foil, cover it, and set it in the oven, bringing the temperature up to 500°F/260°C (some say to 400 or 450°F/205 or 230°C). When it has reached that temperature, you time it for exactly 20 minutes, then turn the oven off. Do not open the oven door! Leave for 3 hours. Repeat the heating again, for 20 minutes. Turn the oven off. Do not open the oven door! Leave for 6 to 8 hours or overnight.

I have done several Smithfield-type hams this way; it works, and it is certainly easier than simmering a ham in all that water. But I shall not do it again for a country ham because the heat was too intense or prolonged or inappropriate for one I did recently that had not been aged—it shredded a bit around the edges. My last aged country ham, a buxom chunky beauty from Kentucky, was, I thought, a little too salty and too firm after this cooking.

Combination simmer-bake. For my next aged country ham I shall try simmering it for 10 minutes per pound (450 g), or half the usual time, then baking it in a tightly closed roaster with half a bottle or so each Madeira wine and dry white French vermouth. I'll bake it slowly at 300–325°F/150–165°C for about 1½ hours or to a meat thermometer reading of 160°F/71°C. Sounds like just the right system, and I hope it is.

Tough Edges and Bottoms:

I have asked several ham authorities why some aged hams have such hard bottom and side surfaces (those not covered by fat or rind). The hardening of the "face," as these parts are called in the trade, is a characteristic of the hams, and comes from salting, drying, and just plain old age. You may wish to trim off these hard surfaces before soaking the ham, or after cooking it. A crusty surface makes carving difficult, certainly, and although it seems as though you are removing a lot of meat as you trim it off, you are saving yourself a good deal of trouble when you come to slice and serve. Save the trimmings for flavoring bean or split pea soups, and those that are not too crusty can be ground up with a little of the ham fat to make a tasty ham spread for sandwiches.

To Carve the Ham:

It is a help in carving to pull out the hip bone from underneath the ham before that meat has cooled. Some carvers prefer the cross-grain cut, going straight down at right angles from the surface of the ham to the bone, after having cut an opening wedge out of the hock (small) end. Or slice parallel to the bone and the surface of the meat; start with a wedge taken out of the hock, then slice on the right then on the left side of the main leg bone.

Aged ham should be cut into the thinnest possible slices. You need a long, sharp knife, and don't saw at the meat; try for long even strokes the length of the blade.

White Beans with Herbs

For almost 2 quarts (2 L), serving 10 to 15 people

1 pound (450 g) dry white beans
2 quarts (2 L) water
1 large onion stuck with 2 cloves
1 herb bouquet (6 parsley sprigs, 2 cloves garlic,
    ¼ tsp thyme, and 1 imported bay leaf tied
    together in washed cheesecloth)
2 tsp salt
1 stick (4 ounces or 115 g) butter (optional)
3 or 4 cloves garlic puréed with 1 tsp salt (page
    374)
5 to 6 Tb minced fresh parsley and/or basil
Bean cooking juices as needed
Salt and pepper

Cook the beans with the water, onion, herb bouquet, and
salt, as described on page 116 (halving the recipe and omitting the pork). Shortly before serving, rewarm them if necessary. Melt the butter in a large serving casserole, stir in
the garlic and let warm a moment, then fold in the beans and
fresh herbs plus a little of the bean cooking juices if you feel
them needed. Season carefully to taste. (If you omit the
butter, simmer the garlic for a few minutes in a little of the
bean cooking juices.)

❷ May be kept warm on an electric hotplate.

Doubling and Tripling the Recipe:

Since a large quantity is often difficult to handle and to season properly, you are probably better off finishing and flavoring the beans in batches about this size, then combining
them.

Fresh Vegetables à la Grecque

A selection of vegetables cooked in an herbal marinade, served cold

Unless one has restaurant facilities and plenty of kitchen help, I think a hot green vegetable is very difficult to serve successfully to a large group. I will always opt, instead, for a copious vegetable salad or something like the platter of cold cooked and marinated vegetables suggested here. They look attractive, they taste good, and since there will also be a fresh green salad on the table, I don't think you need more than a piece or 2 of each vegetable per serving, plus a spoonful of mushrooms.
The idea here is to make a communal cooking bath of spiced liquid, and to cook each batch of vegetables separately in the bath, each for its allotted time. Finally you reduce the liquid to an essence, and baste the vegetables with the resulting sauce—with the exceptions of the bright green vegetables, which are treated differently, as you will see.

For 10 people

Spiced Cooking Liquid à la Grecque:

6 cups (1½ L)

1 cup (¼ L) thinly sliced onions
⅓ cup (¾ dL) olive oil
6 cups (1½ L) water
The zest of 1 lemon (yellow part of peel removed
    with a vegetable peeler)
4 Tb fresh lemon juice
⅛ tsp each mustard seeds, coriander, and
    saffron threads
½ tsp fennel seeds
8 peppercorns
8 to 10 parsley stems (not the leaves)
2 cloves garlic, crushed with their peel
1 tsp salt

For the Vegetable Platter:

Your choice of vegetables
Lemon juice
Fresh olive oil
Salt and freshly ground pepper
Parsley

Equipment:

A wide stainless-steel or enamel saucepan,
casserole, or chicken fryer for cooking the
vegetables; a skimmer or slotted spoon; various
containers, such as glass baking dishes, to hold
the marinating vegetables; 1 or several large
platters to hold the finished product

Preparing the cooking liquid

Simmer the sliced onions for 6 to 8 minutes in the olive oil until tender and translucent, then add the rest of the ingredients and simmer slowly, covered, for 20 minutes. Drain through a sieve into another saucepan, pressing juices out of ingredients.

❶ May be cooked a day or 2 in advance.

Small White Onions:
20 to 30

For easy peeling, drop the onions in a pan of boiling water, bring to the boil again, and boil 1 minute. Drain, shave off tops and bottoms, and slip off the skins. Stab a cross ¼ inch (¾ cm) deep in the root ends with the point of a small knife—to minimize their bursting while cooking. Drop into the cooking liquid, cover, and simmer slowly 20 to 30 minutes or until just tender. Remove with a slotted spoon and spread in a dish.

❶ May be cooked a day or 2 in advance.

Zucchini and Yellow Summer Squash:
3 or 4 of each

Slice off the 2 ends, scrub the vegetables, and cut into cross-wise chunks of about 1 inch (2.5 cm). Toss with 1 teaspoon salt and let drain for 20 minutes to rid them of excess moisture. Bring cooking liquid to the boil and drop in the vegetables; bring rapidly back to the boil and cook about 2 minutes, until barely cooked—still slightly crunchy. Drain and spread in a dish. (Zucchini and other summer squash need attention—too much cooking and they wilt, too little and they do not absorb the sauce.)

❷ Best cooked the day of the dinner.

Mushrooms:
1 quart (1 L)

Trim stem ends off mushrooms, drop the mushrooms into a large bowl of cold water, swish about, and drain immediately. Quarter or halve them if large, leave whole if small. Bring cooking liquid to the boil, drop in the mushrooms, and boil slowly for about 1 minute until barely cooked. Drain; place in a bowl.

❷ May be cooked a day in advance.

Cauliflower:

Cut the head into flowerettes and peel the stems; cook as in the directions for mushrooms.

❷ May be cooked a day in advance.

Leeks and Celery:

These always taste better than they look under such circumstances. You would use just the white part of the leeks, splitting it as shown on page 00 to remove any sand, then quartering or halving it after cooking. Cut celery stalks into 3-inch (8-cm) lengths about ½ inch (1½ cm) wide. Leeks need about 15 minutes of simmering; celery, about 10.

❷ May be cooked a day in advance.

Topinambours or Jerusalem Artichokes:

Scrub and simmer whole in the boiling liquid for about 30 minutes. Peel after cooking.

❷ May be cooked a day in advance.

Carrots:

Particularly attractive for their color, carrots are successful candidates because they do not get mushy. Select really fresh and flavorful baby carrots, or trim mature carrots into attractive small-carrot shapes; peel them before cooking. Simmer about 10 minutes in the liquid, until just tender but still with texture.

❷ May be cooked a day in advance.

Green Beans:

Green beans will discolor if cooked in the spiced liquid. Trim them, leave them whole, and cook in a large kettle of rapidly boiling salted water until barely tender. Drain, and refresh in cold water to stop the cooking and to set color and texture. Chill them, and toss in the reduced cooking liquid (below) 5 to 10 minutes before serving.

◑ Best cooked the day of the dinner.

Broccoli:

The same treatment goes for broccoli. Cut into flowerettes and peel stems; blanch in a large kettle of rapidly boiling salted water for 3 to 4 minutes only; drain; spread out in 1 layer to cool. Chill, and dress just before serving.

◑ Best cooked the day of the dinner.

Reducing the Cooking Liquid to a Sauce:

When all the vegetables are done, boil the cooking liquid down rapidly to about 1 cup (¼ L), and carefully correct seasoning.

Dressing the Vegetables:

Spoon a bit of the sauce over the onions, squash, and mushrooms, as well as the cauliflower, leeks, celery, topinambours, and carrots, if you are using them. Let marinate in the refrigerator for several hours. Dress the beans and broccoli shortly before serving. And just before serving, freshen all vegetables with drops of fresh lemon juice, olive oil, salt, freshly ground pepper, and sprigs or a mince of parsley where needed.

Tossed Green Salad

You may trim and wash the greens the day before, spin them dry, and store in plastic bags. Vinaigrette dressing suggestions are on page 380, including 1 for quantity occasions. Make the dressing in the morning, but dress the salad only at the last minute, eating samples to be sure there is enough dressing and that the seasoning is perfect. (Too often a party salad is not carefully tasted by the cook, and the result is disappointing.)

Orange Bavarian Torte

Molded liqueur-soaked cake layered with Bavarian cream; whipped cream and glazed orange peel topping

For a large party you certainly want a delicious as well as spectacular dessert that needs no last-minute fussing—something like a molded concoction or a cake. The torte described here is a handsome example, with its snowy mountain of whipped cream and pretty strands of glazed orange.

Although the recipe looks long, it consists only of cake that is split into horizontal layers, each of which is flavored with orange syrup, spread with Bavarian cream, and molded in a spring-form pan (or soufflé mold). Bavarian cream is simply a custard sauce made light with beaten egg whites, enriched with a modest amount of whipped cream, and given staying power with gelatin. The torte can be assembled several days before your party, or you can even make it and freeze it; you complete the final decoration the morning of the party.

Manufacturing Notes:

A spring-form mold is what I've suggested here because it is convenient to use in this type of recipe. But if you don't have one you can adapt the system to the bowl-molding technique in the chocolate bombe recipe on page 147, or to a soufflé mold, or even to a casserole lined with wax paper.

The cake layers. The easiest way to form the torte is to have a cake or cakes the diameter of your mold, and slice horizontally into layers. On the other hand, you can cut and patch any size of cake to make layers; your surgery will never show because all is covered by frosting when the torte is served.

When I bake my own, I double the proportions for a 3-egg yellow cake, such as the one for *génoise* on page 487 of *Mastering II*, which fills my spring-form pan by about a third. I have to bake 2 cakes this way to have enough for the Bavarian torte. (Once I tried tripling the recipe instead, to save myself baking 2 cakes, but though the triple-recipe cake looked fine as it emerged from the oven, when sliced horizontally, the center core hadn't cooked through—it was a wet mass of batter.)

How much filling to make. I believe in having more rather than less, and the proportions for the Bavarian cream here will give you about 12 cups (3 quarts or 2¾ L), which will probably be more than you need since the spring-form has a capacity of 4 quarts (3¾ L). However, you can always make the torte higher by pinning a collar of foil around the rim of the pan. Or you can make yourself a little molded dessert out of the excess; store it in the freezer and you'll have something nice on hand for unexpected guests.

The Cake:

10- by 3-inch (25- by 8-cm), serving 12 to 16 people

2 round cakes about 10 by 1 inches or 25 by 2.5 cm (see preceding notes)

The Orange Bavarian Cream:

12 cups or 3 quarts (2¾ L)

The grated rind of 3 oranges
1 cup (¼ L) strained fresh orange juice
4½ Tb (4½ envelopes) plain unflavored
 gelatin
12 egg yolks
1½ cups (9½ ounces or 275 g) sugar
2¼ cups (5½ dL) milk, heated in a small
 saucepan
1 Tb pure vanilla extract (optional)
8 egg whites (1 cup or ¼ L)
½ tsp cream of tartar and ⅛ tsp salt
3 Tb additional sugar
¾ cup (1¾ dL) heavy cream
3 Tb orange liqueur (or concentrated frozen orange
 juice, defrosted)

The Orange Liqueur Syrup:

1 cup (¼ L) water
½ cup (100 g) sugar
4 to 5 Tb orange liqueur (or concentrated frozen
 orange juice)

The Whipped Cream Frosting and Accompanying
Sauce:

3 cups (¾ L) heavy cream
About ½ cup (70 g) sifted confectioners sugar
1 Tb pure vanilla extract
3 Tb orange liqueur
Decorative suggestions: candied orange peel (page
 17), or storebought kumquats in syrup cut into
 strips or designs
Sauce suggestions: sliced fresh strawberries
 flavored with sugar and a little orange liqueur,
 or a purée of sieved raspberries, or the sliced
 oranges (without blueberries) on page 18

Equipment:

A 10-by-3-inch (25-by-8-cm) spring-form pan (or other choices as noted earlier); wax paper; a stainless-steel 2-quart (2-L) saucepan for the custard; beating equipment for the egg whites; a giant-sized rubber spatula for easy folding; a bowl of ice cubes; a large metal bowl for whipping the cream; a round platter or board for serving the torte; a flexible-blade spatula and pastry bag with star tube for decorating

---

Preliminaries

Dot inside of spring-form mold with butter; cut a round of wax paper to fit the bottom and a strip to fit around the inside wall, and press them in place (butter will hold them there). Split the cakes, or cut to fit mold; you should have 3 or 4 layers; wrap in plastic to keep them from drying out. Grate the orange rind into a small saucepan, pour in the orange juice, and sprinkle the gelatin on top to soften. Make the orange sugar syrup: heat the water and sugar in another small pan; when sugar has completely dissolved, remove from heat and stir in the liqueur; cover and set aside.

Custard Sauce—Crème Anglaise:

Place the egg yolks in the stainless-steel saucepan. Using a wire whip, beat in the sugar by 2-tablespoon dollops with 3 to 4 seconds of beating between additions; continue beating for 2 to 3 minutes until mixture has thickened slightly. With a wire whip beat in the warm milk by driblets. Set over moderate heat and stir not too fast with a wooden spoon, reaching all over bottom of pan as custard slowly heats through. Watch carefully that you are not heating the sauce too fast or the yolks will turn granular; keep testing with your finger. When sauce is almost too hot, it is almost ready. Also watch surface of sauce: at first small foamy bubbles collect there, and as they begin to subside the sauce is almost ready. Finally, keep your eye alert for a wisp of steamy vapor rising from the pan—this, again, is an indication that the sauce is almost thickened. Keep on cooking slowly and stirring until the sauce is thick enough to coat the surface of the spoon—if you overheat it, the egg yolks will curdle, but you must heat it enough to thicken. (Time: 5 to 8 minutes in all.)

Immediately remove from heat and continue stirring for a minute to stop the cooking. Stir in the vanilla, if you are using it.

❍ May be cooked a day in advance, and needs no reheating before you continue.

Completing the Bavarian Cream:

(Once the Bavarian cream with its gelatin is completed you must go on to finish the torte or the cream will congeal.)

The gelatin. Set pan with orange and gelatin over moderate heat for a moment, stirring, to dissolve the gelatin completely: look closely to be sure there are no unmelted granules. By dribbles stir the gelatin into the custard.

The egg whites. Set beating bowl with egg whites over hot water for a moment to take off their chill, then start beating at slow speed. When foaming, in a minute or 2, beat in the cream of tartar and salt, and gradually increase speed to fast. When egg whites form soft peaks, beat in the additional sugar by spoonfuls, and continue beating for a few seconds until egg whites form stiff shining peaks. Fold the custard (warm or cold) into the egg whites.

Preliminary chilling. Set the custard bowl in a bowl of ice cubes (with water to cover them), and fold with the giant spatula several times, repeating almost every minute and reaching all around edge of bowl to draw cold custard from outside into the center. When center tests cool (but not chilled) to your finger, remove from ice.

Whipping and folding in the cream. Pour the ¾ cup (1¾ dL) cream into the metal bowl and whip over ice until the cream holds its shape softly (page 370). Fold into the cool custard, ending with the 3 tablespoons orange liqueur. Plan to assemble the torte at once, before the Bavarian cream starts to set. (But if by chance that does happen, fold gently over warm water just until it loosens.)

Assembling the torte

Place a layer of cake, cut side up, in the form, and baste with several spoonfuls of syrup. Ladle on a layer of Bavarian cream and top with a cake layer, cut side up. Baste with syrup, ladle on more cream, and, if there is room, make another layer. (You may have more Bavarian cream than you need; see notes preceding recipe.) Turn the final cake layer cut side up on your work surface, baste with syrup, and place, cut side down, over the final layer of Bavarian cream. Cover with plastic wrap and refrigerate for at least 6 hours to be sure the Bavarian cream and the torte itself have firmly set.

❶ May be arranged 2 or 3 days in advance; may be frozen.

Note: If you are making more than 1 torte, and you have only 1 spring-form, wait for several hours until torte has set, then you can release the form. Slide the torte onto its serving platter or board, but keep the wax paper strip around the side of the cake; cover with a sheet of plastic wrap.

Decorating and serving

Whip the 3 cups (¾ L) cream over ice until quite firm, and it holds in fairly stiff peaks. Sift on and fold in sugar to taste, and droplets of vanilla and orange liqueur—but do not loosen the cream too much. Slip wax paper strips under edge of torte (so as not to mess up serving dish), and spread cream over top and around side of cake with flexible-blade spatula, saving enough for decorative swirls, which you will make with your pastry bag and star tube. Decorate with strands of glazed orange peel, kumquat, or whatever you have chosen.

❶ Cake may be decorated several hours before serving. Keep chilled.

Cut like a regular cake, and serve the sauce on the side, or pass it separately.

❶ Timing

It's probably a good idea to read this chapter through, noting anything you find useful, and make out your own shopping and cooking schedule, spreading it out over several days. Since some of the dishes can be prepared well in advance, you have a good deal of flexibility. All I can provide here are a few mileposts.

An hour before the party, arrange your vegetable platter; but refrigerate it until you present the green salad. If you have only 1 oven, bake the gnocchi now, since they keep warm better than the *pissaladière*. When they're done, raise the oven setting, wait till oven heat is up, and bake the *pissaladière*, first opening and distributing the anchovies. Just about now (an hour before) you can reheat the beef, in the oven if you have 2, otherwise on the stove top, and keep warm. It only takes moments to rewarm the sausages, and they keep well over mild heat, so do it when you like. This is also true of the white beans.

Note: If you own, or can borrow, a slow cooker to warm the beans, your only dirty dish so far is the beef roaster. Refrigerator containers are all small enough for the dishwasher—and, now that their space is vacated, you can put Champagne in the refrigerator in good time for dessert. Jug white wines, of course, take longer to chill: do them in your ice chest.

The morning of the party: if you have enough saucepans and stove top burners, you can do your preparations in an hour. Cook the zucchini and yellow squash, the green beans, and the broccoli, for the vegetable platter. While the beans and broccoli are cooking, prepare the marinade and baste all vegetables except beans and broccoli. Next make your salad dressing; whip the cream and decorate the torte, then refrigerate. Now's the time, if you hadn't freezer space, to buy bagged ice cubes and store in ice chests; it won't hurt jug white wine to sit there for the rest of the day.

Note: Even on a gusty, dusty summer day, with all the windows open, you can set out your table well beforehand. Just cover things; some favor plastic cleaners' bags, but I find they grab at stemmed glasses and cause breakage. On flower arrangements: do them the day before, but in hot weather set them in a cool corner, out of the light; a wine cellar is ideal.

The day before: cook the beef, and finish its sauce. Prepare the salad greens and most of the makings for the cold vegetable platter: the onions, the mushrooms, cauliflower, leeks, celery, and topinambours. Now's a good time to set tables, "tidy all 'round," and fix flowers.

The day before that brown the beef and cook it, and do the sausages and their sauce.

Two or 3 days before, make and refrigerate the *tarama brandade*, and cook the onions for the *pissaladière*.

Any time at all: make and freeze the dough for the *pissaladière*, the gnocchi, and the torte.

Leftovers

If you had 10 guests, you're certain to have leftover beef, ham, and cake. Of the other dishes, all keep well except an already-baked *pissaladière* or browned *gnocchi*—tolerable rewarmed, both of them.

Sausage, beef, and *beans* are easily rewarmed: the sausage nuggets in their sauce, the beef ditto, the beans with added liquid if they seem dry. Puréed, the beans make a delicious soup—add broth. If serving cold, chill, then add cream, lemon, and herbs. A country *ham* will keep several weeks at least, well wrapped, in the refrigerator and is a wonderful resource—excellent in paper-thin slices as an hors d'oeuvre. Or grind scraps and add to sandwich spreads, stuffed eggs, etc. Save the bone for soup—split pea or bean preferred.

The raw *vegetables*: make salad, or cook and dice them for a *macédoine*, or mince them to garnish a consommé. *Vegetables à la grecque*: finish them off next day, no later.

The *torte*, refrigerated of course, will be delicious next day—or scrape off the whipped cream, and freeze the nude remains, then redress. Purée and freeze any leftover sauce to make a strawberry sherbet.

Mail-Order Hams:

I have used the following sources at one time or another:

Callaway Gardens, U.S. Highway 27, Pine Mountain, Georgia 31822

Gwaltney of Smithfield, P.O. Box 489, Smithfield, Virginia 23430

Jordan's Old Virginia Smokehouse, P.O. Box 324, Richmond, Virginia 23202

V. W. Joyner & Co., Smithfield, Virginia 23430

Col. Bill Newsom's Kentucky Country Hams, Princeton, Kentucky 42445

Smithfield Packing Co., Inc., Smithfield, Virginia 23430

E. M. Todd Co., Inc., P.O. Box 5167, Richmond, Virginia 23220

Practical Dishes
for Big Parties

The following table lists a selection of recipes from this book and its predecessor, and rates each dish as to how practical it is to prepare and serve at a large party. A solid dot (●) in any category means "highly recommended," an outline dot (○) means "manageable," and a blank space means either that the category doesn't apply or that the recipe may pose problems in this particular respect. I've skipped dishes that must be eaten as soon as made, but included those involving a lot of handwork (like Gazpacho Salad), provided you can do them well in advance, or have friendly help in your kitchen.

Appetizers	No Last-Minute Jobs	Expandable Recipes**	Easy to Serve	Can Be Reheated	Can Be Frozen	Can Be Made Mostly by Machine	Relatively Little Handwork	Reasonable Price
82 Beet and Cucumber Soup (hot or cold)	●	●	●	○		●	●	●
330 Brandades (dips)	●	●	●			●	●	○
57 Celery Root Rémoulade	●	●	●			○	○	○
297 Chicken Liver Aspic	●	●	●					○
314 Chicken Liver Pâté	●	●	●			●	●	○
71 Consommé	○	●	○	●	○			○
374 Fish Dogs	○	●	○	●				○
239 Fish Terrine	●	●	○			●	●	○
35 Mediterranean Platter (with feta cheese)	●	●	○					●
23 Mussel Salad	●	●	○					○
21 Mussel Soup	○	●	○	○				○
332 Pissaladière (onion tart)	○	○	○		○	○		○
328 Sausage Nuggets	○	○	●	○				○

	No Last-Minute Jobs	Expandable Recipes**	Easy to Serve	Can Be Reheated	Can Be Frozen	Can Be Made Mostly by Machine	Relatively Little Handwork	Reasonable Price
*150 Cheese Appetizers (puff pastry)	○	●	●	●	●	○	○	●
*151 Gravlaks (dilled salmon)	●	●	●	●			○	
*153 Minimeatballs	○	●	●	●	○		○	○
Main Courses								
367 Baked Beans	○	●	●	●	●	●	●	●
336 Beef, Braised Pot Roast (bottom round)	○		○	○			○	
115 Cassoulet (bean and meat casserole)	○	○	○	○				○
192 Crêpe and Vegetable Gâteau	○		●	○				●
168 French Onion Soup	○	●	○	●	○			●
10 Hen Bonne Femme and Variations (chicken)	○		○	○				○
84 Monkfish en Pipérade	○	●	○	○				●
86 Monkfish Variations (cold)	●	●	●					○
294 Pâté en Croûte	●		○					○

#	Dish								
61	Pork, Butterflied Loin	○	○	○				○	
39	Rabbit Pie, Stew, and Variations	○	○	○	○			○	○
315	Salmon Gratin (casserole)	○	●	●	○			●	
291	Salmon Steaks (cold)	●	●	●				○	
*307	Boiled Dinner	○	○					○	○
*244	Chicken Livers, Sautéed	○	●	○	○			○	○
*242	Corned Beef Hash	○	●	○	○			○	○
*303	Eggs in Aspic (ring of)	●	●	○	○			●	●
*61	Fish Chowder	○	●	○	●		○	○	○
*275	Lamb, Butterflied leg of	○	○	○				○	
*92	Paëlla (rice and meat casserole)	○	●	○	○			○	○
*154	Peking Wings (chicken)	○	●	○	○			●	●
*146	Pithiviers (ham tart)	○	○	○	○	●	○	○	○
*369	Turkey Casserole	○	●	●	●			●	●
*218	Turkey Orloff (more elaborate casserole)	○	●	○	○		●	○	○
*308	Turkey Salad	●	●	○	●			●	●
*305	Turkey Wine Stew	○	●	●	●			●	●
*246	Scrapple	○	●	○	○			○	○

Vegetables	No Last-Minute Jobs	Exandable Recipes**	Easy to Serve	Can Be Reheated	Can Be Frozen	Can Be Made Mostly by Machine	Relatively Little Handwork	Reasonable Price
136 Asparagus (boiled, cold)	●	●	●					
69 Butternut Squash with Ginger and Garlic	○	●	●	●			○	●
397 Beans, White, with Herbs	○	●	●	●			●	●
189 Eggplant Persillade	○	●	○	○			○	●
191 Eggplant with Sesame Seeds		●	○	○			○	○
235 Gazpacho Salad	●	●	●		○			○
340 Potato Gnocchi (dumplings)	○	●	○	○				●
279 Potato Gratin	○	●	○	○		○		●
119 Red Cabbage Slaw	●	●	●			●	●	●
379 Rice, Steamed	○	○	●	●			○	●
189 Spaghetti Squash	○	●	●	●				●

Desserts	No Last-Minute Jobs	Exandable Recipes**	Easy to Serve	Can Be Reheated	Can Be Frozen	Can Be Made Mostly by Machine	Relatively Little Handwork	Reasonable Price
198 Bombe aux Trois Chocolats, Chocolate Mousse, & Brownies	●	●	○		●			

No.	Recipe	1	2	3	4	5	6	7
89	Cream Cheese and Lemon Flan	●		○			○	●
67	Gâteau of Apples and Crêpes	●				○	○	●
280	Hazelnut Cookies (flat)	○			●		●	●
196	Ice Cream and Flaming Mincemeat	●	●		●		○	
220	Macaroons	○	●	●	●		●	●
43	Meringue Cases with Ice Cream (vacherins)	●	○		●		●	●
352	Orange Bavarian Torte	○					○	●
121	Pineapple, Fresh				●		○	●
254	Plantation Spice Cookies	●		○	●	○	●	●
306	Savarin and Rum Babas	○		○	○		○	●
*42	Apple Turnover	●	○		●		○	●
*267	Chocolate-Chip Cake	○			●		●	●
*183	Chocolate Truffles				●		●	●
*83	Floating Island	●			●	○	●	●
*104	Indian Pudding	●			●		●	●
*222	Jamaican Ice Cream Goblet	●	●		●		●	
*19	Los Gatos Gâteau Cake (meringue-apricot)	○			●		●	●
*291	Zabaione Batardo Veneziano	○			●		●	●

Q & A Culinary Gazetteer

This is not only a culinary gazetteer; it is a catchall of miscellaneous information to answer questions that often come up about topics like the proper beating of egg whites, flour measuring, and so forth. I've also included here certain base recipes (some repeats from other books) for such items as mayonnaise and vinaigrettes, pie dough, tomato sauces, rice cooking methods, and other processes that reappear so frequently throughout this book it seems sensible to put them all in one place.

Subjects are listed alphabetically. If you do not find what you are looking for here please consult the index, because that particular topic may well have been discussed in one of the menus.

Almonds

To blanch and peel almonds

Drop shelled almonds into a large saucepan of rapidly boiling water and boil 1 minute, to loosen the skins. Slip the skins off 2 by 2 (using both hands), squeezing the nuts between your fingers. There appears to be no faster or easier way.

To toast almonds

Spread blanched almonds in a jelly-roll or roasting pan and set in the middle level of a preheated 350°F/180°C oven, rolling them about with a spatula every 5 minutes, until they are a light toasty brown. Be careful they do not burn; they will take 15 to 20 minutes to toast. (Even if the almonds are to be ground, they have better flavor if you toast them whole first.)

To grind or pulverize almonds

Grind them ½ cup (1 dL) at a time in an electric blender, or 1 cup (¼ L) at a time in a food processor using the on-off flick technique. Be careful that the almonds do not grind too fine and turn oily. It is always safer, if you are using them in a dessert recipe, to grind them with part of the sugar usually called for—they are less likely to turn into an oily mass.

Baked Beans

Baked Beans in a Slow-cooking Electric Pot (revised system):

Since the publication of the first volume, *J.C. & Co.*, I have revised my slow-cooker bean recipe to one that is so simple I can hardly believe it, following a suggestion from a reader in Oregon. "Why go to all the trouble you do?" she writes, and goes on to say she just dumps everything in and starts the cooking. Here's my new recipe.

> For about 2 quarts (2 L) baked beans
> 1 pound (2 cups; 450 g) small white beans
> 5 cups (1¼ L) water
> 6 ounces (¾ cup; 180 g) sliced or diced salt pork
>   (optional), simmered 10 minutes in 1 quart (1 L) water
> 1½ tsp salt
> 1 cup (¼ L) finely sliced onion
> 1 to 2 cloves garlic, minced (optional)
> 3 Tb dark unsulfured molasses
> 2 Tb Dijon-type prepared mustard
> ½ tsp dried thyme
> 2 imported bay leaves
> ½ Tb grated fresh ginger (optional)
> Pepper to taste

Pick over and wash the beans. Mix everything up in the cooker, put on the lid, and turn the heat to high until contents are bubbling. Turn to low, and cook 14 to 16 hours or longer (turn to high once or twice if beans do not seem to be cooking); beans are not done until they have turned a nice darkish reddish brown. Correct seasoning.

Bread

Bread for Cooking—Bread for Crumbs:

There is quite a bit of bread used in these recipes: hard-toasted bread rounds as a topping for onion soup, fresh white crumbs in the stuffing for the poached chicken, crumbs in the fish pâté, on the Cornish hens, in the gazpacho salad, and so forth. Do get yourself the right kind of white bread for all of this: it should not be sweetish squashy bread, the kind you can grab with your hand and press into a sticky lump. It should be bread with natural body, of the Italian, Viennese, or French type; the sandwich bread put out by Pepperidge Farm and Arnold (unless they change their formulas) will also do for crumbs.

Bread crumbs

Cut the crusts off the bread and tear the bread into smallish pieces. Pulverize it a handful at a time either in an electric blender or with the grating disk of a food processor. It's a good idea to do a whole loaf at a time, bag what you don't use, and store it in the freezer.

Bread crusts toasted

If you are making crumbs out of a long loaf, cut the crusts off in neat fairly wide strips. Toast them in the oven with a sprinkling of melted butter and cheese and herbs, if you wish. Good with soups, or to use with dips.

Butter

Butter substitutes

There is no substitute for the taste of good butter in cookery. However, if you are using other spreads, they usually react in the same manner as butter, and you can use them interchangeably.

Clarified Butter:

Since butter is made from cream, a certain residue of milk particles remains in it after churning—more or less, depending on the quality of the butter. It is this milky residue that blackens when the butter is overheated, giving the butter itself and anything that cooks with it a speckled look and a burned taste. Therefore, if you are to brown anything in butter alone, you must clarify it, meaning that you rid the butter of its milky residue. Although you can clarify it by letting it melt and spooning the clear yellow liquid off the residue, which sinks to the bottom of the pan, you are getting only a partial clarification because much of the yellow liquid remains suspended in the residue. You are far better off actually cooking the butter, which coagulates the milk solids and evaporates the water content. Here is how to go about it.

To clarify butter

For about 1½ cups (3½ dL)
1 pound (450 g) butter

Equipment:

> **A 2-quart (2-L) saucepan; a small sieve lined with 3 thicknesses of washed cheesecloth; a screw-topped storage jar**

For even melting, cut the butter into smallish pieces and place in the saucepan over moderate heat. When butter has melted, let it boil slowly, watching that it does not foam up over rim of pan. Listen to it crackle and bubble, and in a few minutes the crackling will almost cease—at this point, too, the butter may rise up in a foam of little bubbles. The clarification has been accomplished: the water content of the milky residue has evaporated, and if you continue to boil it, the butter will start to brown. Remove from heat at once and let cool a few minutes. Then strain through lined sieve into jar. You should have a beautifully clear deep yellow liquid, which will congeal and whiten slightly as it cools.

⊘ Clarified butter will keep for months in the refrigerator in a closed container. Scoop out what you want to use, and you may want to heat and liquefy it before using. (This clarified butter is the same as the *ghee* used in Indian cookery.)

Hot Butter Sauces:

The following 2 sauces are delicious with fish, shellfish, fish mousses, soufflés, asparagus, and broccoli. Both are given in detail in *J.C. & Co.*, and are simply outlined here for convenience.

Lemon Butter Sauce:

For about ¾ cup (1¾ dL)
2 Tb fresh lemon juice
3 Tb dry white French vermouth
Salt
1 stick (4 ounces or 115 g) chilled butter, cut into 12 pieces
White pepper

This sauce takes only minutes to make, and should be served at once. Boil the lemon juice, vermouth, and ¼ teaspoon salt in a small saucepan until reduced to 1 tablespoon. A piece or 2 at a time, over lowest heat, start beating in the chilled butter, adding a fresh piece just as the previous piece has almost melted. You should have a creamy ivory-colored sauce. Remove from heat, season to taste, and serve immediately.

White Butter Sauce—Beurre Blanc:

For 1½ to 1¾ cups (3½ to 4 dL)
4 Tb wine vinegar, preferably white
2 Tb lemon juice
4 Tb dry white French vermouth
2 Tb very finely minced shallots or scallions
Salt and white pepper
2½ sticks (10 ounces or 285 g) chilled butter, cut into 30 pieces
Optional additions: 4 to 8 Tb heavy cream, minced parsley and/or dill

Simmer the vinegar, lemon juice, vermouth, shallots or scallions, ½ teaspoon salt, and a big pinch of pepper in a smallish enameled or stainless-steel saucepan until reduced to about 1½ tablespoons. Then start beating in the butter and continue as directed in the preceding recipe, to make a thick ivory-colored sauce. Remove from heat; beat in optional cream by spoonfuls, then the herbs.

❷ You can make the sauce somewhat ahead: omit the cream, and keep sauce barely warm near a gas pilot light or warm burner, just to keep it from congealing. Heat the cream shortly before serving and beat by driblets into the butter sauce to warm it.

Cheese

Storing and freezing cheese

Always store ripe and ready-to-eat cheese in a cool place or the refrigerator, wrapping up each kind of cheese individually.

Grate leftover hard cheeses like Cheddar, Swiss, and Parmesan, and store them together in a plastic bag in the freezer. A mixture makes a fine topping when dishes are to be gratinéed in the oven, and it is wonderfully convenient to have a ready hoard on hand.

Chocolate

Chocolate Sauce:

For about 1¾ cups (4 dL)
2½ ounces (70 g) best-quality semisweet chocolate
½ ounce (15 g) unsweetened chocolate
¾ cup (1¾ dL) water
3 to 4 Tb heavy cream
A small pinch of salt

Bring the chocolate and water to the simmer in a 4-cup (1-L) saucepan, and cook, stirring, for 4 to 5 minutes, until chocolate has melted and liquid is smoothly blended. Set chocolate pan in another pan of slowly simmering water, cover, and let cook for 15 to 20 minutes, stirring occasionally. Sauce will be quite thick; thin out with tablespoons of cream, and stir in a pinch of salt—to bring out the best chocolate flavor. Serve at room temperature.
❷ May be cooked ahead, and refrigerated. Reheat either gently over direct heat while stirring, or over simmering water, stirring occasionally.

Cream

Lightly Whipped Cream—Crème Chantilly:

For about 2 cups (½ L)
1 cup (¼ L) heavy cream, chilled
½ cup (1 dL) confectioners sugar (optional)
½ tsp pure vanilla extract (optional)

Equipment:

> A 2½-quart (3-L) round-bottomed metal mixing bowl; a larger bowl containing a tray of ice cubes and water to cover them; a large balloon-shaped wire whip, or a hand-held electric beater

Pour cream into metal bowl and set over ice. If you are using a whip, beat with an up-and-down circular motion, to beat as much air into the cream as possible. Or rotate an electric beater around the bowl to achieve the same effect. In 3 or 4 minutes cream will begin to thicken, and has reached the Chantilly or lightly whipped stage when the beater leaves light traces on the surface of the cream—a bit lifted in a spoon will hold its shape softly.

● May be whipped in advance and kept over ice, then whipped lightly again before serving. Or you may refrigerate the cream in a sieve lined with damp washed cheesecloth, set over a bowl; liquid will exude into the bowl as the cream sits—will keep reasonably well for several hours.

If you are serving the cream for dessert, sift on the sugar, add the vanilla, and fold in with a rubber spatula just before using.

Variation:

See the whipped cream lightened with beaten egg whites, on page 283, in the rack of lamb chapter.

Dough

Dough for Pies, Quiches, Tarts, Tartlets, and Flans:

For an 8-inch (20-cm) shell

1¾ cups (8 ounces or 225 g) all-purpose flour, preferably unbleached (measure by scooping dry-measure cups into flour and sweeping off excess)

1 tsp salt

1¼ sticks (5 ounces or 140 g) chilled unsalted butter

2 Tb (1 ounce or 30 g) chilled lard or shortening

5 to 8 Tb iced water

Equipment:

> A mixing bowl and rubber spatula; or bowl and pastry blender or 2 knives and spatula; or food processor with steel blade

Measure the flour and salt into the mixing bowl or bowl of processor. Quarter the chilled butter lengthwise, cut crosswise into ⅜-inch (1-cm) pieces, and add to the bowl or container along with the chilled lard or shortening, cut into small pieces.

Dough by hand

Rapidly, so fat will not soften, either rub it with the flour between the balls of your fingers until the fat is broken into pieces the size of small oatmeal flakes, or cut with pastry blender or knives until fat is the size of very coarse meal. (If fat softens during this process, refrigerate bowl or container for 20 minutes, then continue.) Then, with a rubber spatula, blend in 5 tablespoons iced water, pressing mixture against side of bowl to make a mass. Lift out massed pieces of dough onto your work surface, sprinkle droplets of water on the unmassed bits, press together, and add to rest of dough. Finish as in the final paragraph.

Dough in a food processor

The preceding proportions are right for machines with a 2-quart or 2-liter container; a large container will take double the amount. Turn machine on and off 4 or 5 times to break up the fat. Measure out 5 tablespoons iced water, turn the machine on, and pour it in. Turn machine on and off 5 or 6 times, and dough should begin to mass on the blade; if not, dribble in another tablespoon water and repeat. Repeat again if necessary. Dough is done when it has begun to mass; it should not be overmixed. Remove dough to your work surface.

Finishing the dough

With the heel, not the warm palm, of your hand rapidly and roughly smear dough out 6 to 8 inches (15 to 20 cm) on your work surface by 3-spoonful bits, to make a final blending of fat and flour. If pastry seems stiff, you can at this time sprinkle on droplets more water as you smear. It should be pliable, but not damp and sticky. Knead and press it rapidly into a rough cake, flour lightly, and wrap in a sheet of plastic and a plastic bag. Chill for 1 hour—preferably 2 hours—before using, which will allow dough to relax while the flour particles absorb the liquid.

● Will keep under refrigeration for a day or 2, but if you have used unbleached flour it will gradually turn gray; it is best to store in the freezer, where it will keep perfectly for several months. Let thaw overnight in the refrigerator, or at room temperature and then rechill.

Dough for Pâtés and Meat Pies:

The following proportions are for ½ pound (225 g) flour, to keep them in line with the previous doughs, but you will undoubtedly want more if you are making a *pâté en croûte*—like the fine pâté baked in a pastry crust in "Picnic." The amount is tripled, and the dough is made in a heavy-duty machine, which is useful indeed for large amounts. The proportions and recipe are on page 244, but here is the smaller amount suitable for making it as in the preceding directions.

> 1¾ cups (8 ounces or 225 g) all-purpose flour
> 1¼ tsp salt
> ½ stick (2 ounces or 60 g) chilled unsalted butter
> 3 Tb (1½ ounces or 45 g) chilled lard
> 2 egg yolks plus enough iced water to make 6 to 8 Tb liquid
> Egg Whites

To Beat Egg Whites: Preliminaries

Be sure your beating bowl and beater are perfectly clean and free of oil or grease, which will prevent them from mounting. Before you begin it is useful to wipe bowl and beater with 1 tablespoon each of salt and vinegar, which seem to provide a proper mounting atmosphere. If the egg whites are chilled, set beating bowl in hot water and stir for a few minutes until tepid.

Bowls and beaters

Egg whites mount best when almost the entire mass of them can be kept in motion at once. A beater on a stand should be equipped with a large whip that rotates as it circulates rapidly about the bowl, and the bowl should be narrow, and rounded at the bottom. A hand-held beater works well in a stainless-steel or unlined copper bowl—egg whites collapse down the slippery sides of glass and porcelain; again, choose a bowl with a rounded bottom, and not too big a bowl or you cannot keep the mass of whites circulating as you beat. A giant balloon whip beats egg whites beautifully in an unlined copper bowl, but be sure you have a big enough whip for your bowl.

Beating

Besides having a very clean, grease-free bowl, and room-temperature or tepid egg whites, you must also be sure that there is no particle of yolk in the whites, since this also will prevent them from rising.

For table-model beaters

Start at slow speed until egg whites are foaming throughout, then add a pinch of salt and a large pinch of cream of tartar for every 3 egg whites—these help stabilize the whites after they have risen. Gradually increase your speed to fast, standing right over the mixer to be sure you don't overbeat the whites. Continue until egg whites form little mountains on the surface; stop and test them—the whites should stand up in stiff shining peaks as illustrated. If you are using the whites in a dessert, beat in ½ tablespoon sugar per egg white, which will also help stabilize them. Use the egg whites at once. Time: with an efficient beater, about 3 minutes.

For hand-held electric beaters

Use the same system as for table-model beaters, pretending you are an efficient whirling and rotating electric whip that circulates rapidly all about the bowl. Time: 3 to 4 minutes.

Beating by hand in a copper bowl

Start at slow speed until egg whites are foaming, then beat in a pinch of salt per 3 egg whites. Gradually increase speed to fast, using an up-and-down circular motion alternating at times with several round-the-bowl beats, and continue until the egg whites form stiff shining peaks. Beat in ½ tablespoon sugar per egg white, if you are doing a dessert. Time: 2 to 3 minutes.

Fish Mousse in Sausage Casings—Fish Dogs—Boudins:

When you are making a fish mousse, such as that for the terrine on page 239, put the leftovers into sausage casings for an amusing first course or luncheon dish. Ask your butcher for a few lengths of small hog casings; if you don't plan to use them right away, you can store them by packing them in layers surrounded by coarse salt in a screw-topped jar in the refrigerator.

An hour before you plan to stuff the casings, wash off the salt, and soak them in cold water. Then attach one end of a 3-foot (90-cm) length to the end of your cold water faucet, and run a thin stream of cold water through it to be sure it is whole and unpierced. Attach the end, then, to the end of a wet pastry tube or sausage horn, and slip the rest of the length up onto the tube, leaving a free end of 4 inches (10 cm).

In the illustration here, the sausage mixture is in a pastry bag with tube attached, and the second tube with the casing on it is being held by hand onto the first—not the easiest way to stuff a sausage, but it works. Be sure to keep the filling coming constantly into the casing, to avoid air bubbles. Fill the length of the casing, then tie the free end; twist the casing at 4-inch (10-cm) intervals and tie, to form the sausages. ❷ May be frozen raw, and cooked after thawing.

To cook them prick in 4 or 5 places with a pin, to prevent the casing from bursting as the sausages swell. Place in simmering salted water and cook at below the simmer for 15 minutes. Serve with melted butter or a sauce such as hollandaise or white butter sauce, or the sour cream sauce on page 243.

Measuring:

Be serious when you measure your flour because you can get into real trouble doing cakes and pastries if you get too much or too little; baking recipes are designed for quite accurate amounts. All flour in this book is measured as follows, in dry-measure cups:

Dip dry-measure cup into flour container until cup is overflowing; sweep off excess with the straight edge of a spatula or knife, as illustrated below.

To peel and purée

I think the garlic press is a great invention but sometimes I want to do it by hand, and here is an easy way to peel, mince, or purée garlic. Lay a whole garlic clove on your work surface, set the flat of your big knife upon it, and smash down on the knife with your fist. The garlic will split, loosening the peel, which you can then easily pluck off from the flesh. To purée the garlic, mince finely with your big knife, and when in small pieces, sprinkle with salt. Continue mincing, and then press against the garlic with the flat of the knife, drawing it back and forth across the surface 2 or 3 times; continue mincing, then pressing, and in a few seconds the garlic will be a fine purée. (The salt seems to help soften the garlic, so that it purées quickly.)

Mayonnaise

Mayonnaise:

For a little more than 2 cups (½ L)

Mayonnaise couldn't be easier to make if you just remember these points: beat up the yolks well before you begin, add the oil by droplets at first until the sauce begins to thicken; don't exceed the proportions of 2 cups (½ L) oil to 3 egg yolks; and remember that a turned or thinned-out mayonnaise is very easy to bring back. Here are directions for making mayonnaise by hand, and in a food processor.

> 3 egg yolks (for a processor, 1 egg and 2 yolks)
> ¼ tsp dry mustard
> ½ tsp salt
> Fresh lemon juice and/or wine vinegar to taste
> 2 cups (½ L) best-quality olive oil or a combination of olive oil and salad oil
> More salt, and white pepper

Equipment:

> Either a 2-quart (2-L) mixing bowl with rounded bottom and a large wire whip or hand-held electric mixer, or a food processor with steel blade; a rubber spatula

---

By hand

Set the bowl on a wet potholder to keep it from slipping about. Beat the egg yolks in the bowl for a good 2 minutes, until they turn pale yellow and thicken into a cream. Beat in the mustard and the salt, and 1 teaspoon of lemon juice or vinegar; continue beating a minute longer. Then, by ½-teaspoon driblets, start beating in the oil, making sure it is being constantly absorbed by the egg yolks—stop pouring for a moment every once in a while, and continue beating until about ½ cup (1 dL) oil has gone in and sauce has thickened into a heavy cream. Then add the oil by larger dollops, beating to absorb each addition before adding another. When sauce becomes too thick and heavy, thin out with droplets of lemon juice or vinegar, then continue with as much of the additional oil as you wish. Taste carefully for seasoning, adding more salt, pepper, lemon juice or vinegar.

By food processor

Place the whole egg and 2 yolks in the container and process for 1 minute. Then, with machine running, add the mustard, salt, and 1 teaspoon lemon juice or vinegar. Start adding the oil in a stream of droplets, and continue until you have used half, and sauce is very thick. Thin out with 1 teaspoon of lemon juice or vinegar; continue with the oil. Add seasonings to taste, and if sauce is too thick add more lemon juice or vinegar, or droplets of water.

Storing mayonnaise

Scrape mayonnaise into a screw-topped jar and store in the refrigerator—7 to 10 days.

Turned or thinned-out mayonnaise

If you have added the oil too quickly and the sauce will not thicken, or if it has been refrigerated for some time and the chilled yolks have released the oil from suspension and the mayonnaise has curdled like the example in the photograph, the problem is easily remedied. Place 1 tablespoon prepared Dijon-type mustard and a ½ tablespoon of the sauce in a bowl and beat vigorously with a wire whip or hand-held mixer until mustard and sauce have creamed together; then, by droplets, beat in the turned sauce—it is important that you add it very slowly at first for the rethickening to take place.

Garlic Mayonnaise—Aïoli:

For about 2 cups (½ L)

This marvelous sauce goes well with fish soups, boiled fish, fish in cold sauces (like the monkfish *pipérade* on page 84), with boiled chicken (like our stewing hen on page 143), with poached egg dishes, with boiled potatoes—in fact with anything that could use a strong garlic mayonnaise to perk it up. And how do you get all that garlic off your breath? Everybody et it and no one will notice a thing.

4 to 8 large cloves garlic
½ tsp salt
1 slice homemade-type French or Italian white bread
2 Tb wine vinegar
2 egg yolks
1½ cups (3½ dL) strong olive oil
More salt and vinegar to taste
White pepper and/or drops of hot pepper sauce

Equipment:

**A mortar and pestle or heavy bowl and pounding
instrument of some sort; a wire whip or hand-held
electric mixer**

Either purée the garlic into the mortar or bowl with a garlic press,
or mince very fine and add to the bowl. Pound to a very fine paste with
the salt—a most important step, taking a good minute or more. Cut the
crust off the bread, tear bread into pieces and add to the bowl with the
vinegar, and pound with the garlic into a paste; then pound in the egg
yolks to make a thick sticky mass. By driblets, as though making a
mayonnaise, start pounding and stirring in the oil; when thickened, begin
adding it a little faster and beat it in with a whip or mixer. Sauce should
be thick and heavy. Season to taste with more salt and droplets of
vinegar as needed, and pepper and/or hot pepper sauce. Store as described for mayonnaise; if it turns, give it the same treatment.

Napkin Folding

Just a simple trick like the folding of napkins can make a most attractive
decoration for your table. You'll want them made of a somewhat heavy
material so that they will stand up in shape.

1)Fold the napkin in half, to make a triangle, its point away from
you. 2)Bring the 2 bottom corners from the folded side up to the point
at the top, to make a diamond shape.

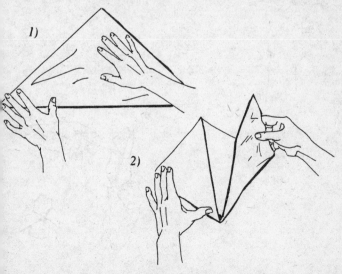

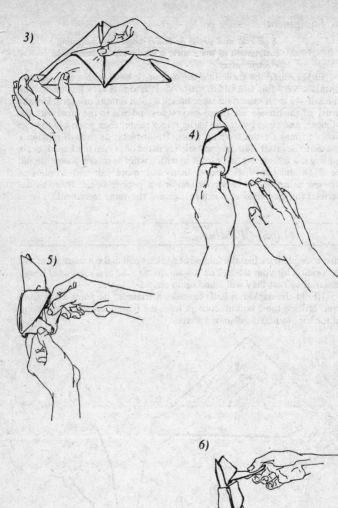

3)

4)

5)

6)

3)Fold the napkin in half, making a smaller triangle, then fold the top corner down as shown. 4)Turn the napkin over, and roll a lower corner to the middle of the bottom fold. 5)Bring the other corner around to the front of the napkin and tuck it under a front fold flap as shown. 6)Stand the napkin upright, and bend down the 2 top corners.

Rice

Cooking Methods:

Plain raw white rice is so easy to cook and to reheat that I see no reason for paying extra money to buy processed rice. Here are 2 methods I use all the time, to produce rice with separate, nongummy grains.

Amounts: 1 cup or ¼ L raw rice makes 3 cups or ¾ L cooked rice.

Steamed Rice:

Steaming is the simplest method and works for long, short, and fat-grain Italian rice. An advantage is that you can cook it ahead and reheat it.

> For 6 cups (1½ L) cooked rice
> **2 cups (½ L) plain raw unwashed white rice**
> **4 quarts (3¾ L) rapidly boiling water**
> **2 Tb salt**

Equipment:

> **A large saucepan or kettle; a colander that will fit into it (see notes in recipe): a well washed and rinsed kitchen towel**

Sprinkle the rice into the rapidly boiling water, and add the salt. Boil slowly, uncovered, for 8 to 9 minutes or more, just until the rice is almost but not quite tender—bite into several grains to be sure. Drain in the colander; wash briefly under hot water to remove starch so that rice grains will not stick together. Pour 2 inches (5 cm) water into the kettle and set the colander with the rice in the kettle; cover with the damp towel. (*Note*: if colander does not fit into kettle down to the level of the rice, turn the rice into the kettle and towel and fold it up over, to keep rice from drying out.) About 10 minutes before serving, steam the rice to finish cooking.

❷ May be completed hours in advance, and may even be steamed in advance, but be careful not to overcook the rice in that case. Leftovers may be rewarmed by steaming, or may be warmed in a saucepan with butter and seasonings.

Overcooked rice

You can tell it is overcooked because the rice grains will have splayed ends rather than rounded ones. You can still use it, but the taste and texture will have suffered.

Plain Boiled Rice:

This produces rice with a little more flavor than steamed rice.

> For 6 cups (1½ L) cooked rice
> 2 cups (½ L) plain raw unwashed white rice, long-grain type
> 4 cups (1 L) water
> 3 Tb butter (optional)
> 2 to 3 tsp salt
> Pepper

Equipment:

> A heavy-bottomed 2-quart (2-L) saucepan with cover; a wooden fork or chopsticks

Bring the rice to the boil with the water, optional butter, and salt; when boil is reached, stir once with fork or chopsticks. Reduce heat, cover the pan, and let rice simmer over moderately low heat, undisturbed, for 12 to 15 minutes, or until it has absorbed the liquid and is just tender. Note the steam holes (I call them clam holes, the kind you find in the wet sand indicating clams are below), showing that the liquid has been absorbed; tilt pan and lift a lower side to be sure. Simmer, covered, a few minutes more if necessary.

Correct seasoning, after you have lifted and fluffed up the rice, and fold in more butter if you wish.

❷ If you are serving shortly, set pan in another pan of almost simmering water to keep warm. Fluff up again, before serving. Or set the rice aside, and reheat over simmering water several hours later, fluffing and turning the rice several times for even heating, and you may need to fold in a little water if rice seems dry.

Salad Dressings

Vinaigrette:

Basic French dressing for salads, cold vegetables, and so forth

For ½ cup (1 dL), enough for 6

> 1 to 2 Tb excellent wine vinegar and/or lemon juice
> ¼ tsp salt
> ¼ tsp dry mustard
> 6 to 8 Tb best-quality olive oil or salad oil or a combination of both
> Several grinds of fresh pepper
> Optional: 1 tsp finely minced shallots or scallions and/or fresh or dried herbs, such as chives, tarragon, basil

Either beat the vinegar, salt, and mustard in a bowl until dissolved, then beat in the oil and seasonings. Or place all ingredients in a screw-topped jar and shake vigorously to blend. Dip a piece of lettuce into the dressing and taste; correct seasoning.

Variations for Cold Fish Salads, Eggs, and Vegetables: Garlic and lemon dressing

Purée a clove of garlic into a bowl, using a garlic press, then mash into a fine paste with the ¼ teaspoon salt and grated peel of ½ lemon. Proceed with vinaigrette as usual.

Vinaigrette with sesame paste

Make the garlic and lemon dressing, and beat in 1 teaspoon or so of sesame paste after you have added the lemon peel.

A creamy dressing

Make the dressing as usual, but also beat in an egg white or an egg yolk, or a tablespoon or 2 heavy cream or sour cream before adding the oil.

Vinaigrette for a Crowd of 30:

For about 3½ cups (almost 1 L)

4 Tb minced shallots or scallions
2 Tb dry mustard
5 or 6 shakes of hot pepper sauce
Grinds of fresh pepper to taste
About 1 Tb salt, or to your taste
5 Tb wine vinegar; more if needed
2 Tb fresh lemon juice
3 cups (¾ L) best-quality olive oil or salad oil or a
   combination of both
Herbs, such as tarragon, basil, or chives

Prepare the dressing as described previously, but you may want to beat it up in an electric mixer.

Spices

Special Spice Mixture:

Here is a special homemade spice mixture that I find wonderfully convenient to have on hand for seasoning pork chops and roasts, pâtés, and so forth. Saves you a lot of trouble, and it will keep for months in a screw-topped jar. If you don't have a special grinder, use an electric blender for those herbs and spices that are not already pulverized.

2 Tb each ground imported bay leaves, cloves, mace,
   nutmeg, paprika, thyme
1 Tb each ground dried basil (if fragrant, or else oregano),
   cinnamon, and savory
5 Tb ground white peppercorns

Raw Tomato Garnish:

Cold chopped tomatoes, particularly in full tomato season, are a delicious accompaniment to many another cold dish, and you may use the tomato garnish as is, or add to it other chopped vegetables as suggested here.

> For about 2 cups (½ L)
> 2½ to 3 cups (½ to ¾ L) fresh tomato pulp
>   (tomatoes peeled, seeded, juiced, and neatly diced; page 000)
> 2 Tb minced shallots or scallions
> 1 tsp or so wine vinegar
> Salt and pepper
> Fresh minced herbs if available, such as parsley, basil, dill, and tarragon (or dried herbs)
>   1 to 2 Tb olive oil (optional)

Toss the tomato pulp in a bowl with the shallots or scallions, vinegar, and salt and pepper to taste. Let stand 10 minutes, then pour into a sieve set over a bowl. Drain several minutes; turn into a serving bowl and fold with the herbs, optional olive oil, and more seasonings to taste.

Tomato Fondue:

> Fresh tomato lightly cooked in butter, herbs, and shallots

> For about 1½ cups (3½ dL)

So often one needs a little something to go with a vegetable custard, a soufflé, or a boiled fish—something a little bit tart, something not too insistent in flavor, something with a bright color—this very simple accompaniment often fills just these requirements. (If you're doing the sauce in full tomato season, when they're bursting with flavor, of course you don't need the help of the canned plum tomatoes for extra taste and color, as suggested below.)

> 2 Tb minced shallots or scallions
> 2 Tb butter
> 2½ cups (6 dL), more or less, fresh tomato pulp, chopped (page 000)
> 4 Tb or more drained and seeded canned Italian plum tomatoes, if needed
> Salt and pepper
> Fresh herbs, such as fresh basil and parsley, or tarragon; or dried herbs to taste (tarragon, oregano, thyme)

Cook the minced shallots or scallions in butter, in a small frying pan or saucepan, for a minute or 2 without browning. Then add the tomato and cook over moderately high heat for several minutes until juices have exuded and tomato pulp has thickened enough to hold its shape lightly in a spoon. Season carefully to taste. Just before serving, fold in the herbs.

Tomato Sauce—with Fresh Tomatoes:

For use with meats, baked custards, fish, pizza toppings, pastas, etc.
For 2½ to 3 cups (½ to ¾ L)
1 cup (¼ L) minced onion
2 Tb olive oil
4 cups (1 L) tomato pulp (See Note)
1 imported bay leaf
½ tsp Italian or Provençal herb mixture
1 or more cloves garlic, puréed
Big pinch saffron threads (optional)
A 2-inch (5-cm) piece dried orange peel
Salt and pepper to taste

Cook the onion and olive oil in a heavy-bottomed saucepan, stirring frequently, until onion is limp and translucent but not browned (5 to 7 minutes). Stir in the tomato pulp, herbs, and seasonings, bring to the simmer, then cover and simmer slowly for 30 minutes, stirring occasionally. Taste, and carefully correct seasoning; if too thin, boil down rapidly, stirring.

Note: Out of tomato season, add a judicious amount of strained canned Italian-style plum tomatoes for color and flavor.

Index

238
and herb stuffing RECIPE,
139, 230
how to make, 367–8
in tomatoes moussakaise
RECIPE, 276–8
uses, 230, 241
crusts: toasted RECIPE, 368
for French onion soup, 167–8
Melba RECIPE, 215
rye: Melba RECIPE, 215
toasted rounds RECIPE, 170, 198
storage, 171, 178
Brillat-Savarin, Jean Anthelme, 292
broccoli, 71, 156, 187
with avocado garnish, 179
cold, à la grecque RECIPE, 351
in gâteau of crêpes RECIPE,
192–4
peeled vs. unpeeled, 135–6, 194
with rabbit, 46
broth, see stocks and bouillons
Brown, Cora, Rose, and Bob, 187
Brown Derby Restaurant, 162
brownies (chocolate), 152
Brussels sprout(s), 71, 156
buffet, 319–58
equipment and planning, 322–3
burnt-almond cream RECIPE, 67–8
leftover, 71
butter: beurre manié, see beurre
manié
black (sauce) RECIPE, 95
clarified, 5, RECIPE, 368–9
in brown poultry stock
RECIPE, 11
for potato galette, 15
for potato gnocchi, 340–3
creaming, 281
lemon (sauce) RECIPE, 369
with asparagus, 137, 312
with lobster tomalley, 211
orange sauce RECIPE, 176
white butter sauce RECIPE, 369
with asparagus, 136; fish, 312
butterflied loin of pork RECIPE,
61–3
buttermilk baking powder biscuits
RECIPE, 41
with herbs RECIPE, 41
dough used for chicken pot pie,
147
butternut squash
in ginger and garlic, 54, RECIPE,

64–5
steaming vs. boiling, 64

cabbage: stuffed with chicken, 157
red: pickled slaw RECIPE, 119–
20, storage, 124; in Reuben
sandwich, 124–5
cakes: chocolate fudge cake
RECIPE, 151–2
orange Bavarian torte RECIPE,
352–7
savarin, 292, RECIPE, 306–11
sponge: with poached pears, 216–
17
strawberry shortcake, biscuit
dough for, 41; savarin for,
310–11
caper(s): in Cobb salad, 172
in gazpacho salad, 238
capon, 131
caramel: sauce RECIPE, 222–3;
with vacherins, 47
-topped pear and chocolate
dessert RECIPE, 218
carp roe: brandade RECIPE, 330–1
carré d'agneau (rack of lamb),
272–4
carrot(s): buttered, 261, RECIPE,
276
buying and storage, 187
with chicken livers in aspic, 297
cold, à la grecque RECIPE, 350
in gâteau of crêpes RECIPE, 192
in vegetable sauté RECIPE, 87,
92
cassoulet, 46, 101–102, RECIPE,
115–18, 125
assembling, 117
controversy, 102
leftover, 124
storage, 117–18
vegetarian, 123
caul fat, 234, 245
in pâté en croûte RECIPE,
245–53
cauliflower: à la grecque RECIPE,
350
Cazalis, Chef, 31
celeriac, see celery root
céleri-rave, see celery root
celery: cold, à la grecque RECIPE,
350
in gazpacho salad RECIPE, 238
celery root, 54

For lovers of good food everywhere...

THE BALLANTINE "GREAT COOKS" COOKBOOK SERIES

The best recipes from America's most respected chefs